British Cabinet C

Second edition

D0862779

Fully revised and updated, this new edition of Simon James's comprehensive and accessible text provides an excellent insight into Cabinet government. It draws on the wealth of new material that has become available in recent years to shed light on the mechanisms and structure of the Cabinet system in Britain from 1945 to the present. Its coverage includes:

- ministers and their departments
- collective decision-making
- the role of the Prime Minister
- the strengths and weaknesses of the Cabinet system
- the future of the Cabinet system

British Cabinet Government will give both A-level students and undergraduates a clear understanding of the realities of this central aspect of British politics.

Simon James was formerly at the Cabinet Office and is now at the Organisation for Economic Co-operation and Development in Paris.

British Cabinet Government

Second edition

Simon James

London and New York

First published 1992
by Routledge
11 New Fetter Lane, London EC4P 4EE

Simultaneously published in the USA and Canada
by Routledge
29 West 35th Street, New York, NY 10001

Second edition 1999

Typeset in Baskerville by Routledge
Printed and bound in Great Britain by
TJ International Ltd, Padstow, Cornwall

British Library Cataloguing in Publication Data
A catalogue record for this book is available from the British
Library

Library of Congress Cataloging in Publication Data
James, Simon
        British cabinet government / Simon James. – 2nd ed.
            p.   cm.
        Includes bibliographical references and index.
        (alk. paper)
        1. Cabinet system–Great Britain.   I. Title.
    JN405J35 1999   98-51387
        320.441–dc21
ISBN 0–415–17976–9 (hbk)
ISBN 0–415–17977–7 (pbk)

Contents

Preface to the second edition

This second edition requires some explanation, since readers may wonder to what extent a book on the Cabinet system written by a civil servant who has just spent eighteen months working in the Cabinet Secretariat is an 'authorised' or 'official' version.

I wrote the first edition while working in local government in the late 1980s. Shortly after the book went to press in 1991, I joined the civil service and spent five years in the Department for Education and Employment. Not wanting to give the impression that the book was written with inside knowledge, I simply made no reference at all to my new profession on the dust jacket, and in subsequent journal articles concealed myself discreetly behind visiting fellowships kindly provided by the University of Newcastle and the Institute of Contemporary British History.

This reticence became less tenable, however, after the general election of 1997 when I transferred to the Cabinet Secretariat to work on the new government's programme of constitutional reform, a move which necessarily pushed me into the sightlines of Britain's political scientists. After discussion with those responsible in the Cabinet Office, I decided to avow my position openly rather than conceal it and risk attracting the attention of conspiracy theorists.

What are the limits within which I have written? Essentially, civil service rules prevent me from offering comments on current government policy – not a great problem since I am writing on process, not policy. I may not use confidential information acquired in the course of my work (which, as a matter of professional ethics, I would not do anyway) and must clear the text with the Director of Personnel. The practical impact of these restrictions has been very limited: I can fairly say that nothing of importance has been omitted as a result. (I should make it clear that the book has been prepared in my own time, and using my own computer.)

This is, therefore, not an 'authorised' book except in the negative sense that it has been checked for unprofessional indiscretions. The content, examples, analysis and argument are mine alone.

In preparing this second edition, I have retained the original structure of the book but have substantially reworked the text. Unexpectedly, these changes owe relatively little to my immersion in civil service life; it was a surprise and relief when I entered Whitehall to discover that the account that I had compiled from the outside stood up pretty well to the test of direct experience (an exception to this is the stress on presentation that now features in chapter 2). Rather, I have taken the opportunity to integrate new material – notably John Major's unveiling of the Cabinet committee system, and useful new books by Lawson and Seldon – and to sharpen up arguments and cut unnecessary material. I have kept the historical perspective reaching back to 1945, although in a textbook like this there is a tension between the claims of narrative and analysis: it is salutary to bear in mind that many of today's undergraduates can scarcely remember the era when Mrs Thatcher was Prime Minister.

With these changes, I hope that the volume remains what I originally intended it to be: a reliable, comprehensive student textbook. It makes no claim to great theoretical originality. In part this is due to scepticism: as Professor Jean Blondel put it when reviewing the first edition, 'we simply do not know how to measure power or how to evaluate precisely the effectiveness of given cabinets or of the ministers and prime ministers of which they are composed'. It is also in part because I regard the historical institutionalist approach to public administration as inherently valid, as long as institutions are not defined narrowly but are taken to include their working practices, their links with their political environment, and the ethics and values of those who work within them. The focus of the book remains firmly on decision-making, since the principal significance of any governmental machinery must surely be its impact on public policy.

A stylistic point: the regrettable truth is that the overwhelming majority of ministers and senior civil servants are men. For that reason and to avoid a cumbersome style I have referred to them as male throughout, but the male pronoun should always be taken to include the female. For the same reason I have used such terms as 'chairman' which are still employed in Whitehall. I have also ruthlessly rationalised references to the Common Market, EEC, and EC, and refer instead to the European Union throughout.

Simon James
London, November 1998

Acknowledgements

The more I write on this subject, the more conscious I am of my debt to other writers. Once again, I record my gratitude to Anthea Bennett and John Barnes for allowing me to attend their seminars and for offering advice and encouragement; to Professor George Jones, Professor Peter Hennessy and Professor Rod Rhodes, on whose work I have drawn heavily; and to colleagues at the Institute for Contemporary British History, notably Dr Peter Caterall and Dr Michael Kandiah, who have done much to foster academic debate on the subject.

I have gone out of my way in this edition to draw on the international comparative literature becoming available on cabinet studies. In particular I must acknowledge my heavy reliance on the work of a consortium of Western European academics convened by Professors Blondel and Muller-Rommel, and hope that I have done something to draw their scholarship into the insular study of the central executive in Britain. To these and the many other writers whose works I have pillaged I must record my apologies and thanks. I take responsibility for all translations from original languages.

I am grateful to the editors of Political Studies, Parliamentary Affairs, Contemporary Record and Politics Review, in whose pages certain sections of this book originally appeared. I am also grateful to have been given the opportunity to test ideas in this book at Peter Hennessy's seminar on Premiership and Cabinet at Queen Mary and Westfield College, at the United Services College, Greenwich, and – on numerous occasions – at John Barnes' seminar at the LSE.

I have made extensive use of the admirable Westminster City Libraries, the Public Records Office at Kew, the British Newspaper Library and the Treasury and Cabinet Office Library, and am indebted to the helpfulness and patience of their staff. David Wilkinson has been helpful far beyond the call of duty. I am grateful to Mark Kavanagh and Goober Fox of Routledge, who saw this revised edition through to publication.

Family and friends have once again put up with a lot, nobody more than Sophie. However, the Job memorial prize for forbearance goes to my brother Adrian, who saved me months of work by salvaging the text of the first edition from a computer system pre-dating Charles Babbage. To him and other kind and tolerant people, my heartfelt thanks.

A note on sources

The only serious criticism of the first edition of this work was of its apparent reliance on ministerial memoirs. In fact, the primary source for the book is the seminar on Cabinet Government and the National Policy Process organised at the London School of Economics by John Barnes and Anthea Bennett, at which serving and former ministers and senior officials talk about their experience of the system, and which I have attended since 1980. However, since the seminar is held under Chatham House rules, information drawn from it was not attributed in the first edition, and wherever possible I inserted a reference to a published source. I have changed that approach on this edition: where an assertion is made based on LSE seminar evidence for which I can find no parallel published source, it is marked with an asterisk (*).

1 Describing the Cabinet system

Cabinet government is a popular model, found in around a quarter of the world's states. Usually it is an integral element of a parliamentary executive – that is, an executive responsible to a parliament, whose ministers are members of that parliament, and where the post of chief minister is separate from that of head of state. Such Cabinet systems are concentrated in Europe – modelled on the historical examples of Britain and Sweden – and in Commonwealth countries, to which Britain exported its creation. There are a few additional examples of executive Cabinets beyond these two categories, principally Israel, Japan and Thailand. Cabinets with executive functions are also found in the world's half dozen 'semi-presidential' systems – notably Finland, France and Poland – where leadership is shared between a president and a prime minister. In contrast, in fully presidential systems the Cabinet is usually so subservient to the president that we cannot speak of Cabinet government (Derbyshire and Derbyshire 1996, Duverger 1986).

Within this international spectrum, the pattern of Cabinet government varies between countries according to political culture, constitutional arrangements, the structure of party politics and – especially – whether or not the government is a coalition. The pattern also varies within countries according to political circumstances and the leading personalities within the Cabinet system (for a typology of Western European cabinets see Andeweg 1993).

From government by Cabinet to a 'Cabinet system'

This book deliberately concentrates on the British Cabinet system since the Second World War. Mackintosh's *The British Cabinet* (1977), for decades the standard text, explored the Cabinet's genesis in the seventeenth century and subsequent evolution. While historically intriguing, this can be unhelpful and even misleading. The post-1945 Cabinet is very different from its ancestors. Between the early nineteenth century, when the Cabinet assumed a form that modern ministers might find familiar, and the First World War, the character of the system remained much the same. The span of business was relatively narrow. There was little administrative, as opposed to pre-legislative, work to be done. A minister's life was comparatively leisurely (Asquith's Agriculture Minister put in two hours at the office each day). The Cabinet was small – an average of fourteen members – and its meetings, held once or twice a week, were informal and discursive. Its members frequented the same clubs, visited the same great houses and were social acquaintances as well as political colleagues. The narrow scope and easy pace of government afforded ministers enough time to consider issues properly. The Cabinet was genuinely the political and administrative high command of the country.

Things changed a little during and after the First World War. The scope of government and complexity of administration grew. A secretariat was established and committees were increasingly, if unsystematically, used to relieve the pressure on the Cabinet in certain key areas such as future legislation, defence and foreign policy. But the Cabinet was still run basically on nineteenth-century lines.

It was the Second World War that demonstrated the inability of this system, which had served Gladstone and Baldwin alike, to cope with the prodigious effort required by total national mobilisation. War, peacetime reconstruction and commitment to economic management and the welfare state markedly changed the character of government. Departments increased in number and size. The volume of work grew enormously in complexity and detail, and the work of individual departments grew more closely interrelated, particularly in the economic and social fields. Ministerial life became frantic and high-pressured: several of Attlee's colleagues literally worked themselves to death. Ministers had less time to study each other's policy proposals, especially since these grew ever more complex. The size of the Cabinet, which had grown slowly since the turn of the century, reached two dozen: too many to allow a thorough discussion of more than a few subjects at any meeting.

A huge network of Cabinet committees developed to cope with the load: some 461 ministerial and official committees under Attlee, which a scandalised Churchill succeeded only in reducing to 246 (Hennessy 1986). Increasingly, ministerial committees took decisions on their own authority without the need for Cabinet ratification. Authority became diffused. The Cabinet's role became confined to discussing the great issues of the moment, noting the more significant decisions taken by committees and resolving disputes between ministers. Although a trend in this direction had been discernible between the wars, the Second World War marked the point when Britain ceased to be governed by the Cabinet and became governed by a Cabinet system of which the Cabinet itself was only the pinnacle. And in the subsequent half century the role of committees has expanded further to the point where they take most decisions and the Cabinet has become a reporting and discursive body – a development analysed at length in Chapter 3.

This does not mean that the Cabinet has ceased to matter. It is still the supreme tier of British government and an aura of importance still surrounds it. Attaining Cabinet rank is an enormously significant step for a minister, the promotion that places him above the salt; there is a huge gulf between the most popular and successful junior minister and the least known, least senior of Cabinet ministers. It gives access to confidential information and a seat at the top table. Attendance at Cabinet takes precedence over all other ministerial duties, except the Privy Council. Membership is exclusive, in the sense that Cabinet ministers alone may attend; a junior minister may be invited for the discussion of a particular item for which he is responsible, but only for the duration of that item. No civil servants are present except for the Cabinet Secretary, the heads of the Cabinet Secretariats, the Prime Minister's Principal Private Secretary and, latterly, the Prime Minister's Press Secretary. It is an exclusive meeting where great matters are discussed.

This pattern of development is not peculiar to Britain. Most Western European countries that operate some variant of a Cabinet system experienced a similar growth in workload and responded much like Britain. The size of Cabinets has grown (though a very recent trend in Western Europe has been for them to shrink again), junior ministers have proliferated, the role of the Prime Minister has been extended and Cabinet committees created – although varying in number and function – to relieve pressure on the Cabinet. This raises the same problems of the erosion, but not elimination, of the collegial system as in Britain (see Blondel and Muller-Rommel 1988).

Legal status and underlying principles of the system

Famously, the British constitution is unwritten and its Cabinet system exists and operates not by statute but by constitutional convention – essentially, established tradition. This concept of convention as constitutional law is a dynamic one because it accepts that institutions change to reflect social reality, and the conventions are adapted accordingly. So, for example, while the Cabinet originated as a committee of the Privy Council, and in theory probably still is (certainly all Cabinet ministers are sworn of the Council), the link with its parent body has withered away. This flexible concept of constitutional convention allows the Crown – in practice, the Prime Minister – great latitude in deciding the structure and *modus operandi* of the Cabinet system. Consequently, arrangements are imprecise, defined largely in terms of historical events, and susceptible to change. For example, it is now accepted that the convention of collective responsibility may be suspended by the Prime Minister, as it was in 1931 when the Cabinet split over tariffs, and again in 1975 when it split over Europe.

However, the functions of the British Cabinet system are spelled out in the Ministerial Code of Conduct (Cabinet Office 1997a). Originally promulgated as Questions of Procedure for Ministers in 1945, this document has quadrupled in length over the years to 135 paragraphs (Baker 1998). It is essentially a practical document, a rather miscellaneous compendium of dos and don'ts, and most of it is concerned with ministers' private and constituency interests, appointments by ministers, and arrangements for the presentation of government policy. However, paragraphs 3 to 18 (Cabinet Office 1997a) spell out some of the operating rules of the Cabinet, and paragraph 3 provides a functional definition:

Cabinet and Ministerial Committee business consists, in the main, of:

a   Questions which significantly engage the collective responsibility of the Government, because they raise major issues of policy or because they are of critical importance to the public;

b   Questions on which there is an unresolved argument between Departments.

This formulation is longer on pragmatism than principle. However, it is possible to identify five characteristics of the British system that combine in different measures elements of constitutional convention and operational habit – elements that between them define the parameters of the system, govern its internal dynamics and explain some of its quirks. These are the unitary nature of the Cabinet, its collegiate ethos, the collective responsibility of all ministers, the dominance of Parliament, and the growing importance of the European Union.

The unitary nature of the Cabinet

In the past decade a small but high quality comparative literature has developed, making it possible to compare the British Cabinet system with its European counterparts (see Blondel and Muller-Rommel 1988 and

1993, Mackie and Hogwood 1985, Jones 1991). For the most part, however, the literature is dominated by the dynamics of coalition government (see notably Laver and Shepsle 1994) that prevails in most European countries (Spain is the most conspicuous exception).

In Britain, by contrast, a long-established two-party system generates single-party governments. Even when the government has lost its majority in the Commons – under the Callaghan administration and in the last year of Major's government – the impact on the inner life of the Cabinet has been limited. The Prime Minister can appoint and dismiss ministers, create a Cabinet committee and merge two departments without brokering it with the leader of other political parties. Ministers can make decisions without having to clear their lines with coalition partners. Policies do not have to be developed within the confines of a written coalition agreement – a feature of Cabinet life particularly dominant in Eastern Europe. There exists no management committee of party leaders to pre-cook or over-rule decisions of Cabinet and its committees. The government still has to operate within the constraints of external political circumstances, and still remains highly sensitive to backbench opinion in the House of Commons, but is not constrained at every turn by the mechanics of coalition government.

This saves a lot of time and trouble when compared with many other European governments, particularly Italy and The Netherlands whose coalitions are unstable and where the Prime Minister's time can be wholly taken up with holding the government together (Jones 1991).

Collegiality

Collegiality is the exercise of authority by a group of people acting jointly rather than one person acting alone. This features strongly in British political culture. Countries with a Napoleonic political and legal culture tend to adopt monocratic instruments of government: prefects, mayors and presidents. British political culture has tended to confide power to collective groups: councils, boards and committees. Collegiality is rarely egalitarian: in most collegiate bodies a small number of its members wield most of the day-to-day influence, and certainly in Cabinet some members wield much more influence than others. Nevertheless, in collegiate bodies the less prominent members are able at very least to counsel their dominant colleagues, and often have the right to approve or reject their actions. The existence of a mechanism for warning and restraint gives legitimacy to the decisions of such bodies – or, more accurately, its absence will be seen as undermining the legitimacy of decisions.

Collegiality has strengths. It combines the abilities and experience of many people. It acts as a check on rash or hasty action. It lessens the risk of power going to the head of one person. In central government's administratively complicated system it dovetails well with the need for policy coordination between ministers. Yet it can cause delay: discussion takes time. Decision by consensus tends also to produce the lowest common denominator, and restrains bolder and more decisive action. This creates a particular tension between Cabinet collegiality and prime ministerial leadership.

These issues surrounding collegiality are to be found in all the European and Commonwealth Cabinet systems mentioned at the start of this chapter. More often than not, collegiality is a strong element even when the Cabinet is susceptible to the pressures of a federal system – like Canada, Germany or, supremely, Switzerland – or of a multi-party coalition, as in much of Europe. Collegiality is a factor in Cabinet life as much in systems where the Prime Minister is dominant – Spain, for example – as in systems where the Prime Minister is weak, such as Italy. There is, however, a spectrum ranging from countries where the collegiate ethos is resilient, as in Scandinavia, through to those like The Netherlands where it is feeble. Also, as in Britain, the situation varies over time, reflecting changes in personality and external circumstances: in the former West German republic collegiality was stronger under Chancellor Erhard than under his authoritarian predecessor Adenauer (Blondel and Muller-Rommel 1988).

Collective responsibility

The principle of collective responsibility is deeply rooted in the British Cabinet's collegiate ethos. It holds that all ministers are equally and jointly responsible for every decision taken by the government. In private within the government they may disagree and argue about the policy, but once a decision is taken they must support and defend it in public. The minister who cannot bring himself to stifle his disagreement in public must resign. This applies to decisions taken in Cabinet, by smaller gatherings of ministers such as Cabinet committees, or by individual ministers, and every minister shares responsibility for every decision whether he was involved in taking it or not.

The rationale for this seeming absurdity is the need for the government to present a united front. If ministers may contradict each other in public and abide by some decisions but not others, confusion and division will soon set in. The position of a minister who is publicly criticised by his colleagues will become untenable, and a government whose policies are under fire from its own members will lose its authority. It is an illogical, even distasteful doctrine, but there is no practical alternative to it. Collective responsibility is an organised hypocrisy, but a necessary one.

There are several corollaries. The first, self-evident, is that what is said at ministerial meetings must remain confidential so that the eventual decision will not be undermined by the publicising of conflicting views. If there is no confidentiality, either collective responsibility is shattered, or ministers cannot speak frankly and the meetings are a waste of time. That is why the government does not divulge how often Cabinet committees have met or what they have discussed (indeed, until 1992 their very existence was officially a secret). As Roy Jenkins reputedly put it, ministers must be able to change their minds in private. Second, ministers' duty to observe collegiate unity implies a right to be consulted and to voice their views on at least the most important and sensitive issues. The Prime Minister, who is responsible for enforcing collective responsibility and for deciding which committee deals with which issue, is also responsible for ensuring that ministers' right to be consulted is observed. They can be involved in only a small proportion of decisions, but the Prime Minister needs to ensure that they do not feel shut out of any decision of great significance or sensitivity.

This doctrine is not a British eccentricity. A similar rule applies in almost all Western European and Commonwealth countries with a Cabinet system, even in countries like The Netherlands where Cabinet control over individual ministers is weak (Blondel and Muller-Rommel 1988). Indeed certain constitutions – those of Sweden, Spain and Portugal amongst them – go so far as to specify that ministers are collectively responsible to Parliament.

The importance of Parliament

Central government's life is dominated by Parliament. Strange though it seems in an era when the governing party's stranglehold over the House of Commons through the party whip has never seemed stronger, both ministers and their officials are preoccupied by Parliament, not to say apprehensive of it. As the former minister Jock Bruce-Gardyne perceptively observed (at a time when the Government had a majority of eighty-three): 'No matter how seemingly impregnable a Government's majority, it always feels itself to be vulnerable to backbench pressures' (Bruce-Gardyne 1986).

It comes down to political culture: Parliament expects ministers to be accountable to it, and parliamentary performance makes and breaks ministerial careers in Britain. Not only does Britain, famously, have no sharp separation of powers between legislature and executive; the link between minister and Parliament is intimate. Ministers must be members of the Commons or Lords, and must frequently account for their actions to Parliament. For the nine months of the year for which it meets, Parliament dictates the timetable of legislation and absorbs much of the energies of ministers. Statements must be made in the House, questions answered every three weeks or so, speeches made in debates, statutory instruments laid, a contribution prepared to the Queen's speech, and ministers and officials must appear at intervals before select committees. And if the department is promoting legislation, for some ministers Parliament must become a working obsession.

An inept parliamentary performance can seriously affect a minister's standing: a bad afternoon at the dispatch box destroyed two of Mrs Thatcher's Cabinet colleagues, John Moore over an NHS funding crisis and Paul Channon over the Lockerbie air disaster. Ministers have continuously to demonstrate to their colleagues that they are on top of their jobs. This is best demonstrated at the end of each day's main debate in the Commons. The last 40 minutes are given over to the closing speeches, first that of the opposition spokesman, then that of the Minister. Slowly during those 40 minutes the Chamber fills up. The floor of the Commons is a surprisingly small and intimate place; MPs cluster on the benches closest to the dispatch box and crowd round either side of the Speaker's chair, watching, cheering, barracking the two main speakers, rather like a prize fight. The minister's spirit in standing up to the Opposition and skill in presenting his case is hugely important to this parliamentary standing and, by extension, his political reputation.

Civil servants usually see Parliament at one remove, but share the sense of responsibility to it: they have to brief the minister for each appearance, and if the minister is poorly briefed this reflects badly on the department. But in recent years senior officials have increasingly been called to give evidence in person before select committees – a remarkably potent factor in impressing on them a healthy respect for Parliament. In addition, it is the Permanent Secretary and not the minister who is 'accounting officer' for the departmental accounts and who must appear at intervals before the Public Accounts Committee to answer for his stewardship – always a nerve-wracking and exhausting experience (Holland 1995).

Many ministers have a love–hate relationship with Parliament; it is their element, where political reputations are made, yet it is full of traps for the unwary or unlucky. Civil servants regard it rather warily, as a hurdle to be clambered over, or a threat to be appeased, or a penance inflicted on the department for the good of its collective soul. It is always, healthily, a potent factor in the minds of those at the top in Whitehall.

The importance of Europe

One constitutional development of immense importance is the encroach-
ment of the European Union (EU) into Whitehall life. Since 1973,
domestic British law has been subordinate to EU law, and the competence
of the EU now extends into most areas of economic life, and increasingly
into new areas such as foreign affairs, border controls, social policy and
education. But European issues are mostly an extension of domestic policy,
conducted in a foreign context, so there is a substantial European dimension to the work of all departments. The most dramatic example is the
Ministry of Agriculture, Fisheries and Food (MAFF), now so dominated by
European concerns that 20 per cent of its spending is decided directly by
the EU Council of Ministers and its internal organisation was reworked in
the 1990s to reflect the EU Commission's internal working processes.
Many other departments, such as Trade and Industry, have had to re-
orientate themselves towards Europe in many of their dealings.

It is surprising, therefore, that the impact on the way British central
government runs itself is comparatively slight. The structure of the Cabinet
system and its underlying ethos and principles remain unaltered. EU
membership has added a new dimension to the work of many departments,
especially the imposition of an additional juridical system with an unBritish
emphasis on legal codes and rules. The EU also requires officials (often quite
junior) and ministers to make frequent visits abroad; and it needs a special
coordinating mechanism in the Cabinet Office (described in Chapter 3). But
all this has been accommodated within the framework of the old system.

There are two significant respects, however, in which the dynamics of
collective decision-making differ in EU matters. First, the status of governmental decisions in EU matters is less definitive. Where once the British
government took a decision and that was the end of the matter, its decisions on EU-related matters can now only be 'this is what our negotiating
position must be'. For example, the Cabinet used to have an annual review
that fixed British agricultural prices and subsidies. Now that responsibility
has shifted to the EU Council of Ministers, the Cabinet simply determines
what attitude its Agriculture Secretary should adopt in the negotiations.
Second, and as a consequence of this, some of the Cabinet's authority has
to be devolved to the minister who carries out the negotiations, acting in
consultation with the Prime Minister. The Cabinet approves a negotiating
stance, but as negotiations in Brussels proceed, the minister on the spot
must decide what to concede and what to stick on. For evident practical
reasons, the Cabinet cannot be convened every time he has to adjust his
negotiating position, so he either takes the responsibility himself or, if the
issue is important, rings the Prime Minister for approval.

Admittedly this has happened in the past in other international fora, for example in dealings with NATO or with the United Nations. It also happened quite frequently in domestic politics in the 1960s and 1970s when the government got involved in settling strikes. But these were comparatively limited areas; in contrast, huge swathes of national life now fall within the curtilage of EU business, and the loosening of Cabinet control is correspondingly more significant.

The unimportance of the party machine

Finally, it is worth noting the very limited impact of the Conservative or Labour party machines on the internal workings of the Cabinet system. The parliamentary party is crucially important; the party in the country far less so. Party is supremely important in providing those preconditions that must be met to achieve and maintain a Cabinet government. The Prime Minister must be elected leader of his party, and retain its confidence. But once these preconditions are fulfilled, the government is free of the party machine. Party does exercise influence on government policy indirectly in the sense that backbench MPs, and to a much lesser extent party workers, voice aspirations or, more often, anxieties to ministers. This 'smoke-detector' influence is potent in setting constraints within which the government feels obliged to operate. At moments of crisis, the government may show great sensitivity to the mood of the party in the country, as Margaret Thatcher did during the Falklands episode and John Major did during the crisis over coal mine closures. But as a general rule, the party in the country is no more than one of many conditioning influences on ministerial behaviour.

The recollections of Edward Short, Chief Whip in Wilson's first government, holds true for all governments:

> the centre of gravity, so far as policy-making and decision taking were concerned, had now moved from [party headquarters] to Whitehall. In spite of all our efforts to inform and consult the [party] officials and the National Executive Committee, there was a feeling of alienation and, dare one say, of jealousy.
>
> (Short 1989)

Prime Ministers like to keep it that way. Attempts by Labour party officials in the late 1960s to oppose moves towards EU membership were brusquely overruled by Wilson, who in the 1970s forbade ministers to associate themselves with the resolutions of party committees that criticised government policy (Wilson 1976). Since the Conservative party machine is notably more subservient to its leader, Tory leaders face even less party pressure.

A glance overseas shows that there is no reason why this should be so. Practice in France and Germany is as in Britain, but in Austria, The Netherlands and Scandinavian countries, consultation between Cabinet and party is the norm, and in Belgium and Italy parties often exercise strong influence on Cabinet decisions (de Winter 1993, Laver and Shepsle 1994).

Summary

Britain today is not governed by the Cabinet but by a Cabinet system, an elaborate pyramid of which the Cabinet is only the pinnacle. The control centre of government is a highly articulated but diffuse mechanism and all the layers in between them make up 'Cabinet government'.

Despite these changes certain fundamental characteristics persist. The ethos of the system remains collegiate. Parliament remains crucially important and its demands dominate departmental life. Ministers remain collectively responsible to Parliament for all government decisions. Joining the EU has made the decisions of the cabinet in many ways less definitive.

That is the framework. The rest of this book examines how the Cabinet system works in practice. The second chapter looks at the internal departmental policy-making roles of ministers and their officials, and the third at policy coordination between departments, with particular reference to the Cabinet and its committees. The fourth considers the Prime Minister's role, and the fifth the respective roles of premier, Cabinet and ministers in various spheres of policy. The last three chapters examine problems in the workings of the system and possible ways of remedying them.

2 Ministers and their departments

One of the crucial dynamics of the British Cabinet system is that policy-making is very much in the hands of individual departments. It is the departmental minister who initiates change by imposing new initiatives and altering the course of existing policies. The 'lead' department for a subject controls the subsequent development and implementation of policy, and is invariably the focus of discussion and consultation with interested outside organisations. Consequently, the minister in charge of a department in Britain enjoys a level of autonomy in policy matters greater than in almost any other country. As Professor Jones has observed, British government is essentially 'ministerial government', although this is counter-balanced by a Cabinet whose collegiate ethos is stronger than in most countries. But while many of the outputs of the policy process are well publicised – through parliamentary debate and the extensive presentational efforts of departments – and while many of the inputs are publicly visible – pressure in Parliament, the advocacy of interest groups, the advice of government inquiries, the statistical or scientific data on which decisions are based – it is extremely difficult for the outsider to penetrate the stage at which the decision is actually taken: the stage often referred to by political observers and professional lobbyists as the 'black box' of policy-making. This chapter examines a facet of that process which crucially affects the operation of the Cabinet system: the relationship between departmental ministers and their civil servants.

Ministers: 'just passing through'

Britain is governed by the creative friction generated by putting temporary ministers in charge of more permanent civil servants. Whitehall departments are large, expert, monolithic to the outside eye, and staffed by experienced officials. Onto the top of these organisations are parachuted ministers, largely unversed in administration or departmental subject matter, yet given ultimate command and responsibility for a sizeable slice of public life.

They arrive in the knowledge that they will not be staying long. It is usual for ministers to stay in each job only for two or three years before a reshuffle or change of government moves them on, although the most senior members of the Cabinet – Prime Minister, Foreign Secretary, Chancellor of the Exchequer and Home Secretary – tend to serve longer than the average. This is not a feature unique to Britain: two or three years is the norm in France, Canada and Australia, while unstable coalition governments like those of Belgium and Italy usually last only one or two. The former West Germany, with an average tenure of four to five years in one post, is untypically high for a democratic Cabinet system (Blondel 1985).

As Alderman has argued, there are advantages to the government as a whole in frequent ministerial turnover. It stops ministers from becoming over-absorbed in the business of one department. It gives ministers a broad range of experience, which suits the ambitious. And, in Mrs Thatcher's words, it makes them 'more likely to pursue government policies rather than departmental policies' (quoted in Alderman 1995). Within the department, frequent turnover avoids the problem of too close a symbiosis developing between the minister and his officials. Denis Healey was Defence Secretary for six years in the 1960s and one of his junior ministers became convinced that he became too closely identified with the department's traditional interests (Owen 1991). Also, there is in any government a limited number of ministers with drive and creative impulse, and they have to be moved around from field to field according to need.

Ministers' lack of subject expertise

Ministers rarely know much of the departments to which they are appointed. Few have worked as civil servants themselves: the French system by which officials flit from civil service to politics and back is alien to Britain's severe insistence on an apolitical bureaucracy. Few ministers can boast long previous experience in outside professions apart from the early stages of a career in law, teaching, business or journalism. Yet previous experience of their departments' subject area is not necessarily an advantage; the expert minister may be too close to the subject matter to be willing to challenge his officials or balance the competing demands of technical and political considerations. James Prior, a farmer, and Douglas Hurd, a former diplomat, took office at Agriculture and the Foreign Office respectively with a body of previous experience, but proved unradical. The snail's pace of legal reform in post-war Britain may owe something to the high proportion of lawyers in every Cabinet.

In practice, the skills and expertise required of a minister can be deduced from the main functions of the job. The key internal duties are policy innovation, policy management and departmental administration. The key external duties are parliamentary duties; acting as the department's advocate at Cabinet, Cabinet committees and the EU Council of Ministers; acting as departmental ambassador to the wider world; and public presentation of policy.

Policy innovation

This is the activity that can make a minister memorable. Left to their own devices, officials will concentrate on running the existing arrangements competently: a small reform here, an improvement there, but basically pursuing what Richard Rose has termed 'government by directionless consensus' (1974). Above all, a minister is appointed to a department to provide strong policy leadership and inject his party's outlook and values into its departmental policies. The Blair government elected in 1997 gave innumerable examples of departments being told by new ministers to re-order their priorities and habits, for example by overhauling the welfare system or creating a freedom of information regime.

The innovative minister will be remembered when the capable administrator is forgotten. The latter part of this chapter will concentrate on policy innovation as the overwhelmingly significant part of the minister's function. For the moment it is worth noting, first, that the innovative role in a department is played mainly by the Secretary of State rather than by junior ministers; and second, that for all its importance, policy innovation only takes up a minority of such a minister's time.

Policy management

So what takes up the bulk of a minister's day? For a start, the management of existing policy. At any given time a department will have numerous policies in the process of implementation, and even the most radical government will want to change only a few of them. But each regularly generates decisions to be taken by ministers. For example, legislation creating the National Curriculum was passed in 1988, but the sheer complexity of devising and implementing a curriculum and the associated tests for ten subjects took another decade. Many decisions were highly sensitive – What will be taught in each subject? Will we have written or practical tests? How fast can we push through each element of the reform? – and had to be taken by ministers because of the public sensitivity.

Executive work

This takes up a surprising amount of time, for many decisions within departments must be taken by ministers. Much of this stems from the vast expansion in secondary legislation, which delegates to ministers quasi-judicial powers – for instance, on immigration cases – and extensive powers to issue regulations and guidance; the Children Act of 1989 required the Health Secretary to issue innumerable sets of complex guidance and regulations. Ministers spend a lot of time going through papers from officials on proposals to close schools, approve or reject planning appeals, merge health authorities, approve pay settlements, and so on. Increasingly, Secretaries of State devolve such detailed work to junior ministers, but must still be aware of the main decisions being taken, for which they must answer to Parliament and the public. The volume of correspondence is particularly daunting: ministers must reply to letters from MPs and peers, and Edwina Currie recalls regularly signing 300 letters to MPs a week when she was a junior health minister (Currie 1989).

Parliamentary duties

Turning to ministerial duties outside the department, the minister's parliamentary role has become familiar to the public through the broadcasting of Parliament. A department's ministers must answer oral questions – usually every three weeks in the Commons – and a host of written questions, speak in major debates, answer adjournment debates, and occasionally appear before select committees. If the department is trying to enact legislation many hours must be spent piloting it through long debates, a task that falls mainly to junior ministers.

For every such occasion, as for any ministerial engagement, preparation takes longer than the event itself: a 30-minute speech will take hours to draft and redraft, and elaborate preparations are made for oral question time. In addition, a wise minister will spend some time in the bars and tearoom of the Commons, keeping his contacts with backbenchers in good repair, listening to their views, helping with their problems, attending party meetings, meeting party backbench committees and the like.

The departmental advocate

This role involves seeking the agreement of ministers in other departments to policy proposals, sometimes in bilateral meetings, sometimes at Cabinet committees. Ministers must attend the EU Council of Ministers in Brussels to negotiate for the UK interest. The Secretary of State must secure for his department a share of parliamentary time to steer through any legislation – Barbara Castle's diaries for 1975 record her struggle to secure time for her Pay Beds Bill and Child Benefits Bill (Castle 1980). The Secretary of State must also secure adequate funding for the department's programmes: an onerous task, as described in detail in Chapter 5, but of crucial importance as shown in 1987–8 when John Moore, then Social Security Secretary, damaged his career by accepting too low a settlement for his programmes, thus precipitating a crisis (Seldon 1997).

The departmental ambassador

The ambassadorial role involves a lot of work meeting innumerable deputations from interest groups operating within the department's sphere of responsibility: private companies, trade unions, health authorities, local councils, quangos, nationalised corporations, professional associations and so on. Many such meetings are delegated to junior ministers. There are also visits to establishments around the country: prisons, hospitals, universities, factories or whatever the department's responsibilities may encompass, and formal occasions like receptions and dinners. While some of these engagements are a chore, and are invariably used as opportunities for lobbying by those the minister meets, visits in particular give the minister a valuable opportunity to meet people directly affected by departmental decisions and to see conditions at first hand.

Public presentation of policy

Today, presentation is seen as an essential facet of any policy, and some politicians' concern with public relations borders on obsession. Nicholas Ridley, at Trade and Industry in the late 1980s, was not exaggerating wildly when he said that he spent one-quarter of his time taking decisions and three-quarters of his time explaining them (Cole 1995). Near-instantaneous reactions to any event will be given by news commentators and opposition politicians, and ministers cannot afford to be left behind. Presentation is now seen as an integral part of policy-making. A 1997 review of the Government Information Service observed:

> The effective communication and explanation of policy and decisions should not be an afterthought, but an integral part of a Government's duty to govern with consent…However well-conceived and developed, many Government policies will fail if they are not capable of being explained convincingly to, and accepted by, the citizen.
>
> (Cabinet Office 1997d)

The government now intervenes in areas of life where it has no direct control, like arts or sport, or where a policy's success depends on public acceptance, like road safety, pay restraint or health education. In these fields persuasion is essential.

The emphasis on presentation can be over-done. Douglas Hurd, after leaving Major's cabinet, disparaged the 'huge amount of time given to fretting over the media' (*Daily Telegraph* 24 June 1996). Certainly, there are limits to what presentation can do for a policy. Kenneth Baker's promotion to Home Secretary owed much to his presentational skills, but when his Dangerous Dogs Act blew up in his face, being good on television could do no more than mitigate the damage. And there is the danger, as one former Permanent Secretary has observed, of

> a confusion between 'presentation' and announcements and action and real effect. It is touching to see Ministers' faith that when they have announced something at the dispatch box, it has happened. Of course it has not. The job is only just beginning.
>
> (Holland 1995)

The skills required of ministers

So ministers do not require expertise in a particular policy field, but rather a set of skills transferable from one field to another. Principal amongst these are:

* *Communication skills* – the ability to present a case clearly, in speeches, in discussion and on the airwaves. Critical here is the ability to win over that most difficult of audiences, the House of Commons.
* *Negotiating skills* – crucial for fighting the department's battles in negotiations with other departments, especially the Treasury, and at EU meetings.
* *Administrative skills* – the ability to get through the huge volume of paperwork generated by the department (for example, submissions, draft press releases, letters, decisions on casework) and the judgement to decide what to delegate to junior ministers and officials.
* *Skills of decision* – the most difficult of skills to define: knowing when to act, when to wait on events, when to demand more information, when to accept the written advice of officials and when to call them in for a meeting to probe their recommendations.

Of all these, the skill that matters most in gaining preferment is parliamentary skill, and in particular the skill of accounting persuasively to parliament: that is, persuading parliament that it is being given a candid explanation of the government's actions, and defending those actions convincingly against critics. Almost all post-war ministers have been long-term professional politicians who have spent up to fifteen years in Parliament before gaining office. The difficult art of managing the Commons is reckoned far more valuable than either expert knowledge of the subject in hand or experience in running a large organisation. Britain is not unique in this regard: in most Western European and democratic Commonwealth countries the majority of ministers are recruited from a parliamentary background, although some – notably France, The Netherlands and Austria – also draw heavily on civil servants as a reservoir of ministerial talent (Blondel 1985).

In practice, most MPs come from a limited range of professions: lawyers, academics, teachers, journalists and a scattering of business people and accountants. On the face of it, this is a narrow cadre, but it provides not a bad match to the skills described above, for such professions require clear communication, the knack of dealing diplomatically with people, the ability to master a brief at short notice, and powers of decision. The few attempts to bring in expert ministers have not been great successes. John Davies, former head of the Confederation of British Industry, was a failure in the Commons; so too, in retrospect, was Mrs Thatcher's protégé David Young, despite being sent to the shelter of the House of Lords. Trade union experience seems to be no greater asset if the failure of Frank Cousins and Ray Gunter in Wilson's first government is any measure. An expert background is as much help to a minister as a good speaking voice or a memory for detail; useful but not essential.

Over a century on, Walter Bagehot's classic formulation holds true: ministers need 'sufficient intelligence, quite enough various knowledge, quite enough miscellaneous experience, to represent general sense in opposition to bureaucratic sense' (Bagehot [1867] 1964). Ministers are not required to immerse themselves in minutiae. They need to grasp the basic issues, inject the government's political priorities into departments' thinking and subject officials' proposals to the litmus test of political acceptability. David Young admits that when he was a special adviser at the Department of Industry he initially felt contempt for ministers because of their lack of managerial experience, but

> after a while I developed a healthy respect for them and the system. Time after time they would show that they had the political feel for the possible that I lacked. They really were the interface between the possible and the people.
>
> (Young 1990)

John Prescott put it more pithily a month after becoming Deputy Prime Minister:

> There's some great mystique because you haven't been trained to govern. I have to tell you it's pure common sense, good political judgement and making sure you know your facts. And, I think, a damn good civil service.
>
> (*Financial Times* 16 June 1997)

Junior ministers

Students should beware of being misled by the diaries of Castle, Benn and Crossman, which describe Whitehall life as it was between twenty and thirty years ago. They tend to personalise policy-making into a face-to-face relationship between the Secretary of State and the Permanent Secretary. This was perpetuated by the television series 'Yes Minister', which for dramatic purposes focused on that relationship. This may have been true in the past, but in practice today policy is made by a wider cast. Most notably, a greater role is now accorded to junior ministers.

There are two tiers of junior ministers: ministers of state and the more junior under-secretaries of state. The number of junior ministers has doubled from thirty-two in 1945 to sixty-six in 1998. They are appointed by the Prime Minister rather than by the Secretary of State, although the Prime Minister will sometimes consult his more senior colleagues on the juniors he proposes to assign to them. Junior ministers have no formal powers; their authority 'is essentially informal and indeterminate, depending upon personal and political, not statutory factors' (Theakston 1987). The convention of ministerial responsibility holds the Secretary of State responsible to Parliament; junior ministers are responsible to the Secretary of State. Their slightly ambivalent position within the policy-making hierarchy is illustrated by the Ministerial Code:

> The authority of Ministers outside the Cabinet is delegated from the Minister in charge of the Department; the Permanent Secretary is not subject to the direction of junior Ministers. Equally, junior Ministers are not subject to the directions of the Permanent Secretary.
>
> (Cabinet Office 1997a)

As recently as the 1960s, relatively little of importance was confided to junior ministers. A lot of their work was parliamentary: answering questions and adjournment debates, and piloting legislation through Parliament. But this was a waste of a valuable resource, especially as

Cabinet ministers became increasingly overworked. In 1970 Edward Heath made a determined effort to delegate substantial blocks of work to Ministers of State (the more senior tier of junior ministers). [1] This made particular sense given the simultaneous trend to create larger departments through mergers, like the Department of the Environment. While the extent of delegation to junior ministers varies enormously between departments, quite a few Minister of State posts now allow their occupants substantial autonomy and personal responsibility, often recognised by illustrative titles such as Minister for Sport, Minister for Public Transport, Minister for Disabled People, and so on. The Scott report on arms to Iraq tweaked back the curtain to show junior ministers at the Foreign Office, Defence and Trade and Industry taking decisions regarding weapons exports without reference to their Secretaries of State – understandably, since 98,000 export licences a year had to be approved (Scott 1996). Yet the ultimate responsibility lies with the Secretary of State. When big decisions are pending, or when there is trouble in the Commons, he is expected to take charge (Theakston 1987), as indeed the Secretaries of State did when the arms to Iraq scandal broke.

There are three main determinants of the degree of delegation. First, it varies according to the department; before it was split, the Department of Health and Social Security was so vast that Secretary of State Norman Fowler, who had to devote a lot of time to AIDS, left most health service and social security matters to his juniors (Seldon 1997). Second, the political sensitivity of the issue matters a lot. When Shirley Williams became Education Secretary in 1977, a huge surplus of teacher training places compelled her to close training colleges. Initially the outcry was so great that she had to handle the closures herself; as it subsided, she left them to junior ministers, allowing her to turn her attention to higher education (Williams 1996). But what matters above all is the junior minister's relations with his boss: whether the Secretary of State is a good delegator and whether he trusts or likes the junior ministers assigned to him by the Prime Minister. As usual at the top in Whitehall, it is all very personal. Heath was a poor delegator at Trade in the 1960s (Campbell 1993). A decade later, so was Tony Benn at Industry, despite having junior ministers congenial to his left-wing views. Conversely, Nicholas Ridley and Peter Walker, despite occasionally having juniors assigned to them with whom they were out of sympathy, delegated effectively. A distinctly unhealthy arrangement is when the junior minister has a direct line to the Prime Minister, like Jennie Lee who as Minister for the Arts in the 1960s used her friendship with Harold Wilson to overrule her Secretary of State, Tony Crosland, on funding issues (Williams 1996).

Civil servants observe the balance of forces and operate accordingly.

They gauge whether the junior minister has his boss's confidence or whether he is, in Malcolm Rifkind's metaphor 'a transit lounge that must be passed through before the actual decision is taken on any matter of substance by the Secretary of State himself' (Theakston 1987).

Junior ministers should not be confused with parliamentary private secretaries. Each Cabinet minister has his PPS, while his junior ministers will share one. Tam Dalyell, who was PPS to Crossman, compared himself to Sancho Panza, nurturing the minister's links with the Commons, arranging pairs for his votes, keeping in touch with opinion, planting questions with sympathetic MPs at question time, and making himself useful when the department was promoting legislation (Dalyell 1989). PPSs see something of the department's work, attending briefings for question time and the like, but only sometimes do they develop the confidential relationship with ministers that gives access to key meetings and papers. Dalyell achieved this and was periodically asked to comment by Crossman on papers (letter to *The Times* 17 July 1994). It is essentially an auxiliary post that helps the minister, gives the PPS an insight into departmental life and significantly adds to the government's 'payroll vote', for the Ministerial Code decrees that no PPS may vote against the government.

The European Community

The impact on departmental work

From the outset, Whitehall has integrated EU business into the daily work of departments rather than treat it as a separate activity. As in most EU countries, no separate Department for European Affairs has been set up; instead the Cabinet Office coordinates cross-departmental policy when necessary (see Chapter 7). While many departments have their own international division, EU work is diffused throughout departments on a functional basis; in some, notably MAFF, it colours almost all their activities.

It generates a lot of work. Statistics are surprisingly hard to come by, but the burden must have increased greatly since 1980, when Agriculture sent 2,500 civil servants to attend 1,200 meetings in Brussels and Trade and Industry sent 1,200 (Stack 1983). The tide has come a long way up the river: even quite detailed aspects of policy must be cleared at European level. A good example is competition policy. The phasing out of subsidies for pig-farming and for temporary employment measures under pressure from the Commission in the 1970s was a foretaste of the extensive vetting by Brussels of subsidies to British Steel, the Airbus project, the setting up of the new Nissan car operation and the clearance of many takeovers, most famously the British Aerospace takeover of Rover (Tebbit 1988, Young 1990). This is all quite modest compared to the way in which the EU Commission forced the French Socialist government in the early 1980s to abandon its protectionist economic programme.

Whitehall departments keep a close eye on the Commission's doings. The Commission is much less secretive than Whitehall, and the UK permanent representative in Brussels (UKRep) – a small outpost of officials linking Brussels to London – send back reports that are widely distributed around Whitehall, so that departments are forewarned of the Commission's plans, or can lobby it to initiate some plan Britain favours.

The EU Council of Ministers

The Council of Ministers is a hybrid body: it has both executive responsibility, which it shares with the EU Commission, and legislative responsibility, which it shares (notionally) with the European Parliament. In theory, there is one Council, comprising a minister from each country. In practice, the Council meets with different memberships for each subject area: a Council of Energy Ministers, a Council of Transport Ministers, and so on. Foremost amongst these are the General Affairs Council, composed of Foreign Ministers (which deals with constitutional questions and a number of key issues like the Regional Fund); the Council of Agriculture Ministers (agriculture is of crucial importance in EU politics); and ECOFIN, the Council of Finance Ministers. These meet approximately monthly, the agriculture ministers perhaps more often in the spring when prices are fixed. Other Councils – on Industry, Transport, Social Affairs and so on – convene quarterly or less often. The members of each Council get to know each other well, holding bilateral meetings and speaking by telephone between Council meetings. Something of a club atmosphere can develop.

The Council of Ministers is like the British Cabinet system in three crucial respects. First, its work is prepared beforehand by officials in the Committee of Permanent Representatives (see Chapter 3). Second, it is essentially a negotiating body, with a great deal of give and take. Third, it is largely reactive to proposals from elsewhere in the policy-making system. On most issues the Treaty of Rome stipulates that the Commission has the exclusive right to originate proposals (except in the EU's new areas of competence – foreign affairs, security and home affairs). But although in most spheres only the Commission can propose, in all spheres only the Council of Ministers can decide, which makes it the EU's crucial decision-making forum from Whitehall's point of view.

For a British minister a Council meeting runs something like this.

Beforehand he is presented with a sizeable brief by his department that explains the issues, the British government's objectives, the likely stance of other countries and proposes a line to take. This is supplemented by one or two meetings with officials. On the day of the meeting he flies to Brussels, or occasionally Luxembourg, and is further briefed by the UK permanent representative on the latest developments and on how the Council's President and other ministers are expected to handle matters. This last minute update is useful: some countries coordinate their EU negotiating stance poorly and the intentions of, say, Germany, often become clear only at the last moment.

The Council then gathers for lunch, the occasion of much lobbying of other ministers and the Commission. Ministers eat separately from officials and the President usually tries to get quite a lot agreed over the meal. The Council then commences: a huge gathering with many experts to support each minister, and consequently much noise and coming and going. A list of issues agreed at official level and not opposed by any minister – so-called 'A' points, explained in Chapter 3 – is read and agreed. Some 85–90 per cent of business is transacted as 'A' points. Any relevant resolutions of the European Parliament are noted (although often subsequently ignored). The Council then turns to 'B' points – the contentious items. Almost always these appear as draft decisions of the Council, and debate focuses on the detail of the proposed text, often with little discussion of the general principles involved.

One improvement of recent years is the demise of the deadly ritual of the 'tour de table' in which each delegate in turn gave his view. The enlargement of the EU to fifteen members made this (usually unproductive) practice quite interminable, and instead there now tends to be a freer discussion. If a fair degree of consensus emerges, the President may sum up and refer the issue back to officials to progress it. If there are substantial differences the talk goes on and horse-trading begins. The majority put pressure on the minority; a few concessions are made. The Commission appeals for consensus. There may be adjournments during which the President may speak to individual ministers, while others go downstairs to brief the waiting press.

Often the most recaltricant minister must be seen for domestic reasons to put up a fight: the President must give him time and patiently detach his allies from him. If things get really difficult he may order a restricted session, excluding all but one minister and one adviser from each country, or even a super-restricted session (ministers only) on the sensible grounds that accommodations and compromise are easier to obtain in small meetings than in large ones. Meetings can last long into the night. When he judges the moment right, the President can put forward his own compromise proposal and try to push it through. The Single European Act and Treaty on European Union have extended the range of issues that can be resolved by a weighted majority vote and, because the same Council can find itself dealing with issues to only some of which this procedure applies, they tend to behave as if it applies to them all. Yet, there is a reluctance to force votes that isolate the losers: it creates resentment, can perpetuate divisions and could cause coalition governments in some EU countries to fall. If at all possible, the Council proceeds by consensus.

The bottom line is that ministers have to agree sometime. If the Council breaks up without a decision, the issue, after further consideration by the permanent representatives, will reappear at their next meeting. As Sir Michael Butler, Britain's permanent representative in Brussels in the early 1980s, observes:

> They have got to agree in the end. They are condemned to achieve a successful outcome to a community negotiation, even if they sometimes make it difficult for themselves to present success in the Community other than as failure at home.
>
> (1986)

Tony Benn has complained of the

> continual temptation to compromise and not be difficult, to agree to something in principle and get the experts to look at it, instead of standing firm for what you want. This slithering along towards compromise and concession is something I find very hard to accept.
>
> (Benn 1989)

But, in truth, that is how the British Cabinet and its committees operate: a slow working towards agreement, narrowing the differences by discussion until the remaining points have to be forced to a decision, painful for some. The difference is that the EU lacks the final decisive element of a Prime Minister's authority, which makes reaching decisions more difficult.

The presidency of the EU Council of Ministers

Matters are complicated by the presidency of the Council of Ministers, occupied by each of the fifteen EU member states for six months, in rotation. The burden is heavy, involving chairing the Council, organising its business, providing some strategic direction to the EU's development, visiting the European Parliament to report on the Council's work and answer questions, and meeting Commissioners and key ministers. The timetable for the UK's 1992 presidency saw two heads of government meetings, seven additional meetings of the Council of Ministers (dubbed 'informal' because held in the presidency country, not Brussels), six other ministerial meetings and five reports by the presidency to the European Parliament. All this can be wearisome and difficult: as one Foreign Office Minister put it, the presidency is a hard slog through dull technical detail (Garel-Jones 1993).

The Council has its own secretariat, independent of the Commission. Its role is essentially to service Council meetings, but it does play a discreet advisory and brokering role. The Secretary-General and his staff provide the presiding minister with a summary of the position of each member country on the issue at question, suggesting where the areas of compromise might lie and helping to draft 'compromise texts'. The presidency has been compelled increasingly by the volume and complexity of business and the long gaps between each country's presidency to rely on the Secretariat's help – for example, in devising a solution caused by the crisis when Denmark's voters rejected the Maastricht Treaty (Ludlow 1993). However, the Secretariat still prefers to see itself as serving the entire Council of Ministers, not just the presidency, and for much of their policy advice Presidents tend to rely – partly from necessity, partly from choice – on their national officials (Hayes-Renshaw and Wallace 1996, Middlemass 1995, Butler 1986, Edwards 1985, Conlon 1998).

Occupying the Presidency can be a mixed blessing. It involves a lot of work for ministers and officials. It is difficult simultaneously to defend one's own country and maintain authority over the meeting. On the other hand it can be strategically useful: it is almost impossible to get a decision out of a Council against its President's wishes. Kaufman as President of the Research Council cheerfully recalls a meeting that went very badly against Britain but which, as President, he kept going until dawn when it broke up, in bad temper, without agreement (Kaufman 1980).

Some ministers have felt thoroughly ill at ease in Europe. Tony Benn spoke for quite a few when he said: 'this huge area of community business has opened up and I am not in charge of it' (Benn 1989). It is understandable. The EC has its own jargon of envelopes, directives, margins, and *reserves de fond*. Simultaneous translation does not quite compensate for business being transacted in several different languages. The procedures and the issues are complex and confusing, the culture alien and legalistic: even a proficient Europhile like Nigel Lawson chafed at 'the cumbersome and jargon-ridden nature of its proceedings, the self-conscious moral authority of the Commission' (Lawson 1992). It is far more difficult for the minister to apply his general political experience to abstruse matters of Community policy than to matters he might encounter on the British

Cabinet agenda. He must rely on his officials to do it. As they watch their officials organising and horse-trading, ministers can easily feel left out of it, perched on top of a juggernaut out of their control.

The British civil service

What is the character of the civil service through which ministers must work? Whitehall officials are not typical of their species. Most civil servants carry out executive work: tax collectors, social security staff, scientists, vehicle inspectors, prison officers and so on. Most are based outside London. Consequently, the civil servants with whom ministers deal daily are the tiniest but most senior tranche of their profession. There are perhaps some 4,000 policy-makers in Whitehall (those at grade 7 and above). These conform much more to the television stereotype. In 1996, only 12.5 per cent of civil servants in the senior civil service were women, compared to 49 per cent for the non-industrial civil service as a whole (*Civil Service Yearbook* 1997, second edition). Most are white, a situation that has improved little over recent years. Many join through the 'high flyer' administrative trainee route of successive short-term postings leading to accelerated promotion.

They are in their own phrase 'generalists', from all academic disciplines, and are not hired to specialise in any one area. Officials usually spend most of their careers in one department, although secondments to other departments are increasingly encouraged, with secondment to the Treasury or Cabinet Office particularly prized. However, they are expected to be able to take on any policy job in virtually any subject. What matters is not specialised knowledge, but administrative skills: the capacity to absorb detail at speed, to analyse an unfamiliar problem at short notice, to clarify and summarise it, to present options and consequences lucidly, and to tender sound advice in precise and clear papers.

This creates a highly cohesive, rather closed society with its own character, thought processes and professional values. Interchange with the outside world is limited. Outsiders are recruited from other walks of life to middle ranking positions, but in small numbers. Temporary secondments to industry or other sectors are encouraged, but still proportionately few in number – and those seconded do not always come back since the private sector pays better.

This system and the ethos it generates have great strengths. The senior civil service is intellectually high-powered and infinitely adaptable. It can cope with just about anything the world throws at it. It is honest (not all countries can boast the same). It is loyal, hard-working and has a strong sense of collegiality. Above all, it is supremely capable of keeping the complicated show of governing the country on the road. But left to itself the civil service would roll along on autopilot. To repeat Rose's perceptive phrase, the civil service left to its own devices will provide 'government by directionless consensus'. This is a good thing, for it causes the civil service to be highly geared up to the directions of its ministers. As a result, the personal opinions and preferences of an individual minister – especially a Secretary of State – carry enormous weight.

Criticisms of the civil service

In recent decades this generalist, omnicompetent character has faced four serious criticisms: inefficiency, lack of technical skills, politicisation and resistance to change. The complaint of inefficiency takes two forms: that the civil service is too large, and that it is poorly managed. The size of the civil service was the focus of a determined attack by the Thatcher government; by a combination of staff cuts, IT automation and market testing, civil service numbers have fallen since 1979 by approximately a quarter, to 461,000 by late 1997 (the outright privatisation of over a million public sector jobs has largely affected non-civil service sectors, notably formerly nationalised industries).

On the management front, the first criticism has been that civil servants lack the management skills needed to run vast departments and spending programmes. The 1980s saw an efficiency drive headed by Lord Rayner of Marks and Spencer, who found an ally in the Cabinet Secretary and Head of the Civil Service, Sir Robert Armstrong. They introduced devolved budget management, greater cost consciousness, efficiency scrutinies of specific government activities, delegation of recruitment and pay arrangements, training in management techniques, the hiving off of executive sections of the civil service into independent 'Next Steps' agencies and external advertising of roughly half of the most senior posts (see Hennessy 1989, Butler 1993 and, for a critical approach, Dowding 1995). By the end of the decade Armstrong could claim, with some justification, that 'the civil service on the whole stands comparison with the best of the private sector and outdistances much of it' (Armstrong 1988), although he might have added that management in much of the private sector is not all it is cracked up to be. These reforms are open to the criticism – voiced by trade unions – that in adopting performance-related pay and de-layering the top management of departments, the civil service is adopting techniques already tried and abandoned by parts of the private sector. Whatever the value of individual initiatives, however, the key point is that the civil service has been seized by the spirit of managerial reform.

A second criticism is that the civil service is amateurish and incapable of giving the advice needed in the increasingly technical business of government. This attack was most famously formulated in the 1968 report of the Fulton committee, which argued that the generalist and technical branches of the service should be unified, and that recruits should specialise in either social policy or economics (Fulton 1968). In retrospect the claims of the 1960s for social science were over-optimistic; it is doubtful that recruiting more graduates in economics or social administration would have seen Britain better through the last twenty years. At the time, officialdom skilfully blocked the proposals (Hennessy 1989), in the process also obstructing the report's prescient recommendations for better management and training. In time, some of the recommendations have been implemented; in particular, the technical and generalist wings of the service have been combined in a 'unified grading structure'. However, specialists are still not often promoted to posts previously held by generalists – a situation possibly worsened by hiving off functions to agencies, which encourages specialisation (Dowding 1995).

Politicisation

A third criticism is that in the 1980s the civil service lost its political impartiality. The origin of this complaint was the appointment of Peter Middleton as Permanent Secretary to the Treasury at the comparatively early age of 48. The Opposition claimed to detect a political element in the appointment. By genuine coincidence, almost half of all Permanent Secretaries (twenty-two of fifty-one) were due to retire within a short period. The huge reshuffle and consequent promotions at lower levels created scope for manoeuvring people of sympathetic views into key posts, and John Hoskyns, then Head of the Prime Minister's Policy Unit, pressed on Mrs Thatcher lists of 'suitable' and 'unsuitable' candidates. But in retrospect it is clear that wholesale politicisation did not take place. A 1987 study for the Royal Institute of Public Administration by a group of academics, ex-ministers and former civil servants concluded:

> We do not believe that appointments and promotions are based on the candidate's support for or commitment to particular political ideologies or objectives; style rather than political belief is important. The Prime Minister is thought to favour an active and decisive approach, rather than the traditional style which lays greater emphasis on the analysis of options.
>
> (RIPA 1987)

The closing years of the Major government saw a different complaint:

that ministers were seeking a degree of political engagement from officials. A report by the House of Commons Treasury and Civil Service Committee (1994) reported fears – voiced by amongst others the former Prime Minister Callaghan – of 'a greater willingness to contemplate actions which are improper, an unhealthy closeness between Ministers and civil servants'. While the Committee found the evidence inconclusive, it recommended introducing a Civil Service Code to protect the civil service's neutrality, which the Government duly did in 1995.

Yet, during the run-up to the 1997 election the senior civil servants' union reported a spate of complaints – twenty-five from eleven departments – from its members that they had been asked to undertake political work, including preparing material for the Conservative election manifesto and preparing political briefing on opposition policies – complaints rejected by the Deputy Prime Minister, Michael Heseltine (*FDA News* August 1996). Evidently, some civil servants still felt themselves to be under pressure but they were still wedded to their ethos of neutrality. When Labour returned to power the following year, there was a singular lack of allegations of partisanship; for instance, a 'fly on the wall' television documentary observing three new ministers getting to grips with their departments did not identify this as a problem (Channel 4 1997).

When the cry of 'politicisation' arose under Blair, it was due to an increase in the number of special advisers, and dramatised by a television documentary about the new ministerial team at the Treasury. This documentary showed the dominance in the Chancellor's counsels of his two special advisers, responsible respectively for press relations and economic advice (Scottish Television 1997) – a programme followed by press suggestions that senior Treasury officials were being 'cut out of the policy loop' (for example, *The Economist* 11 October 1997). There was also a much-remarked-on turnover of chief press officers in Whitehall departments, eight of these being replaced in the early months of the government. While some had long planned to change posts, others voiced their unhappiness at being urged to move on. Their posts were not politicised, in the sense that they were not replaced by special advisers but by existing civil servants or by external media personnel who then signed civil service contracts, but this turnover attracted extensive public comment (national press 29 May to 3 June 1997 *passim*). Undoubtedly, some of this sat ill with traditional civil service values. The outgoing Head of the Civil Service expressed himself not too worried, believing that 'the "meshing" with the civil service will occur in time, not least after ministers are moved around in reshuffles' (*The Times* 29 October 1997). Perhaps he recalled past conflicts caused by the economists Balogh and Kaldor in the Treasury in the 1960s. Significantly, the senior civil servants' trade union, the First

Division Association took it quietly. But the Deputy Prime Minister, for one, admitted that the activities of spin doctors had 'created tension' (Channel 4 1998) and in July 1997 the Government propagated new guidelines for the Government Information and Communication Service reminding it of long-standing requirements not to become involved in attacking the Opposition nor to engage in the image-building of ministers (Cabinet Office 1997c). And the difficulties over press officers were serious enough to cause the First Civil Service Commissioner, Sir Michael Betts, to warn that that the number of political appointments should not increase further (*Guardian* 29 May 1997).

Resistance to change

A fourth and more subtle criticism is that officials are conservative: not politically, but in the sense of resisting change. This has been voiced by politicians of all parties, such as Labour's Richard Crossman who portrayed himself in his diaries as battling prodigiously against formidable entrenched views, and Keith Joseph who encountered great resistance to his plans to cut subventions to industry. Such complaints have deep consti-tutional implications. Hallowed convention maintains that officials advise, ministers decide and officials then do as they are told. If they resist, they are breaking the rules.

In practice, life is more complicated. Officials' caution is rooted in two aspects of their work. First, most policy work is incremental rather than radical: over the years practices are adjusted to meet new developments but not often radically reviewed – apart from anything else, because of time constraints. To this extent, official conservatism is institutional, often subconscious, and on that account deserves to be challenged. Second, it is very much civil servants' business to ensure that what ministers are proposing is feasible. The political philosophy behind an idea is not their concern, but it is their duty to ensure that translating that philosophy into practice does not produce an outcome that is unworkable, or will contra-dict some other government policy. When Department of Industry officials set their faces against Benn's proposals for massive state intervention in industry in the 1970s, and against Joseph's wish to end such intervention a decade later, they genuinely feared that industry, far from benefiting, would suffer as a result. In each case they won their argument and extensively diluted the proposals. Similarly, officials in the Department of the Environment who urged Mrs Thatcher's government to reform the Greater London Council rather than abolish it genuinely foresaw the prob-lems that the loss of a London-wide body would cause.*

David Lipsey, special adviser at the Department of the Environment in the 1970s' Labour government, describes the official reaction to the manifesto:

> Most of these policies were ones the department's officials had traditionally opposed. Their arguments were not just of administrative convenience (which is not to decry such arguments: many policies come to grief because they are unworkable). They were arguments of substance. Security for furnished tenants? Yes, Minister, but what about the danger to the supply of relets? Abolish agricultural tied cottages? But how are the cowmen to tend a stricken beast in the middle of the night when the buses aren't running? Public ownership of land? But what do the private builders build on while they are having to wait for the compulsory purchase orders to go through? In each case, we decided that the benefits outweighed the costs and the policies went ahead...I, at any rate, did not hold it against civil servants when they argued the contrary case. Their views have their legitimacy, too. They, like the country, will have to live with the perhaps irreversible consequences.
>
> (Lipsey 1980)

When Chancellor Dalton fulminated against them as 'congenital snag-hunters' he was right: it is their duty to hunt out the snags before the machine is set running. Geoffrey Holland, a former Permanent Secretary, put it bluntly:

> Because the average tenure of a Minister is so short, all want to make their mark. As one said to me: "you are running a marathon; I am in a 100 metre sprint". So they must introduce – and introduce very quickly – something new, their own initiative, the development for which, if and when they come to write their memoirs, they will claim personal credit and a significant influence on the nation's affairs. This leads to Ministers often ignoring previous Ministers' "things" (whilst paying lip service to them), to the all too evident tendency to pull up tender plants before they have begun to take root, to lack of interest in anything other than "my thing" and, not least, to an obsession with the short term.
>
> (Holland 1995)

Civil servants, who have to live with the consequences, need to ensure that the new policy will not stall or break down after a few months.

The obverse is that when civil servants believe that the system is working badly or that some innovation is worthwhile they will tirelessly pursue the cause of change. They were keen to see shipbuilding nation-alised in the 1970s on purely practical grounds (Kaufman 1980) and were keener than many Conservative ministers to see action taken against AIDS.*

The 'departmental view'

Often, scepticism towards innovation or enthusiasm for change is linked to civil servants' own views or sometimes the department's collective view. Officials stick closely to the principle of political neutrality, but inevitably intelligent people working intensively on a certain policy may develop strong views about it. Although they were little known to the outside world, within 1960s Whitehall Con O'Neill was strongly identified with the pro-EU faction in the Foreign Office, Elizabeth Ackroyd at the Board of Trade with the push to abolish resale price maintenance, and Derek Morrell with a series of social initiatives at the Home Office. This often goes wider, and there may develop on an issue a 'departmental view' – a phrase attributed to the head of the Civil Service in the 1950s, Edward Bridges. Most departments derive from the work they do a set of priorities or values that they take for granted, and which outsiders – particularly ministers – can find incomprehensible or perverse. Denis Healey referred to this as 'institu-tional hardened arteries' (BBC 1990b). Thus the old Board of Trade was incurably wedded to the idea of free trade. The Department of Health, because it runs the NHS, is understandably preoccupied with the interests of public rather than private provision. The Ministry of Agriculture, Fisheries and Food has for decades enjoyed a close relationship with the National Farmers' Union, which makes it difficult for it also to champion the interests of the food consumer – an institutional problem solved in institutional terms by the Blair government, which decided to transfer its food safety functions to an agency reporting to health ministers.

The structure of a department

Although each Whitehall department deals with a different subject area, the basic structure of each department is much the same. Its political head is a Cabinet minister with between two and seven junior ministers to assist him, each responsible for overseeing a broad area of policy. Its civil service head is a permanent under-secretary (usually and confusingly referred to as the Permanent Secretary), beneath whom the department's work is divided and sub-divided by subject area. So, for example, the DTI is divided into six policy directorates:

1   corporate and consumer affairs;
2   energy;
3   regional policy and small and medium enterprises;
4   industry;
5   export promotion;
6   trade policy.

The energy directorate in turn is subdivided into divisions dealing with: coal; electricity; energy technologies; the Engineering Inspectorate; energy policy; nuclear industries; and oil and gas (*Civil Service Yearbook* 1997, second edition).

In addition to these areas of policy, there will be branches of the department dealing with finance, personnel and support services, together with the press office and the staff of the parliamentary clerk, who coordinates all dealings with the Lords and Commons. Of these, a minister will deal most frequently with the press office, the parliamentary clerk and officials in whichever policy areas preoccupy the minister at the time.

As observed above, ministerial diaries and 'Yes Minister' misleadingly suggest that the main policy-making axis of the department lies between the Secretary of State and the Permanent Secretary. Just as junior ministers have taken on a share of the Secretary of State's role leaving him to focus on the really big issues, so the Permanent Secretary's involvement in policy is now confined to the very greatest themes – although this will vary according to personalities, and in a crisis the Permanent Secretary will be drawn in. The growth of managerialism and the creation of super-departments such as the Department of the Environment, Transport and the Regions has shifted the Permanent Secretary's role towards resource and personnel issues. Today the Permanent Secretary can usually have no more than a passing involvement even in the biggest issues.

That legendary race of formidable Permanent Secretaries who tried to dominate their Secretaries of State, like Dame Evelyn Sharp in the Crossman diaries, seems to have died out. The key policy coordination role is more likely to be played by their deputy secretaries, who have become chief executives for their policy areas. But as the volume of business has mounted and efficiency reviews have thinned out the upper ranks of officials, even they have to lean heavily on the staff below them. The consequence is that ministers are getting an increasing amount of advice from the middle band of officials in the department: the grade 5s and 7s, who are the most likely to be called up to see the minister if he wants to discuss an issue in any detail.

Private secretaries, diaries and boxes

One other aspect of departmental life that crops up in all ministerial memoirs is the private office. Each minister's private secretary leads a team of between six and a dozen junior officials (fewer for a junior minister). They are the conduit linking him to the department and the outside world. They sift out from the hundreds of documents and people clamouring for his attention the most important and most relevant. They arrange his meetings and unobtrusively attend to take notes. They fix his attendance at outside functions and beforehand commission from within the department a briefing on whom he will meet, what he should say and – equally impor- tant – not say. Theirs is a high pressure life, in which the mobile phone and the fax machine play a large part, and in which adrenaline and the interest of the work are expected to compensate for the ludicrously long hours of work.

The diary and the boxes

The private office organises two routines that dominate ministerial life. First, every private office has its diary secretary, a junior official responsible for arranging the ministerial schedule: meetings, visits, receiving deputa- tions and the like. The former Labour minister Gerald Kaufman, in his revealing and witty book on ministerial life, warns with feeling against allowing officials to put anything into a minister's diary without his permis- sion, otherwise it gets filled with formal appointments, not all necessary, and constituency or party engagements are squeezed out (Kaufman 1980). Ministers live to hectic schedules: their time is a scarce commodity and control of the diary is crucial.

Second, the boxes. At the end of each day the private office loads into red dispatch boxes all the papers the minister must look at before the next day: briefs for meetings, folders of letters to approve and sign, policy submissions from officials, papers for Cabinet committees, assorted admin- istrative documents, executive matters requiring a ministerial decision like compulsory purchase orders and school closures, and so on. In most departments two boxes will not be unusual; three means a bad night.

The papers must be signed, or initialled, or comments scrawled in the margin by the next morning when the official car collects both the minister and the boxes. Whitehall is at pains to ensure that ministers 'do their boxes', otherwise the system clogs up. The practical effect is that a lot of ministerial decisions are taken in the small hours after a long day, and that many ministers work twelve to fourteen hours at a stretch. It is a rather inhumane system, and not surprisingly some ministers rebel against it, refusing to take papers home and working in the office for fixed hours instead.

The dual loyalties of private secretaries

Cabinet ministers generally speak well of their private offices, and seem keenly aware that their staff work long hours and take on high responsibility. Denis Healey's specification for a private secretary is a first class brain, inexhaustible tact, demonic energy and an understanding spouse (Healey 1989). A personal closeness usually develops, the minister being the focus of the private office's working life, the minister in turn relying on it to provide a professional life support system.

Nonetheless, the private secretary's position is delicate. Although the minister's assistant, he (or increasingly often she – a good sign) is still part of the department. Other officials expect him to make sure the minister doesn't say anything embarrassing, doesn't depart too far from his departmental brief, or get awkward about the policy submission that it has taken the department months to work up in time for next week's EU Council of Ministers. This causes some ministers to see the private secretary primarily as a manifestation of the department, a cross between a prison warder and a nurse (Bruce-Gardyne 1986, Crossman 1975).

In truth, the private secretary has a dual loyalty. He must explain the demands of the department to the minister and the political needs of his minister to other officials. He must gently break the news to more senior colleagues that the minister is unhappy with their paper, or that he wants them to speed up some work. Conversely, officials may press him to get a submission approved quickly, or to persuade the minister to drop an idea thought to be unworkable. Both sides may use the private secretary as a sounding board, officials to fathom the minister's mind, the minister to discover what is brewing in the department. The private secretary must face both ways without seeming two-faced. The television series 'Yes Minister' caught the relationship well, especially the delicate relations between the Secretary of State's principal private secretary and the Permanent Secretary.

Despite their pivotal position, private secretaries are not policy advisers. Their role in brokering access to the minister makes them influential in handling the flow of business, and they become more sensitive than the rest of the department to the broader political picture, including party opinion and the minister's overall standing in the government. But they are not there to offer a separate line of advice to the minister, and if they did their relations with the rest of the department would rapidly sour. They might informally prompt the minister to bear in mind such and such a factor, or to probe a piece of advice a bit further, but that is the limit of their policy influence.

The making of policy

Civil service expectations of ministers

Whatever ministers may expect from their departments, civil servants have a very clear idea of what they want from ministers: effectiveness outside the department and decisiveness within it. They need their minister to be good at doing those things they cannot do for themselves: taking those decisions that require ministerial sanction, speaking for the department in Parliament and fighting its corner in Cabinet, committee and the EU Council of Ministers. This illustrates well the interdependence of ministers and officials. Although most of the time ministers may feel that they are swept along by the machine and must struggle to assert themselves, in these few areas officials are totally dependent upon them. If the Secretary of State cannot get the department's proposals through Cabinet committees, does not secure the necessary share of public spending or will not take decisions, the department is stranded. In short, they need strong ministers.

It follows that the department's nightmare is a minister who can't make up his mind. The machine seizes up. Administration stalls. A minister who persistently overturns officials' advice is infinitely preferable to one who just dithers. Michael Heseltine saw it at first hand:

> Decisions have to be taken: if a minister cannot make up his mind, his officials may in despair try to help the process even to the point, if need be, of making it up for him. I would never belittle this process. It carries many a department through periods of indifferent political direction.
>
> (Heseltine 1987)

Almost as bad is the minister who keeps changing his mind. Sir Keith Joseph was notorious for this when at Industry, as when he approved – after much agonising – a plan for further subsidies to BL motors and then spoke against the plan at Cabinet committee. This did Joseph no good – his colleagues overruled him – and only caused confusion and delay (Prior 1986).

Ministers' expectations

Ministers' expectations of their civil servants are usually less clear-cut. They often come to their posts ill-prepared. If their party has just won an election policy preparation will have been sketchy: party research capacities in opposition are very limited, with little access to Whitehall data, and ideas are worked up by ill-paid juniors or volunteer academics in their spare time (Hennessy 1989). The gap between manifesto and reality is often wide. Shortly after taking office, Crossman complained:

> though the Labour party has been committed for five years to the repeal of the Enoch Powell Rent Act, there is only one slim series of notes by Michael Stewart on the kind of way to do it in the files at Transport House. That's all there is. Everything else has to be thought up on the spot.
>
> (1975)

After an election, ministers are often posted to departments with whose work they are quite unfamiliar, and in later reshuffles they have no advance inkling of where they might go. In these circumstances the minister switched abruptly to a new department will have only a general idea of his party's attitude towards policy in this field and little idea of how he wants to set about his job or of what he expects from officials.

So ministers either expect civil servants to amplify the skimpy proposals in the manifesto into a workable programme, or – if in mid-Parliament – to pick up the threads of what their predecessors have done. There is little evidence in politicians' writings that they try beforehand to think out how their partnership with officials will work. They just expect workable advice to appear.

Ministers as policy-makers

In his pioneering study of Cabinet ministers, Bruce Headey identified three possible ministerial roles in policy determination (Headey 1974). They are:

1 *The policy legitimator* who simply rubber-stamps what officials suggest, and defends the decision as his own to Parliament and the public. On many questions, especially minor or routine ones, this is often the sensible course; but the minister who does it all the time, on matters great and small, will not last long. Wilson in 1964 appointed two ministers who almost always did as their officials proposed, Soskice at the Home Office – easily talked into abandoning the idea of a pardon for Timothy Evans, wrongly hanged for murder – and Fraser at Transport, who made no progress with the idea of an integrated transport policy. Political criticism mounted, and both were removed within a year.

2   *The policy selector,* who considers the various options outlined by the civil servants and makes up his own mind. This requires the minister sometimes to be awkward, to overturn officials' preferred course of action, and to ask for more details of options they have discounted. Nonetheless, the policy selector works within the framework of the official machine. He accepts its presumptions about which issues are urgent, and accepts by implication its existing objectives and priorities, which may be heavily marked by the outlook of a ministerial predecessor of different political outlook.

3   *The policy initiator,* who challenges the department's assumptions, imposes other priorities and establishes new policy goals. Dramatic examples of ministers who have done this include Macleod's acceleration of decolonisation in the 1950s, Jenkins' radical liberalism at the Home Office in the 1960s, and the extensive reforms of education, health and local government by Conservative ministers in the 1980s. Policy initiation is the most radical mode of ministerial operation. It is also the most political, and ministers are above all put in charge of a department to give it political direction.

(For ministers' perception of their roles in other Western European countries, see Blondel and Muller-Rommel 1993.)

While Headey's three-fold distinction holds good, these are not mutually exclusive alternatives: rather there is a gradation. All ministers will on occasion rubber stamp officials' recommendations because there is no real alternative, or because the matter is comparatively trivial. All ministers also act as policy selectors because the machine usually offers them sensible choices. But a majority also impose their own policy initiatives on departments, and it is in this last manner that a minister will make his name. The dynamics of policy selection and policy initiation merit further analysis.

Policy selection

How proposals for change originate

The impulse for officials to put policy proposals to ministers generally come from one of four sources. First, some decisions are cyclical: certain annual events – pay negotiations, the renewal of legislation against terrorism, the funding of local councils – require regular decisions.

Second, in the course of daily administration officials may conclude that outdated provisions must be updated, or that machinery that is not working should be overhauled. The Health and Safety at Work Act, familiar to most British workers, was enacted because an under-secretary in the Ministry of Labour, C H Sisson (better known to the public as a distinguished poet) was horrified by the catalogue of industrial accidents in the annual report of the Chief Inspector of Factories and persuaded ministers to act (Holland 1995).

Third, a spur to action is pressure from an influential outside group which persuades officials that a reform is needed: pressure from medical groups led to steps against smoking and agitation from environmentalists moved the government to favour lead-free petrol. An inquiry or royal commission may report: the report of the Annan committee on broadcasting led to prolonged debate on the shape of the fourth television channel. Action may be needed to meet an international obligation – most frequently, EU legislation. Public opinion may compel action: terrorist attacks in 1974 compelled Whitehall belatedly to make the IRA illegal in mainland Britain, and near-hysterical food scares in 1989 led to an overhaul of food safety legislation.

Fourth, Whitehall has to develop policy to deal with new problems. The 1980s saw the appearance on the public agenda of such hitherto unknown or unregarded phenomena as AIDS, satellite television and child abuse; in each case officials had to put up new proposals.

The criteria for ministerial involvement

How do civil servants decide which issues should go to the minister for approval? As a matter of law, a civil servant of an appropriate grade, working within a framework endorsed by the minister, is empowered to take all but the most important decisions on that minister's behalf: the courts have variously held that an official may, on the minister's behalf, take decisions on issues as significant as requisitioning a factory and approving the equipment used to breathalyse motorists. The number of decisions that require the personal imprimatur of a minister is small – it includes approving secondary legislation and certain immigration decisions (Wade and Bradley 1996). But do officials need to refer to their minister an adjustment to the Forestry Commission's financial targets or a minor change in the procedure for appointing boards of prison visitors? In his study of Cabinet ministers, Bruce Headey identified four criteria by which to judge this.

1   *Does the issue require primarily a normative judgement,* or have politicians already made their values, objectives and priorities clear so that only decisions about programmes, organisations, staffing, etc., remain?

2   *Is it obvious what the minister would decide* in view of his (and his party predecessors') past decisions, or would an official have to exercise an unduly wide margin of discretion in order to resolve the issue himself?

3   *How intrinsically important is the issue*; i.e., what quantity of resources would be committed by a decision, how many people would be affected, how serious would the consequences be if things went wrong, how great is the probability of error, etc.?
4   *How politically sensitive is the issue*; i.e., how likely is it that parliamentary controversy (debates, questions) will be aroused?

(Headey 1974)

Inevitably all these considerations are subjective, but they are good guidelines. But because ministers are held responsible for everything that happens in their departments civil servants must be impelled to play safe and refer borderline cases to the minister – which can only add to the workloads of already overburdened ministers.

How civil servants may press a proposal on a minister

If it is decided to put the matter to the minister, a 'submission' covering the main arguments is prepared. Junior officials prepare detailed drafts for their seniors, who in turn clear the broad lines of the proposal with their superiors. The personnel and finance branches are squared. The press office advises on the presentational aspects; the lawyers are asked if there is any danger of a legal challenge. Whitehall likes to get its act together before it puts anything to ministers, to think through the detailed implications of all courses of action, to anticipate the minister's query 'Yes, but what if…?'

In his diary, Crossman complained that Whitehall used to overdo the meticulous preparation. Often, he said, the first he knew of a proposal was when a sizeable submission turned up in his overnight box. Understandably, he felt that he was being bounced. Certainly, by the time an idea has been discussed all round the department – and possibly with other departments – it may have gained a momentum of its own. The experience of other ministers seems mixed. Some report the same experience as Crossman, others report officials broaching the broad principles of a proposal first, with more detail later if the minister is interested. Some have experienced both.* Much seems to depend on the working methods of the official leading the policy's development, and the department's own tradition of policy management.

The constitutional theory underlying civil servants' advice is well known. Civil servants give ministers the options, the information and their own advice. Ministers decide. The civil service then carries out the decision. That is the theory. In practice, it would demand a superhuman detachment for civil servants, individually or collectively, to be quite so cold-bloodedly objective. First, as pointed out above, civil servants are by

instinct and experience cautious and approach radical options, of whatever political stripe, warily. Their work tends to be incremental rather than
radical. Second, departments sometimes develop a collegiate view on a
subject, a phenomenon examined below. Third, officials discuss ideas at
length between themselves before they are put to ministers. Inevitably they
start coming down in favour of one approach rather than another: it is
impractical and wearisome to keep an open mind for too long. Thus a
series of options put to ministers will be refracted through the preconceptions and instincts – perhaps unconscious – of civil servants, no matter
how hard they may strive to keep an impartial mind.

Joel Barnett, a former Labour Treasury minister charitably inclined
towards officials, judged:

> I have no doubt that most officials, because they felt they were
> working in what they conceived of as the national interest, would
> come to their own conclusions about each policy and then seek by
> every means at their disposal to carry their minister with them.
>
> (Barnett 1982)

Usually, the minister's decision will be the end of it. However, if civil
servants have developed a strong view they may resubmit the papers, plead
with the minister, bombard him with ingenious explanations. They have
the considerable advantage that there are many of them, while ministers
are few and overworked. Faced with such persistence, the minister may just
get fed up and give in.

Ministers do overrule civil servants

However, the bottom line is that if the proposal is initiated by officials
and requires ministerial consent, the minister is in a strong tactical position if he says no. The odds are always stacked in favour of the status
quo. If the minister sits tight, there is probably little the civil servants can
do. So when Lord Carrington refused to back the European Monetary
System (Bruce-Gardyne 1986) or Kaufman declined to amend the rent
freeze to compensate landlords for heating costs, officialdom was snook-
ered.

Once the minister has pronounced, officials make a virtuous parade of
necessity by faithfully doing as they are told – not as quickly or keenly as
they might have done if the minister had ruled their way, but faithfully all
the same. When in 1975 Scottish Office ministers rejected their officials'
advice not to bail out the loss-making Chrysler UK plant at Linwood, it
was to stop the flight of Labour voters to the Scottish Nationalists (Dell

1992). Despite this disreputable motive, officials loyally executed their ministers' policy. This applied even to the redoubtable Dame Evelyn Sharpe, immortalised in Crossman's diaries. Charles Hill, Crossman's predecessor, once overruled her strong representations on some issue and, assuming she would not want to draft the resulting paper to Cabinet, commissioned his private secretary to write it instead. She was livid and took over, composing a powerfully argued statement of Hill's case quite at odds with her personal views (Hill 1964).

Policy initiation

How initiatives originate

So far, this chapter has concentrated on policy originated by civil servants, of which there is a lot. But the more radical changes in policy are inspired by ministers, especially following a change of governing party. The new administration brings in commitments to change and different attitudes towards future decisions. There will be upheavals in great matters – to nationalise or denationalise, to increase or decrease trade union powers – and in small – even obscure areas such as land drainage or entertainment licensing may be affected by little-advertised pledges on rural development or noise control.

In the early 1960s Wilson's first Cabinet found Whitehall rather slow to square up to the new government's policies, the first change of governing party in thirteen years. Today the preparations for a change of government are more thorough. Party manifestos – inevitably skimpy and rather vague – are combed for meaning; civil servants are amongst the few people to read them thoroughly. The department assembles a separate brief for each party, and the incoming minister receives the relevant set of proposals for turning the manifesto proposals into practice.

Certainly when Labour returned to power in 1997, they found a civil service almost startlingly keen to prove that they had not been politicised by eighteen years of Conservative rule. After his first week in office, Tony Blair wrote to express

> my gratitude for the quite superlative way in which the Civil Service have handled the first change of Government in this country for 18 years. I and my colleagues have all been deeply impressed by the way staff were ready to work through the Bank Holiday weekend to help us make a rapid start in implementing our programme. And we have all been grateful for the professional way in which this has been done: my experience is that staff at all levels have worked constructively and

with good humour, while at the same time being willing to speak frankly where they felt that necessary.

(open letter to the Head of the Civil Service 12 May 1997)

General elections are not the only mainspring of policy change. Inevitably, in the course of a government's life ministers must face up to problems for which the manifesto did not cater. A good example of such a mid-term policy review was the Conservative government's 1985 review of social security (James 1997). A new minister in mid-Parliament may provide the impetus for change. He may radically alter a department's activities: the appointment of Ian Macleod to the Colonial Office and of Kenneth Baker to Education brought radicalism and energy to traditionally cautious organisations. More often, a new minister will alter attitudes towards a limited number of questions. As Secretaries of State for Trade and Industry, Norman Tebbit, Leon Brittan and Paul Channon pursued broadly similar policies. Nonetheless, when record manufacturers asked for a levy on blank tapes to compensate them for 'home taping' of records they got Tebbit's support, but Brittan dropped the scheme, only for it to be revived by his successor, Channon (Bruce-Gardyne 1986).

Civil service reactions to policy innovation

Officials will not necessarily be hostile to all innovation. It was widely reported that Sir Keith Joseph, the philosopher-minister sent to Industry when Mrs Thatcher first won power, presented officials with a reading list of free-market tracts. The reports omitted to mention that civil servants had asked him to provide it. Some new policies officials will welcome with open arms: for example Heath's commitment to joining the EU, and later his economic U-turn. But as described above, they will look at others askance because they think they are not feasible. In 1964 Crossman's staff resisted his plans for rent controls not out of antipathy but because they feared they would be difficult to administer in the courts (Dalyell 1989). They were proved wrong, but their colleagues at the new Ministry of Land were proved right when they queried the viability of the new Land Commission. Sometimes officials are wary of change because they believe that the government proposing it will not last: Labour Treasury ministers at the fag end of the Callaghan government found officials quietly distancing themselves from what they perceived, accurately, as a dying administration (Barnett 1982).

And sometimes, as the former Head of the Civil Service openly confirms, 'these arguments are about whether or not a particular policy should be pursued' (Young and Sloman 1982). On what basis do civil servants challenge the policy of democratically elected politicians? They usually term it tempering ideology with realism – a favourite term amongst civil servants. Sir Brian Cubbon, former Permanent Secretary at the Home Office, speaks for this attitude:

> Over the years we're all to some extent anaesthetised by the practicalities of our work and we therefore tend to see the practical aspects of idealistic policies rather clearly and it's right, I think that that view, that corrective, should be applied…[but] I certainly wouldn't wish the use of the word 'corrective' to be interpreted in any sense as the beginning of obstruction.
>
> (Young and Sloman 1982)

This overlooks the existence of a departmental ethos and view. Sir Brian's own former department provides an interesting example of official reaction to an incoming government's manifesto. When Mrs Thatcher first took office the Home Office welcomed Conservative moves to improve police pay and morale, which it saw as a problem neglected by Labour. However the department's basically liberal instincts made officials flinch from Conservative proposals for tighter immigration control, particularly a register of immigrants' dependants, an idea eventually judged to be unworkable (Stephenson 1980).

And there are occasions when civil servants oppose a policy out of collective prejudice. It is rare – Norman Fowler recalled only one incident in eleven years in which officials continued the fight after he had overruled them – but it happens (Fowler 1991). In 1979 the Home Office opposed the 'short, sharp shock' proposals for young offenders partly because it judged from past experience that it was doomed to fail – and the experiment was in time abandoned – but also because it disliked the regime as oppressive and reactionary. In 1974 Roy Jenkins, initiating proposals to outlaw sex discrimination, ran into 'more departmental opposition at upper-middle level than I had ever previously encountered' and in the end asked his special adviser, Anthony Lester, to write the White Paper (Jenkins 1991). Lester later reckoned that officials regarded the minority Labour government as lacking a proper mandate and likely to lose the following election. 'It was not typical; it did not happen for very long, but it was quite deplorable' (Lords debates 9 July 1997, cols. 690–1).

Yet, if a minister makes it absolutely clear that he is going to push through a policy despite official misgivings and has the determination to see it through, he will win. In the struggle to turn round the department he may be helped by two little-remarked factors. The first is that officials have become sensitive to the charge that they obstruct ministers and undermine party manifestos. They watch 'Yes Minister'; they are sensitive to the criticisms of those who, like Tony Benn, allege themselves betrayed by the machine. Barbara Castle's 1972 lecture on 'mandarin power' had impact (Castle 1973). Put this in the context of a profession much criticised since the mid-1970s and the civil service becomes much more self-conscious. Second, the civil service's faith in the superiority of its own scepticism was badly shaken by the experience of the first Thatcher administration. Many officials expected the government to abandon its radical approach in the face of external pressures and revert to the policies of earlier governments. Mrs Thatcher stuck to her guns (in most areas) and forced home radical policies across Whitehall. The Thatcher government's biggest impact on Whitehall may have been to alter attitudes by proving how much can be achieved by sheer political will.

Conflicts between ministers and civil servants

It is worth repeating that policy clashes are the exception, not the rule.

> In the great majority of cases, there is no difficulty because the decision is fairly straightforward, and I had no difficulty in agreeing with the recommendation put before me. It is in the small, but vitally important, number of cases where the decision is a very difficult one that a minister can have major problems with his officials.
>
> (Barnett 1982)

It is also worth reiterating the distinction drawn above between civil servants opposing a proposal because they believe it genuinely won't work, and opposing it because it runs against received departmental wisdom. In the latter case, no doubt officials are certain that they are acting in what they believe to be the public interest by defying their ministers.

James Prior, an experienced minister, lists four main tactics available to officials manoeuvring against a policy they dislike:

> They could slow it down by raising constant objections, saying that every single policy issue, however small, had to be cleared in a minute sort of way, and having endless discussions on it. [Second,] they could stir up other departments to raise all sorts of objections when it went to Cabinet Committee or Cabinet. The third thing they could do, and undoubtedly this would happen, would be to have some discreet briefing of organisations in the country to raise problems of 'Was this right?' and so on and so forth. And then lastly, of course, it somehow does get into the newspapers. I'm not saying that there would be

deliberate leaks, but there would certainly be nods and winks given that the policy the minister was pursuing was perhaps rather dangerous and not according to the advice he was receiving.

(Young and Sloman 1982)

Under these circumstances, what does a minister do? He plays the civil servants at their own game. This requires time and perseverance, and officials may spin out the game in the hope that he will either run out of patience, lose interest, give up in disgust or be moved to another job. But persistence pays off. Joel Barnett recounts one such episode when he wanted a change to the levy paid by commercial television companies. His Treasury officials prevaricated: the moment was not opportune, etc. Barnett gave them a fortnight's deadline and the department knuckled under. However Home Office officials then took against the idea and, since their minister would not overrule them, fought a determined rearguard action lasting three months. But Barnett stuck to his guns and won (Barnett 1982).

The minister can also resort to the political network. Kaufman tells of the financial rescue of a paper mill that his officials at Industry simply did not want to help. He overruled them, only to be told the Treasury would not agree, meaning (Kaufman reckoned) that the official whose advice he had rejected had persuaded his Treasury counterpart to block it.

He is now hoping that you will do one of two things: either accept defeat with good grace or, if that is too much to expect, ask him to draft you a letter of protest to the Chief Secretary...all that will happen is that your letter will go straight to the Treasury official who is conniving with your own official to do you down. He will then draft a rather nasty refusal which will in due course be submitted to the Chief Secretary, who will almost certainly sign it, since he has several dozen such matters clamouring for his attention at any one time. Instead what you will do if you are wise is to say offhandedly that you will think about it and then, in the division lobby at the House of Commons that night, get hold of the Chief Secretary, tell him the problem and persuade him to agree to your course of action.

(Kaufman 1980)

Action on the political network very effectively short-circuits the official network, for it is a medium to which civil servants have no access: they cannot control what happens when politicians gather and gossip, and are singularly frustrated when deals are struck over their heads.

This does not mean that ministers should spend their lives in conflict with officials. The most important quality for a minister to attain is to be taken seriously by officials, so that when he says 'It will be so' or 'Parliament won't stand for it' they do not waste time in guerrilla warfare. Conversely, he must learn to accept their advice, to know when to trust their expertise that this is not feasible or that that way is a better approach. An occasional run-in is unavoidable, but working with the machine towards the same end is the most economical way.

There has been only one publicised example of a complete breakdown in relations between a minister and his officials: in 1974, when Department of Industry officials fiercely opposed the radical, interventionist policies of Tony Benn. The Permanent Secretary, Sir Antony Part, went far beyond his remit in his opposition, encouraged by the Prime Minister's barely-concealed hostility to Benn. There were a number of highly unprofessional leaks to the press. The upshot, however, was that officials did knuckle under and produce the Green Paper as Benn wanted it – only to see the rest of the Cabinet expunge the radicalism from it. Within a year, the Prime Minister had demoted Benn and Part had retired after a heart attack (for a fuller account see James 1997).

Conclusion

Some friction between ministers and officials is unavoidable, even posi-tively desirable, because they are different types of people who perform different functions. Ministers are temporary and, as far as departmental business goes, amateur. Civil servants are permanent and professional. Ministers' forte is parliamentary and public performance and political brokerage. Officials' expertise lies in the smooth administration of public business. Ministers are concerned with the public acceptability of policy, civil servants with its administrative rationality. In this sense there is, as the current Cabinet Secretary Sir Richard Wilson approvingly put it, a gulf between them (*Observer* 18 January 1998). So it would be surprising if there were not occasionally conflict over policy decisions.

These conflicts are played out within a peculiar framework. In theory the minister's word is supreme and officials are subordinate to him. In practice this is tempered by the fact that there are few ministers, usually overworked, and many officials who tend – often unconsciously – to develop a collective view of their own. Yet their relationship must be one of mutual dependence. Ministers need civil service expertise to amplify their programmes into administrative practice and to keep the machine running. Civil servants need ministers to fight their battles in Cabinet and committees, in Parliament and at Brussels, and to act as the department's public spokesman and advocate. An implicit bargain has to be struck, in which the Permanent Secretary and private office are important mediators. But the system only works if both ministers and senior officials make unceasing efforts to understand each other's motives and needs.

3 Collective decision-making
Cabinet committees and the Cabinet

Collective decision-making operates at three levels:

1 Bilateral discussions between departments, at both official and ministerial level.
2 Cabinet committees of ministers (or, increasingly frequently, ad hoc meetings of ministers) 'shadowed' by committees of officials who prepare the ground for discussion.
3 The Cabinet.

This system has five main characteristics:

1 *Collegiality.* It is collegiate in the sense described in the first chapter, and is based on the premise that all ministers must accept collective responsibility for government decisions. Consequently, it seeks solutions that conciliate all interests as far as possible and that ministers can be expected to support. This requires compromise and flexibility from all involved.
2 *Issues are settled at as low a level as possible.* Given ministers' heavy workloads, their time is a scarce commodity and the system has to be geared to place as light a burden on them as possible. Consequently, there is strong pressure not to take matters to Cabinet if they can be settled at committee, nor to committee if they can be settled by correspondence or discussion between departments.
3 *A strong emphasis on administrative coordination.* Most cross-departmental transactions are concerned simply to clear the lead department's lines with other departments, to ensure it is not doing anything that would cut across their policies. For instance, when in the 1970s the Department of Energy launched a survey of the fuel efficiency of British cars, it checked first that this would not adversely affect the Department of Industry's sponsorship of the car industry (Kaufman 1980). The Ministry of

Aviation was 'lead department' for Concorde but the project also affected the Departments of Industry and Trade, the Treasury, the Foreign Office, because it was a joint enterprise with the French, and the law officers because of the treaty with France.

4   *Sensitivity to an issue's intrinsic importance.* All departments may agree on it and it may be politically unexciting, but it may cost so much or have such momentous consequences that it needs to be referred a long way up the chain. For instance, Mrs Thatcher's government was agreed on the construction of the Channel tunnel but it still went to Cabinet for ratification.*

5   *Sensitivity to the political implications of an issue.* Subjects that may not be intrinsically very important may nonetheless be publicly controversial or set political teeth on edge, and for that reason may be referred up to Cabinet or committee. This may conflict with the emphasis, mentioned above, of settling business at as low a level as possible: even if all departments concerned are in accord, it may be pushed further up the ladder for ministers to assess its political flammability.

Policy coordination between departments

Clearance by correspondence and bilateral negotiations

Whitehall officials spend a lot of time in touch with their opposite numbers in other departments, clearing with them aspects of policy which cross departmental boundaries. So, for example, there is a long-established network of officials who deal with local government finance, coordinated by the Department of the Environment, Transport and the Regions but involving all the other departments whose work local government funds: Education, Health (for social services), the Home Office (fire and police services), and Culture (arts and libraries). If a new problem bursts on the government, a new network will spring up impromptu across departments, initially by telephone, to coordinate the response.

So when a department initiates a proposal that impacts on other departments' responsibilities, the existing network will be used to sound out reactions: 'If we suggested this, what would your likely reaction be?' If there is no objection or the matter is a minor one – many are – the agreement will be recorded in a letter between officials. But where there are snags, or the issue raises a substantial question of policy, the lead minister will write to all ministers on the Cabinet committee within whose remit it falls, send a copy to the Cabinet Office (which has to keep track of the more significant inter-departmental proposals and draft a decision letter for the chairman) and a copy to No. 10.

This procedure is efficient and relieves the pressure on committees. Much business is transacted in this way, with the encouragement of the Cabinet Office; and the huge volume of correspondence between ministers that results is as much part of the apparatus of taking decisions as the Cabinet itself. Therefore – and this is a most significant point – ministerial committees act more as a network for clearing decisions by post than as 'real' bodies meeting round a table. Indeed the Cabinet Office routinely speaks of 'clearing a decision round the X committee net'.

If there are still objections, further bilateral contacts may smooth over the problem. For instance, it was a personal minute from the Foreign Secretary to the Chancellor of the Exchequer that softened Treasury opposition to British participation in the JET energy research project (Callaghan 1987). If, instead of writing, the minister rings his counterpart, their private secretaries will listen in to note any promises made or agreements reached: this saves time debriefing the minister and ensures that undertakings are not forgotten. Perhaps a face-to-face meeting will be necessary, provoking a flurry of telephone calls between officials on either side followed by assiduous briefing of their respective ministers. In any event there will be strenuous attempts to reach agreement without having to call a meeting, because ministers are so busy.

Official meetings

In theory, shadowing each ministerial cabinet committee there is a committee of officials, drawn from the same departments and serviced by the Cabinet Office, which prepares the ground for the ministerial meeting.

> For example, EDI(P)(O) prepares a monthly monitoring report on public sector pay. EDS(O) oversees the development of science policy. Both report to the Ministerial Committee on Competitiveness, EDC.
>
> (Cabinet Office 1995)

Unlike ministerial committees, the existence, membership and terms of reference of official committees are not made public until thirty years after the event, as part of the usual publication of public records. This tends to encourage speculation and suspicion about their role, fuelled by the slightly paranoid allegations of Richard Crossman who, in the 1960s, was convinced that such committees constituted a 'network of Whitehall control', used by officials to fix a policy line which was then pressed by each department upon its ministers (Crossman 1972 and 1975, see also Castle 1993).

In fact, the world has moved on since the days of Crossman and Castle.

Official committees exist in, as it were, a Platonic form to support each ministerial committee but, in these days of email, faxes and easy document copying, these committees often do not meet formally, instead transacting – like ministerial committees – a lot of business by post. Furthermore, they can be constituted at different levels of seniority. A few committees of Permanent Secretaries do exist – one shadows the Defence and Overseas Policy Committee * – but meet rarely and only to deal with what could be termed stratospheric policy. Committees of deputy or under-secretaries are more numerous and transact business more often. However, the most common type is the committee of assistant secretaries, or possibly principals, which deals with a less exalted level of problem. All told, it is more accurate to speak of 'official networks' than 'official committees'.

A key task of these networks is to save ministers' time. John Hunt, then Cabinet Secretary, wrote in the 1970s: 'The job of official committees is to reach agreement if possible but otherwise to bring out the differences to ministers' (Hunt 1977). They identify areas of agreement and pare down unresolved disagreements to a minimum, highlighting the points that remain for ministers to resolve.

This sharp definition of the areas of disagreement is important. Few decisions are straightforward. Most involve a host of subsidiary considerations. For instance, if the government has committed itself to privatising the water industry, many attendant problems emerge. Should the water authorities be sold individually or as a block? What apparatus should be created to guarantee health and safety? Should the maintenance of public waterways go to a separate body? What about the pension rights of existing employees? Should old debts to the government be wiped out? Should foreign shareholders be allowed to take control of British water companies? What will the timetable for privatisation be? What use will be made of the proceeds of the sale? Should the opportunity be taken to create a national water grid? These and dozens of other ramifications of the main policy must be sorted out.

The official network ensures that when ministers meet they do not waste time arguing about whose figures are correct or what precisely different departments' objections are. Ministerial time is one of the scarcest commodities in Whitehall and the official machine is geared up to preparing material with such precision that ministers are presented with fairly straightforward choices – preparation so meticulous that ministers (Crossman for one) have sometimes complained that options they would have liked to explore have been shut off. Thus, a matter that took months to germinate in a department and weeks to filter through inter-departmental consultation may take only an hour at Cabinet committee and, if it goes further, perhaps a matter of minutes at Cabinet.

One aspect of official coordination that has occasionally attracted the attention of conspiracy theorists is the weekly meeting of Permanent Secretaries every Wednesday morning. Limited strictly to an hour, this is an opportunity for a Permanent Secretary to raise an issue of concern to him which may have a wider application, or to explain some major aspect of his department's policy, for example, why local government is being reorganised again. It does not 'pre-cook' the Cabinet agenda and does not shadow the Cabinet's discussions in the same way that official committees shadow ministerial committees; its agenda tends to reflect Permanent Secretaries' greater concern these days with managerial matters. But it is a manifestation of a very influential network, for Permanent Secretaries are very much a collective body who know each other well and whose contacts can smooth business and propose initiatives, often in support of their ministers but also on those managerial issues of greater interest to officials than to politicians. It may be that the most important functions of the Wednesday morning meetings are to keep this network in good repair and to enable business to be transacted in the margins.*

Two conclusions emerge from this examination of official networks. First, they are concerned with administrative coordination. Ministers only need to meet when there is an essentially political judgement to be made, or when two ministers are at loggerheads. Second, this focus on administrative coordination tends to produce agreement on the lowest common denominator. The Whitehall machine is highly efficient at ensuring that one department does not pursue its interest at the cost of cutting across the plans of another department. There is a strong element of give and take that contrasts sharply with, for example, the French tradition of competition between (and indeed within) departments that can be quite brutal (see Wright 1989). However, because the departmental hold on policy is so strong, when several departments are in contention, or where a policy requires a pooling of resources, coordination tends to be confined to the minimum possible to avoid needless conflict. This is a problem explored in more depth in Chapter 6.

Dealing with urgent problems

Although the process described above is the way in which most issues progress upwards, urgent problems can blow up suddenly out of nowhere. Whitehall copes with these with great flexibility, improvising abbreviations of the usual procedures to combine coordination, speed, thoroughness, collective responsibility and expediency. The early stages of the Westland affair provide an illustration. The Westland helicopter company's problems had been sporadically discussed between the Department of Trade and

Industry and the Ministry of Defence at official and later ministerial level throughout 1985, with occasional involvement by the Foreign Office, the Prime Minister (because of an attempt to sell helicopters to India) and the Treasury. It was all done by telephone and letter, with only one or two face-to-face discussions. When matters came to a head, the Defence and Trade and Industry Secretaries disagreed over what should be done. Swiftly two ad hoc ministerial meetings were convened under the Prime Minister's chairmanship. Only when these failed to conciliate the main participants was the problem referred to the Economic Affairs Committee (Linklater and Leigh 1986, Defence Committee 1986).

In matters of great urgency the departmental minister will consult with the Prime Minister and those leading colleagues who can be contacted, by telephone if need be. This has happened quite often over the years on Northern Ireland.

European Union policy coordination

Coordinating Britain's policy towards the European Union is a rather different matter since, as explained in Chapter 1, the decisions are taken in Brussels and the Whitehall machinery can only prepare a negotiating position. The system for getting Britain's act together is well-developed and essentially the same as for domestic policy issues. There is the same pattern of inter-departmental correspondence, and of meetings feeding upwards into official committees, topped by a ministerial sub-committee on European questions – known as (E)DOP under the Blair government – chaired by the Foreign Secretary.

There are two main differences. First, given the highly technical nature of many EU proposals, the vast majority of issues are dealt with by official committees, of which there are many, and only a small volume of business is referred up to (E)DOP. Second, while normally in Whitehall the policy flow is mainly one way – from the departments towards the centre – in EU policy the flow runs both ways. Most EU policy initiatives must come from the Commission. These and other news from the Community are communicated by the UK's permanent representative in Brussels, who delights in the unlovely title UKRep, to the Foreign Office, which then distributes the information around Whitehall. The Cabinet Office, whose European Affairs Secretariat acts as the main coordinating unit for policy formulation, then pulls together a response from departments through its network of official committees. Key amongst these is EQO (European Questions, Official), which deals with significant issues affecting a number of departments, and its specialist sub-committees – EQO(L), EQO(P) and EQO(E) – dealing with legal, personnel and EU enlargement matters respectively

(Cabinet Office 1997b, Burch and Halliday 1996 illustrate graphically the working of the EU network).

In addition to this, the 120 UKRep staff in Brussels carry on a constant process of liaison and negotiation with other member states through the Committee of Permanent Representatives (COREPER) which, like the Council of Ministers meets in several different formations. It holds several long meetings each week and transacts detailed business through a multi-plicity of sub-groups: in the six months of the 1998 UK presidency, there were 1,500 sub-group meetings and 150 COREPER meetings (Conlon 1998). It prepares for the meetings of the EU Council of Ministers, thrashes out agreements if it can, failing which it refines the areas of disagreement to be referred up to ministers – very like a Whitehall official committee (Hayes-Renshaw and Wallace 1996).

Here lies a problem. Chapter 2 described the difficulty within Whitehall of negotiations between officials tending to develop a momentum of their own. With officials working at one remove in Brussels, often up against tight deadlines, meeting frequently both formally and informally, there is a risk that 'what if' discussions between permanent representatives progress so far that they begin in participants' minds to set into a firm agreement. Particularly delicate is the issue of discussing a concession on issue X in exchange for gains on issue Y – especially if the minister responsible for Y objects. Although few ministers have gone into print on the issue, the former junior minister Alan Clark spoke for many when he complained: 'Everything is decided, horse-traded off, by officials at COREPER....The ministers arrive on the scene at the last moment...read out their piece and depart' (Clark 1993).

However, UKRep sees itself very much as a representative body, acting as advocate for Whitehall departments – to whom it leaves the function of attending most of the working groups in Brussels. UKRep staff are forever commuting between London and Brussels to consult their home govern-ment (Eurostar and video-conferencing have proved a boon). The vast majority of meetings in Brussels are attended by officials from home departments as well as, or instead of, UKRep staff. The Cabinet Office sets out detailed negotiating mandates for officials and briefs them carefully on what reservations they must enter and when. If their position becomes untenable, they can seek an adjournment to allow for what is euphemisti-cally termed 'reflection by telephone'. Indeed, a by-product of Britain's precise organisation of its negotiating machinery is that it places much tighter restrictions on its negotiators than other member states.

Some of the ministerial mistrust of the EU negotiating machinery can be attributed to dislike of the whole impenetrable universe of the Community and all its works. In time, politicians have learned to play the system and even – like Norman Tebbit and Peter Walker – enjoy it (Tebbit 1988, Young and Sloman 1982). Even in the 1970s anti-marketeers like John Silkin and Tony Benn got rather carried away with it all. Silkin recalled being lobbied by Benn as he departed to a Council meeting on fisheries:

> He was, he explained, going to Brussels the next day to negotiate on the siting of the Joint European Torus nuclear fusion reactor, which he wished to have in Britain. Could I please not do anything, like using the veto, to annoy the other countries?
>
> (Silkin 1987)

It should be added that the British coordinating and negotiating machine is highly respected by other EU countries. It appears to be better than that of Italy, whose representatives indulge in brilliant improvisation, or The Netherlands where, in the absence of collective responsibility in coalition governments, ministers speak for their own departments or parties rather than their governments. The German system of coordination is poor:

> On a regular basis, it has failed to prevent the Permanent Representative being put in the position of advocating as German policy the often ill-coordinated views of at least four main departments, overlaid by the personal rivalries of Bonn and certain of the more vociferous *Länder*.
>
> (Middlemas 1995)

The British system even rivals France's tenacious and redoubtable negotiating machine, the SCGI, a free-standing secretariat a little like the Cabinet Office, but six times the size. Indeed, the French use the UK model to train their civil servants.

Cabinet committees

Cabinet committee business

The Cabinet Office's 'Cabinet Committee Business: A Guide for Departments' (1997b) – a singularly helpful and lucid document written primarily for Whitehall insiders – says:

> Cabinet Committees provide a framework for collective consideration of and decisions on major policy issues and issues of significant public

interest. The Committees meet to resolve disputes and make difficult decisions. Non-contentious decisions can usually be agreed in correspondence. The business of Cabinet and Ministerial Committee is mainly made up of:

> the coordination of particularly complex Government business, such as the legislative programme, constitutional issues and public expenditure;
> consideration of major issues of policy or issues likely to lead to significant public comment or criticism;
> questions where there is an unresolved disagreement between departments.

Cabinet Committees relieve the pressure on Cabinet itself by settling business in a smaller forum or at a lower level when possible, or at least by clarifying issues and defining points of disagreement. Committees enable decisions to be fully considered by those Ministers most closely concerned in a way that ensures that Government as a whole can be expected to accept responsibility for them. They act by implied devolution of authority from the Cabinet and their decisions therefore have the same formal status as decisions of the full Cabinet.

The Code for Ministers makes clear that:

> Matters wholly within the responsibility of a single Minister and which do not significantly engage collectivity ... need not be brought to the Cabinet or to a Ministerial Committee unless the Minister wishes to have the advice of colleagues. A precise definition of such matters cannot be given; in borderline cases a Minister is advised to seek collective consideration.
>
> (Cabinet Office 1997a)

Most ministers bring anything substantial to committee, although a minister who brings too many issues before his colleagues for their concurrence risks gaining the reputation of being unable to run his department on his own.* So, for all practical purposes, Cabinet committees are the Cabinet in microcosm. Like the Cabinet they strive for a clear decision that commands as wide a measure of support as possible round the table.

Cabinet Committee Business identifies four kinds of Ministerial meeting: committees; sub-committees; ad hoc committees and ad hoc meetings. Over the years, the Cabinet Office has developed a pattern of five standing committees that, between them, span the full range of government. Each is known by its initials (which these days tend to remain the same from one government to another): the Defence and Overseas Policy Committee (DOP), the Economic Affairs Committee (EA), the Home and Social Affairs Committee (HS) covering non-economic domestic issues, and two standing committees on legislation: the Committee on Future Legislation (QFL) which deals with the overall content of the forthcoming parliamentary programme, and the Queen's Speech; and the Legislation Committee (LEG) which vets all bills before introduction. Figure 1 sets out the standing committee and sub-committee structure established by the Blair government in May 1997.

The distinction between standing committees and sub-committees is not always clear. Sub-committees, according to Cabinet Committee Business, 'do not normally take final decisions on policy, but they enable collective discussion of issues ranging across several departments' responsi-

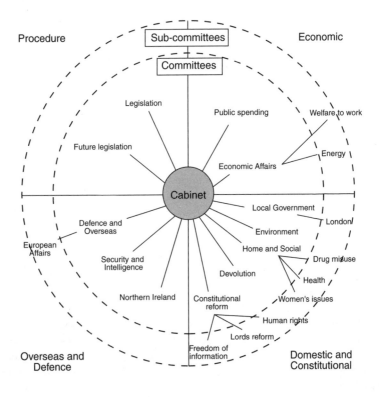

Figure 1 The structure of standing committees and sub-committees in May 1997

bilities'. In practice, the degree of autonomy varies. Since the 1980s the Home Affairs Committee has had sub-committees on women's issues, drugs and health that seem to been subservient to the parent committee, while the European sub-committee of the Defence and Overseas Policy Committee has long taken decisions on its own initiative, and the clear message conveyed by Lord Chancellor Irvine is that the sub-committees he chaired in the Blair government on freedom of information, human rights and devolution acted more or less autonomously (*The Times* 12 July 1997). A more realistic distinction may be between sub-committees consisting mainly of junior ministers, which are not seen as senior enough to take decisions binding the Cabinet, and sub-committees comprising mainly Cabinet ministers, which can be taken as having that authority.

Similarly the status of ad hoc committees is a bit murky. In theory they are temporary bodies, set up to carry out a particular task (Cabinet Office 1997b). In practice they can become long-lived, like Wilson's secretive Rhodesia X committee in the 1960s. The memoirs of Joel Barnett and Barbara Castle show that ad hoc committees covered topics as diverse as gas prices, selling BP shares, extending the job release scheme, the British Library extension, the rival merits of two types of nuclear reactor, the report of a Royal Commission on industrial democracy and dozens of other issues. Ad hoc committees are denoted by the prefix GEN or MISC, the prefix changing from one Prime Minister to the next, and a number. Thus Major's committee on sanctions against Yugoslavia was GEN 27 and Blair's on food safety was MISC 1.

MISCs and GENs proliferated like mushrooms between the 1960s and 1980s, and there is strong evidence that Wilson in particular used them to exclude ministers who sat on the appropriate standing committee or sub-committee from discussion (for example, Castle 1984). The decision in 1992 to publish the details of the committee system coincided with a sharp fall in the number of ad hocs. Trying to elucidate their numbers is complicated by the fact that many official committees were classified as MISCs and GENs until as recently as 1997. Even so, the fall from 160 ad hocs (ministerial and official) created in Callaghan's three years in office (Hennessy 1986) compared with four (ministerial) in Blair's first year indicates that their use has declined sharply. This may have been self protection made necessary by publication of the committee list: to acknowledge the existence of an ad hoc is to highlight the fact that the Government has an issue under discussion. But more significantly, there has evidently been a wish to shift business either back into standing committees and sub-committees or – for one-off issues – to use unnumbered ad hoc meetings.

Ad hoc meetings (as opposed to MISC and GEN committees) used to be a sensitive matter; until the early 1990s, the Cabinet Office was coy about their existence. They are gatherings of a sub-set of a committee's membership, chaired like a committee by a senior minister, to address a specific question not important enough to warrant a meeting of the full Committee (Cabinet Office 1997b). They have a long lineage – Catterall and Brady (forthcoming) have traced examples back to the days of Lloyd George and Chamberlain. Macmillan, usually punctilious about Cabinet procedure, used them to resolve problems: for instance, he allowed a 1961 meeting between the Minister of Agriculture, President of the Board of Trade and Chief Secretary, chaired by the Home Secretary, to agree action to be taken against the dumping of cheap East European food exports. Sometimes he used them to shape and guide the development of policy, as for example the small group that he urged his Chancellor to withdraw from the (extensive) membership of the Economic Policy Committee 'to discuss the larger questions of policy'. However, Macmillan, solicitous about the implications for collegiality, insisted that such meetings could not take decisions on their own authority: for instance, he insisted that the outcome of the meeting on food dumping be referred to Cabinet for approval (PREM 11/3225).

Such informal gatherings acquired a controversial reputation in the days of Mrs Thatcher who transacted much business in informal groups outside the committee system, whose membership she arranged to suit her purpose, and whose decisions often did not go to more formal gatherings for approval. An example was the group that undertook a fundamental review of the health service in 1988 under her chairmanship, consisting only of Treasury and Health ministers (Lawson 1992). Such groups under her leadership in the mid-1980s variously took decisions to launch a new initiative on technical and vocational education, to block the purchase of a US subsidiary by British Steel, to extend the youth training scheme to two years and to set up the 'Restart' scheme for the unemployed. When Michael Heseltine put forward an ambitious programme of investment in decaying inner cities after the 1981 riots it was an ad hoc group, chaired by Mrs Thatcher and its membership stacked heavily against him, that rejected the idea (Young 1990, Hennessy 1989). The practice of taking decisions at ad hoc meetings – though not loaded in this way – has persisted under her successors (see Cabinet Office 1997b). It was at such a gathering that the Major government took the decision not to replace the royal yacht Brittania (Seldon 1997).

In 1987 Lord Hailsham, worrying about their increased use by Mrs Thatcher, acknowledged their convenience and speed but questioned the wisdom of over-hasty decisions and the impact on collegiality (Hailsham 1987). As Foster observes in his dissection of the Scott Report, one reason for the confusion over government policy on arms exports to Iraq was that responsibility was shared between three ministers in different departments who coordinated their activities only informally (Foster 1996). A department's interests can be overlooked by a small gathering, as illustrated by an episode during the 'three day week' of 1973–4. A ministerial meeting approved an order taking various measures to save fuel. One effect was to reduce heating in schools. Mrs Thatcher, then Education Secretary, furiously complained that she had not been consulted. For that reason the order was changed (Prior 1986). Informal decision-making can also lead to politically insensitive decisions: the withdrawal of trade union membership from GCHQ staff, which caused a public row and led to a court case that proved a pyrrhic victory for the government, was taken by an ad hoc group and was not reported to Cabinet before it was announced, to the retrospective regret of the minister responsible (Howe 1994).

Mrs Thatcher's informal proceedings seem rather to have perturbed the Cabinet Office which, after her departure, moved to restore more ordered business methods; according to Percy Cradock, there was an end to 'Mrs Thatcher's highly personal methods of consulting' with 'records by the Private Secretary circulated to some but not all' (Cradock 1997). Certainly Wakeham's impression was that under Major 'the balance has shifted back towards greater reliance on the Standing Committees' (Wakeham 1993). But under Blair a great many decisions are still taken in such groups (Dobson, quoted in Channel 4 1998), although methods of business are more formal than in Mrs Thatcher's day, with a letter setting out the outcome sent by the chairman to the parent committee and the Prime Minister (for an example, see the letter reporting the outcome of an ad hoc group on representation of women in the Scottish Parliament, reprinted in the *Guardian* 3 March 1998).

Appeals to Cabinet and arbitration by the Prime Minister

In theory, ministers defeated in committee still have the right of appeal to Cabinet, subject – since the 1960s – to the chairman's agreement. However, exceptionally, since 1975 Treasury ministers have not needed the chairman's permission if defeated on public spending in committee (Barnett 1982, Pliatsky 1981). Many other countries' Cabinet systems operate a similar rule (Mackie and Hogwood 1985). The consequences of allowing an unlimited right of appeal to Cabinet are shown by The Netherlands, where as a result the Cabinet meets two or three times a week, while each of its dozen committees meets on average only six times a year. This has prompted Dutch Prime Ministers to compensate by creating informal groups of three or four ministers to decide key issues such as policy on terrorism and the government's socio-economic policy, to the annoyance of other colleagues (Andeweg 1985). In Britain, even with the chairman's permission rule, from 1945 to 1979 appeals made up the bulk of the Cabinet's workload, although even so only a small proportion of committee decisions could ever be referred upwards.

However, the right of appeal is now virtually extinct. The 1997 Code for Ministers repeats the words of its predecessor documents:

> If the Ministerial Committee system is to function effectively, appeals to the Cabinet must clearly be infrequent. Chairmen of Committees are required to exercise their discretion whether to advise the Prime Minister to allow them. The only automatic right of appeal is if Treasury Ministers are unwilling to accept expenditure as a charge on the reserve; otherwise the Prime Minister will entertain appeals to the Cabinet only after consultation with the Chairman of the Committee concerned.

This right of appeal was genuine up to 1979. But under Mrs Thatcher, while they were still theoretically possible (Armstrong 1994), they became very rare: Nicholas Ridley (1991) could recall only two in the period 1983–90. Like the House of Lords' power to reject Commons legislation, this right is now invoked only in the most extreme circumstances and signals a crisis. Significantly, Cabinet Committee Business makes no reference to the possibility of appeals to Cabinet. Instead, as Wakeham announced in 1993:

> On rare occasions, where opinion is evenly divided, the issue will be referred to the Prime Minister for decision. I try hard not to do that. He has enough to do, and it puts him in an invidious position. But sometimes there is simply no option.
>
> (Wakeham 1993)

In short, most government decisions are now taken either by correspondence or by committee.

Analysing the Cabinet committee system

Our understanding of the history of Cabinet committees may be altered by research currently being undertaken by the Institute of Contemporary History (early conclusions appear in Catterall and Brady forthcoming) that suggests greater use of committees before 1939 than was suggested in earlier publications (notably Wilson 1975). But the crucial turning point in the committee system's history remains 1945, because that was the point at which a comprehensive peacetime committee system was adopted and the assumption became that all items of business would go initially to committee, with only a small proportion then going on to Cabinet. At that point was the modern Cabinet system born. Committees became indispensable and the only Prime Minister who tried to dispense with them, Churchill, simply choked up the Cabinet system (Seldon 1981).

Today's ministerial committee system is rather leaner than that in some post-war governments, but committees are still numerous. When Major first published details of the committee system in 1992, twenty-five were listed; this figure remained pretty constant throughout his premiership, a few new ad hocs being balanced by the pruning of a few redundant sub-committees. Blair started at twenty-one, creating five constitutional reform committees but collapsing all foreign committees into one.

This proliferation of committees is not just a British phenomenon: Australia, New Zealand and Canada all have elaborate committee networks, and so do most Western European Cabinet systems, all similar in purpose and activity to their British counterpart. Ireland and Sweden are rare exceptions, having virtually no committees; as a result the Irish Cabinet is seriously overloaded and the Swedish Cabinet has to meet very frequently (Farrell 1988, Larsson 1988). Nonetheless, at a superficial count, Britain's system is a great deal more extensive in both the number of committees and the amount of time that ministers spend in committee meetings – rivalled only by France and Austria, whose full Cabinet meetings are mere formalities (Thiébault 1993). Few countries combine both Britain's strong collegiate practices and the wide outside commitments it imposes on ministers, such as their parliamentary duties (Mackie and Hogwood 1985).

Bald numbers of committees cannot tell the whole story, however. It is important to realise that the committee structure is predictive: it is based on the Cabinet Secretary's best guess of the likely pattern of business over the next few years. However, events usually create the need for new committees: in the first nine months of the Blair government, an additional seven committees were added to the initial twenty-one, on energy, freedom of information, House of Lords reform, youth justice, utility regulation, the millennium date change and the Joint Consultative Committee with the Liberal Democrats (Commons written answer, 21 January 1998, cols. 568–71). Redundant committees inevitably linger on the books, dormant, until the need for them can safely be declared to be past. Furthermore, the level of activity will vary enormously from one committee to another. Some committees will scarcely ever have to meet while, at the other end of the scale, the Blair government's devolution committee met twenty-two times between May and December 1997, with most of the meetings crammed into the first three months, considering some fifty papers and taking several hundred decisions (Irvine 1998). And, as mentioned above, a large volume of business is now cleared by correspondence.

These factors seriously undermine any attempt to measure the influence of individual ministers by drawing up league tables of the numbers of committees in which they serve. Patrick Dunleavey has made such an attempt to measure what he termed ministers' 'committee influence' by weighting committees according to their formal position in the committee hierarchy and according individual ministers scores based on the committees on which they serve and whether they act as chairman (Dunleavy 1994). The approach is problematic. First, it is difficult to define 'committee influence' in any meaningful way. Second, given the predictive nature of the committee system structure, such an analysis can mean little unless it can measure the workload of committees (including clearance by correspondence) and the importance of the business transacted by each. Third, Catterall and Brady maintain that the influence of a committee depends on its membership, not the influence of the members on the committee (an arguable point, but at least three-quarters true). As it is, Dunleavy's analysis of Major's committees generates some rather implausible results, reckoning the Defence Secretary (in terms of 'committee influence') to be the third most influential member of the Cabinet – ahead of the Chancellor of the Exchequer – and according Major's Attorney-General four times the influence of his Lord Chancellor. Until the public records are opened, the only conclusions that can safely be deduced from committee memberships are broad ones, along the lines of the press reports in 1997 that the presence of John Prescott and Peter Mandelson on a dozen committees each gave both a considerable potential influence on decision-making (national press 10 June 1997). Rather more can be deduced from committee chairmanships, a point discussed in more detail below.

More important than the theoretical gradings of committees is the fact that they operate differently in different spheres of Cabinet life. In the field of foreign affairs and defence, committees have long tended to be small and specialised (Wakeham 1993) – Major had seven of these, averaging seven members – and have met rarely, not least because the Prime Minister and Foreign Secretary have crowded diaries and are often abroad. Tony Blair brought most of the business under a single committee, DOP. In the European sphere – fast-moving and highly technical – much of the business is transacted at official level and cleared by ministers through correspondence. In the domestic and economic sphere committees tend to be larger but the frequency of meetings will vary enormously. Often those that meet most frequently are the transient sub-committees or MISC meetings created for a specific purpose, which have a spell of frequent meet-ings, then wither away. The Home and Social Affairs Committee goes through phases under different governments: it is known to have met weekly in the 1950s and in the 1980s, acting as a clearing house for all manner of issues from speed limits and prostitution to dog licences and leasehold reform. More recently it seems to have met less frequently and the volume of business done by correspondence, large at any time and usually concerned with one-off issues, has grown even further.* One sphere in which ministerial committees have met with great frequency under the Blair government has been that of constitutional reform, because of the need for political clearance against tight timetables of complex issues, such as devolution and freedom of information.

The purpose of Cabinet committees

Committees may be set up for a variety of reasons. These may be:

1 *Organisational:* for example the need to relieve pressure on the Cabinet by delegating an area of work. The major standing committees on foreign policy, economics and home affairs handle a lot of day-to-day business in these fields.
2 *Pressure of events:* speed of events forces the Cabinet to delegate day-to-day management of specific problems to committees. Under Callaghan, scrutiny of major pay claims was left to EY(P) – a sub-committee of the economic affairs committee – which met almost weekly at times of crisis, deciding matters crucial to the government's survival (Page 1978). Under Mrs Thatcher the handling of a steel strike and two coal strikes was left to ad hoc committees which she chaired and which, given the speed of developments, took most major decisions including settling the steel strike.
3 *Initiating change:* for example to implement manifesto commitments. Hence committees on nationalisation under Labour and privatisation under the Conservatives, and a well-publicised raft of committees instituted by the Blair government to carry through its programme of constitutional reform.
4 *Problem-solving:* there may be failure to agree at Cabinet on an issue that is then remitted to a committee. This happened on the issue of Concorde in 1974. Whitehall may identify a problem and tackle it through a committee; one such chaired by the Environment Secretary led to the birth of the urban programme. Public pressure for action on a problem may generate a committee to coordinate action, like the 1989 committee on food safety following several food poisoning outbreaks.

5   *Asserting collective control over an area of policy:* Attlee imposed a committee on Aneurin Bevan to ensure that the costs of the health service were held down, and Wilson chaired a 1974 committee to redraft Benn's White Paper on industry in order to take the policy out of the hands of a minister at odds with the rest of the Cabinet (Wilson 1976). In December 1997, after press reports of Cabinet disagreements over welfare reform, the Prime Minister announced that he would chair an ad hoc group on welfare reform (national press 21, 22 and 23 December 1997).

6   *Policy coordination:* the supreme example of this is EQ, the committee on European questions, which reconciles the interests of different departments into a British EU negotiating position. But committees are also appointed to bring coherence to an area of policy, especially if it crosses departmental boundaries, such as the committee to coordinate policy towards the family announced at the 1997 Labour Party conference.

7   *Resource allocation:* notably the Committee on Future Legislation, which allocates space in the legislative programme, and successive committees (the Star Chamber, EDX and PX) which have allocated public expenditure.

8   *Management:* the main example of this is the Legislation Committee, which examines all draft bills to verify they reflect the decisions of policy committees, and consider the parliamentary handling of legislation. Also into this category falls one of the more unusual committees of recent years, the Major government's EDCP, which met daily under the chairmanship of Michael Heseltine 'to consider the coordination and presentation of government policy'.

9   *Procrastination:* occasionally a committee's origins may be rooted in political manoeuvring. When the recommendations of the Committee of Inquiry on Industrial Democracy divided the Cabinet, Callaghan created a committee as the best way of burying them – with total success (Page 1978).

10 *Consultation:* under the Blair government a new species of Cabinet committee has emerged, not taking decisions but providing a forum for consultations with other interests outside the government. A Joint Consultative Committee with the Liberal Democrats was established in 1997

> chaired by the Prime Minister, with other Ministers and Liberal Democrat spokesmen attending as necessary. It will consider policy issues of joint interest to the Government and the Liberal Democrats. While Liberal Democrats are not subject to collective responsibility

for decisions taken by the Government on issues discussed in the Committee, they are expected to support positions it agrees.

(Cabinet Office 1997b)

In its first year of operation the committee met five times (amid press coverage) and concentrated almost exclusively on constitutional reform. The following year the government announced that as part of its devolution arrangements it would establish a Joint Ministerial Committee including UK ministers and members of the Scottish Executive, National Assembly for Wales and Northern Ireland administration to allow consultation on issues for which the UK government remained responsible but which affected devolved issues, and vice versa (Lords debates 28 July 1998, cols. 1487–9).

Membership of Cabinet committees

The Prime Minister chooses the members of Cabinet committees. Unlike European coalitions, where memberships often have to reflect party strengths and like considerations, he has a reasonably free hand. There are five potential reasons for appointing a minister to a committee: functional, collegial, personal, regional representation and political balance.

Functional reasons

This is the primary factor determining committee membership. A committee must include any minister with a direct stake in what is being discussed. Therefore the first three or four members of any committee choose themselves: for instance, Blair's Northern Ireland Committee included the Foreign Secretary (for relations with the Republic of Ireland), the Chancellor of the Exchequer (given the economic dimension) and the Home Secretary (because of the impact of terrorism on the British mainland) as well as the Northern Ireland Secretary and the Defence Secretary. There will always be a Treasury minister, since almost any decision has financial implications. If there is a legal angle, a law officer attends. Some ministers have had open access to all committees because of their political posts, such as the Chief Whip in the 1970s Labour governments and Norman Tebbit and Kenneth Baker as Conservative Party Chairmen under Mrs Thatcher.

Collegial reasons

In the Labour governments of the 1960s and 1970s, however, another consideration came in to play. Up to that time, committees seem to have been appointed almost exclusively on functional grounds – as witness, for example, the committee structure created after Macmillan's 1959 election victory (PREM 11/2912). Harold Wilson, however, maintained:

> It really is my job to see that the committee that works for the Cabinet is sufficiently representative, not only in numbers but in, shall I say, opinions and shades of opinion, so that everyone who is really depart-mentally concerned and one or two who are not will be involved. It is really the Cabinet in microcosm.
>
> (Wilson 1967)

Consequently, he added some ministers not directly involved in the question at issue to give the view of an intelligent outsider, and to ensure that discussion was not confined solely to rivalries between departments, as a substitute for the Cabinet's collegial role. Callaghan did the same and so – in theory at least – did Mrs Thatcher, up to the mid-1980s (Armstrong 1986).

So, at various times the Foreign Secretary, Home Secretary, Leader of the Commons and Lord Chancellor turned up on Wilson and Callaghan's economic committees, while the energy committee included at different stages the Leader of the Lords, the Education Secretary and the Defence Secretary (Benn 1989). In the Callaghan Cabinet Shirley Williams, temperamentally disposed to reconcile conflicting opinions, was often appointed to non-economic committees; by the end of three years she was serving on some twenty of them, mostly dealing with matters outside her departmental remit (Williams 1980).

Doubtless there was a sincere concern for collegiality in this approach. But it also allowed the Prime Minister considerable discretion to fix the political balance of a committee by adding as the 'impartial' members colleagues of a certain view to weight it in a particular direction. Wilson was famed for such manipulation of committee memberships. One of numerous examples was his 1970 committee on a renewed EU member-ship application where there was an ad hoc committee composed entirely of pro-EU ministers, whose existence was unknown to the rest of the Cabinet (Shore 1993). Ten years later Callaghan packed committees on broadcasting and on reform of the official secrets legislation with ministers who agreed with him (Page 1978, Donoughue 1987).

Mrs Thatcher, as she often did, imitated her predecessors' tactics but without their dissimulation. Although in the early years of her government many ministers opposed her economic policy, her Economic Strategy Committee rarely met and membership of the Economic Affairs Sub-Committee (EA) – which dealt with major economic casework – was confined to her supporters, with only one token dissident. This assumed particular importance since the Cabinet was excluded from discussing the economy throughout 1979 (Young 1989). In time she came under pressure to expand its membership and it came to number half the Cabinet. She compensated by transferring responsibility for key areas like nationalised industries and public sector pay to even smaller sub-committees with a more reliable membership (Prior 1986).

Such 'collegial' appointments seem to have been widespread only in the governments of Wilson, Callaghan and Thatcher. They are occasionally to be found in other governments, but are infrequent and are usually of a single senior minister. For instance, Macmillan appointed his Home Secretary, Butler, to the Defence Committee and the Africa Committee, and in the Blair government the Chancellor and Foreign Secretary serve on the Committee on Constitutional Reform Policy, while his Deputy Prime Minister – whose departmental brief is the environment – is a member of the Defence and Overseas Policy Committee.

Personal reasons

Occasionally ministers are added to committees because of their personal knowledge of the subject. Harold Lever, Chancellor of the Duchy of Lancaster and economic adviser to Wilson and Callaghan in the 1970s, turned up on any committee concerned with economics, finance or industry. In the same period, the economist Antony Crosland, responsible for first the environment and later foreign affairs, was occasionally added to economic committees because of his background as an academic economist and his considerable intelligence.

Regional representation

This is a factor in Britain only to the extent that the Scottish, Welsh and Northern Ireland Secretaries will join any committee affecting their fields of work; but this can equally well be seen as a functional consideration, and the creation of devolved administrations in Scotland, Wales and Northern Ireland may alter it. There is no requirement – unlike strongly federal countries like Canada (Campbell 1985) – for committee member-ships to reflect carefully the interests of different provinces.

Political balance

This, too, is a comparatively minor consideration in Britain when compared to coalition governments in Europe, where party considerations are a primary consideration in choosing committee members. Factions within Cabinets are less clearly marked and seem not to affect committee appointments unless the issue is unusually controversial. There have been exceptions: Wilson's committee on European issues before the 1975 referendum on EU membership scrupulously balanced pro-Europeans, anti-Europeans and the ambivalent (Castle 1980). Mrs Thatcher took care always to include one 'wet' opponent on her standing economic committee: first Prior, then Walker. Major retained the right-winger Howard on the economic affairs committee even after moving him to the Home Office. However these appear to have been rare exceptions to the rule.

Of these five reasons, the functional reason is dominant. This, and the decline in the practice of adding colleagues for 'collegial' reasons, now make it difficult for Prime Ministers to engage in wholesale rigging of committee memberships. Personal expertise and political balance are an occasional consideration, and regional balance hardly matters.

Though mixed committees of ministers and officials are quite common in other Western European countries (Thiébault 1993) they are not popular in Britain. Wilson and Heath both experimented with mixed committees of junior ministers and senior officials (Wilson 1967, *Sunday Times* 22 February 1976) but neither experiment was happy. Civil servants do not attend ministerial committees except occasionally to advise on particularly complex issues – exceptions have been the Governor of the Bank of England who, before the 'operational independence' bestowed on the Bank in 1997 by the Blair government, often attended committees discussing currency matters (Keegan and Pennant-Rea 1979) and the attendance of the Permanent Secretary of the Foreign Office at the 'War Cabinet' that handled the military campaign in Kuwait and Iraq.

Chairmanship of Cabinet committees

The Prime Minister has complete freedom to decide who chairs which committee. As Burch (1993) observes, this freedom is unique amongst Western European countries, most of which impose regulations for the appointment of chairmen or require approval by the full Cabinet. This power is particularly significant because the British system makes greater use of committees than most and because, although the premier will chair any committee he attends, he has time to attend only perhaps two or three a week (Donoughue 1988). Since at minimum all premiers chair (invariably) the Overseas and Defence Committee and (more often than not) the Committee on Economic Affairs, he can only chair a limited number of other gatherings. Therefore, to chair most committees, he appoints senior colleagues, chosen for one of five reasons: functional, collegial, oversight, personal, or political reliability.

Functional

The logical move would be to appoint as chairman the 'lead' departmental minister, who is most involved in the subject. However he is open to the temptation of using his chairmanship to favour his own ends. As Home Secretary Roy Jenkins blatantly used his chairmanship of the Home Affairs Committee in 1974 to crush the objections of the Lord Chancellor and Foreign Secretary to granting an amnesty to illegal immigrants by administrative rather than legislative means; adding insult to injury, he refused them leave to appeal to Cabinet (Castle 1980). Similarly, the Agriculture Secretary deeply regretted Prime Minister Wilson's relinquishing of the chair of the European Affairs Committee to his Foreign Secretary, greatly increasing the latter's tactical strength *vis-à-vis* Agriculture (Silkin 1987). Consequently, lead ministers usually chair only minor or uncontroversial committees; for instance the Environment Secretary, responsible for public buildings, chaired a committee on the projected Queen Elizabeth II conference centre in Westminster.

Collegial reasons

Consequently, for reasons of fairness and collegial harmony, the near-universal rule is that major committees are chaired by senior colleagues, often with lighter departmental responsibilities, such as the Lord Chancellor, or non-departmental ministers such as the Leaders of the Lords or Commons. In the Major and Blair governments three-quarters of committees were chaired by such 'neutral' ministers. The main permanent exceptions were the Foreign Secretary's chairmanship of the sub-committee on Europe and the Chancellor's chairmanship of the committee on public spending. Wilson recalled of his first government:

> I had always maintained that the strength of a government lay in its non-departmental ministers. They are the half-back line of modern administration; they get few chances to score goals or secure massive publicity, but without them the team could never prosper.
>
> (Wilson (1971)

Every Prime Minister needs several trustworthy lieutenants to fulfil this role. Under Eden and Macmillan Butler became so vital that, in Enoch Powell's words, when he was absent from the chair of the Home Affairs

Committee 'It was as if government itself came to a standstill!' (Horne 1988). Heath relied on his Home Secretaries, first Maudling, later Carr. In his last stint Wilson found in Edward Short a successor to Bowden. Mrs Thatcher relied above all on Whitelaw, a gifted chairman with a keen nose for trouble and a knack of coaxing consensus out of his colleagues. He was one of the few colleagues whose judgement Mrs Thatcher deeply respected: 'time and time again he provided that mixture of ballast and yeast which secured second thoughts – and often ensured that they were fruitful' (Howe 1994). The importance of these key chairmen was demonstrated when Whitelaw retired: the allocation of his chairmanships between colleagues made front page news and the beneficiaries were tagged the rising stars of the Cabinet (for example, *Daily Telegraph* 5 February 1988).

Oversight reasons

Occasionally this role is developed further and a senior minister is given the oversight of a set of committees spanning a whole policy field. This was true of Michael Heseltine during his period as Deputy Prime Minister from 1995 to 1997 when, with responsibility for competitiveness policy and the coordination and presentation of government policy, he chaired committees on competitiveness, presentation, the environment and local government. Similarly, under Blair, Lord Chancellor Irvine was given responsibility for overseeing the Government's ambitious constitutional reforms, and used his chairmanship of committees on devolution, human rights, freedom of information and reform of the house of Lords to drive forward the programme with remarkable speed.

Personal reasons

Occasionally a minister is made chairman because of his particular skills and expertise. Whitelaw presided over committees when Home Secretary even when his department had a substantial stake in the outcome, and Lever chaired some committees on micro-economic issues because of his expertise and ingenuity in the field. The availability of such personalities is, however, uncommon.

Political reasons

Inevitably, political considerations override all else at times. Wilson neutralised Tony Benn in 1975 not only by moving him from Industry to Energy but by keeping on as chairman of the Energy Committee Eric Varley, who had swapped places with Benn and taken his place at Industry

(Page 1978). Mrs Thatcher weighted committees on privatisation, pay policy and nationalised industries in the Treasury's favour by appointing the Chancellor as chairman (Hennessy 1986).

A committee chairman is required to embody the underlying principles of the system: the ever present – if unspoken – concern to preserve the collegiate ethos, the stress on collective responsibility, a determination to settle matters at committee rather than congest the Cabinet agenda with them, and yet sensitivity to an issue's political delicacy. A good chairman must be efficient in the dispatch of business and able to guide arguing colleagues to a decision by which all can abide. But consensus at any price is not enough. Like the Prime Minister in Cabinet, the chairman must keep a weather eye for the broader implications of any decision and be sensitive to political consequences that individual ministers, immersed in their departments, might overlook. Therefore chairmen, particularly of committees covering a wide span of policy, must be familiar with developments within their sphere and question the implications of any proposal. Edward Short would question relentlessly the minister advancing a paper (Kaufman 1980) and Whitelaw was not shy on occasion to voice his fears and, if necessary, insist on his own authority that a matter go to Cabinet.*

Cabinet committees at work

Committees do not meet to any pre-prepared rota, but as and when business requires. The Cabinet Secretariat carefully coordinates the flow of business and every week the Cabinet Secretary meets with his deputies to discuss a projection of business for the next three weeks, together with a more speculative forecast for the medium term.* But to a large extent their planning must be reactive, driven by the business put forward by individual departments.

Any meeting chaired by the Prime Minister will meet in the Cabinet Room at No. 10. Otherwise Cabinet committees usually meet in the Cabinet Office, which boasts several fine eighteenth century conference rooms, notably the Old Treasury Board Room, a magnificent Palladian apartment with furniture (and a throne) dating from the reign of George II. If Parliament is sitting, the committee may meet in one of the (rather drab) Ministerial conference rooms beneath the House of Commons. Proceedings are pretty formal in tone, although in the Labour governments of the 1970s, and again since 1997, ministers have addressed each other by their Christian names. There is a formal structure of agenda, papers and minutes, and discussion is confined to the specific issues outlined on the agenda, and will not range over a wider field, except perhaps for a discussion of the public presentation of the decision.

However, the nature of the discussion is often different in committees. They have the time to go into subjects in greater depth than the Cabinet. The discussion may be more technical because a higher proportion of those present are departmentally involved. More time may be spent on the technical aspects and less on the political. The atmosphere is also different. There are fewer present than at Cabinet, and it is an observable law of meetings that a higher number of people speak at small meetings than at large ones. Small meetings also tend to encourage better discussion. Certain memorable chairmen, such as Butler and Whitelaw, were often more relaxed in style than their Prime Ministers.

Before the committee meets, the ministers in contention may well lobby friendly colleagues whose voices may swing the balance in discussion. Key amongst these is the chairman. If he is senior and influential, he is the person to get on your side – in the 1980s, the minister who squared William Whitelaw was usually reckoned to have sewn up the meeting – but the tougher the fight a minister expects, the wider he can be expected to lobby, phoning colleagues, waylaying them in the Commons, perhaps reminding them that they owe him a favour, or offering in exchange his support for one of their proposals. In short, there is the same sort of trafficking that precedes many political meetings outside government.

Committees provide an opportunity for junior Cabinet ministers to make their mark, particularly as the importance of the Cabinet as a decision-making body has declined. If a Cabinet minister can establish himself as a voice to be reckoned with at committee, his colleagues will have to seek his support, which gives him a supply of credit to call on when next he needs their help. Since the 1970s ministerial reputations have been made in committee rather than in Cabinet. Under Mrs Thatcher in particular, committees provided an outlet for the ambitions and energies of younger politicians who were surprised and disappointed by the Cabinet's limitations as a decision-making forum.*

The Cabinet

It is not easy to generalise about the Cabinet. Its mode of operation varies according to the Prime Minister, the balance of personalities amongst senior ministers, the stage in the electoral cycle and the pressures of external events. However, it is possible to make general observations about the Cabinet's operations from 1945 to 1979, during which period the system remained fairly stable, and since 1979, a period in which it has undergone a long change that may not yet be complete. Essentially, up to 1979 Cabinet meetings were quite long and consisted mainly of specific issues referred up by committees. Since 1979 the Cabinet has taken fewer decisions on specific issues and its meetings have become a broader but less structured discussion of current developments. The two periods are best examined separately.

The Cabinet from 1945 to 1979

The Cabinet has always been an immensely flexible body: if required, meetings can be – and have been – held on any day or at any time, can be convened at a few hours' notice by telephone calls, or held wherever is most convenient (although these days the Prime Minister is more likely to convene an ad hoc gathering of key players in emergencies, rather than the full Cabinet). All that is needed to call a Cabinet is a summons issued on the Prime Minister's instructions by the Cabinet Secretary. Meetings are usually held at No. 10 Downing Street; occasionally during the parliamentary session they may be held at the Prime Minister's room at the House of Commons but this room is small and ill-suited to the purpose.

Ministers sit round a long, coffin-shaped table, the Prime Minister at the centre of the side facing the windows over the No. 10 garden, his back to the famous portrait of Walpole, with the Cabinet Secretary immediately on his right. His most senior colleagues sit on his left and opposite him. Other ministers are allocated seats according to seniority: the more senior a minister is, the closer he sits to the centre, with the most junior at the far extremities of the table.

In the period 1945–79 the Cabinet held at least one regular weekly meeting, usually on a Thursday from roughly ten o'clock until one. However these were often supplemented by extra meetings, normally on Tuesday, if the volume of business required it – which during the parliamentary session it often did – or if a crisis or major issue required a series of special meetings. Two meetings a week placed a severe burden on ministers and Wilson tried to restrict the frequency to one a week, not always successfully. Wilson also held occasional all day meetings at Chequers on special subjects such as the applications to join the EU in the 1960s and on government strategy and devolution in the 1970s, but insisted on treating these as 'second reading' discussions with any conclusions confirmed by a regular Cabinet meeting (Walker 1972, Wilson 1976).

It is significant that although the volume of business grew steadily after the war, it proved impossible to increase the frequency of Cabinet meetings commensurately. Between 1919 and 1938 the Cabinet averaged seventy meetings a year (calculated from Wilson 1972). In the 1950s and 1960s the annual average was up to ninety (Walker 1972) and in the 1970s this average fell slightly. The growth in size of the Cabinet, mentioned in Chapter 1, was also a significant factor; if every member of a Cabinet of twenty-two speaks for just three minutes on an issue, the discussion will last well over an hour. In consequence, a much smaller proportion of decisions was settled by Cabinet and much more was remitted to committees. Admittedly the efficiency with which business has been dispatched has improved as the century has progressed, but not sufficiently to compensate for the reduction in meetings.

Items of report

Until 1979 a normal Cabinet had an agenda of four or five items and fell into two parts: standing items on which there were oral reports, and individual policy items on which there were papers. The standing items were always parliamentary business and foreign affairs. (Heath added EU business and Northern Ireland as standing items: his Labour successors abandoned this.) First, the Leaders of both Houses detailed business for the coming week and the Chief Whip stated whether a two, three or four-line whip would be imposed. Ministers did little more than note what was said and perhaps agree the government speakers for major debates (Walker 1972, Wilson 1976). Then the Foreign Secretary gave a brief 'tour d'horizon', fairly superficially given the scope of the topic and the pressures of time. He and the Prime Minister usually decided beforehand what to disclose and what to keep quiet (Walker 1972). The Foreign Secretary's report is too brief and sketchy to be of much use to ministers: Lawson complained that it 'seldom revealed anything that was not already well known to the attentive newspaper reader' (Lawson 1992), and Edward Boyle judged that 'Foreign affairs can be the least invigorating part of Cabinet business…it is very seldom that one has a really good foreign affairs debate' (Kogan 1971). But this report lasts long enough to cut substantially into the time available for other business.

What purpose did these discussions serve? They were not executive; in all four spheres if a substantive discussion was needed the subject would be taken as a separate agenda item with a paper circulated in advance. They were items for information, discursive rather than decisive. They gave practical expression to the principle of collective responsibility: leading ministers reported developments to their colleagues, answered questions and listened to comments. Yet collective Cabinet opinion must usually have had little impact on these questions: these items were brief and ministers were heavily discouraged from raising new subjects. Still, the views voiced gave the reporting minister a sense of how colleagues saw issues, warned them of reservations and gave them a feel for the political atmosphere amongst their colleagues. The Cabinet was acting here as a sounding board, setting the general boundaries of political tolerability within which the policy must develop. It was exercising influence rather than control.

Items for decision

The second part of the agenda consisted of items, with papers, for decision. These appeared either because, despite agreement at committee, they were intrinsically or politically important enough to need higher-level discussion, or because ministers disagreed at committee and an appeal had been allowed. The first kind included certain regular annual items often taking up most of a Cabinet meeting: fixing annual public expenditure limits, approval of the Queen's Speech at the opening of Parliament, and so on. White and Green Papers, bills and major announcements usually came to Cabinet under Wilson and Callaghan who insisted on going through them page by page to ensure that no minister could subsequently deny collective responsibility for their contents (Wilson 1976, Barnett 1982).

Some of these items might be decisions agreed at committee but that ministers felt must come to Cabinet because they were important or controversial. Antony Crosland, in two years at Education, took only two items to Cabinet: a circular on comprehensive education and the Public Schools Commission. Neither caused much disagreement at committee but both went to Cabinet because they were bound to cause rows in Parliament (Kogan 1971). Occasionally items of intrinsic importance but no political interest ended up at Cabinet – for example Crossman recorded his impatience at sitting through a discussion on the membership of police authorities, a matter of legal importance but in the 1960s of no political sensitivity (Crossman 1976). It sometimes happened that a course of action was forced by events on the government such as the decision to send the Special Air Service to South Armagh in 1975 in response to terrorist attacks. If no other realistic alternative was available the Cabinet would assent without much comment.

Such undisputed questions, reported mainly to keep colleagues informed of major or sensitive issues, and to bind them to the decision, might not generate much discussion, and what talk there was might concentrate more on presentation than on substance. Consequently some highly important items could go through more or less on the nod. Castle's diary for March to September 1974 records the Cabinet dealing in such a perfunctory way with the Sex Discrimination Bill, White Papers on land policy and Northern Ireland, plans for a national superannuation scheme, a major statement of policy on North Sea oil and proposals for a voluntary pay policy. Not only was there little discussion but when the sponsoring ministers explained their proposals at any length their colleagues complained (Castle 1980).

Occasionally the usual agenda would be disrupted by a sudden crisis requiring special meetings or forcing the Cabinet to scrap its scheduled business, for instance an overseas crisis: Suez, the USSR's invasion of Czechoslovakia and the Six Day War all required long discussions at short notice. Economic crisis can also occasion hastily convened meetings to agree emergency measures to prop up the currency. In 1967 Wilson had a dummy agenda circulated, only to scrap it at the meeting and announce that he wished to devalue sterling (Castle 1984).

Cabinet discussions

However the bulk of the Cabinet agenda in the period 1945–79 comprised appeals by defeated ministers against committee decisions. Such discussions followed a set pattern. A paper was circulated with the agenda by the lead minister: usually a short summary – two pages or so – with detailed supporting information relegated to appendices. The Prime Minister asked either the chairman of the Cabinet committee or the lead minister to introduce the subject, preferably as tersely as possible. He would then invite opposing ministers, who may also have put in papers, to speak. If there were public spending implications and the Chancellor was not one of the main protagonists, he would be invited to speak next. After these set piece contributions the Prime Minister would invite the views of other colleagues.

The crucial moment came when the ministers not party to the dispute gave their views. This was the stage that gave meaning to the concept of collective responsibility. They were not being asked for their expert opinion. Probably they would know little more than was set out in the Cabinet papers. The Defence Secretary would lack intimate knowledge of local government finance in Scotland, unless he was a Scottish MP. Nor would the Scottish Secretary know much about the rival merits of different types of naval patrol vessel, unless he chanced to be a former Defence minister. Neither had been a party to the protracted inter-departmental negotiations that preceded the appeal to the Cabinet, and in all probability each had had time only to skim through the papers on the agenda.

These ministers were expected to screen the proposal for its good sense and public acceptability. They provided a litmus test of a policy's political competence. Often they would ask 'How will we explain this to our constituents?' – a good reason for requiring ministers to be also members of Parliament. This process allowed a minister to test his ideas, in the privacy of the Cabinet room, against the instincts and political experience of his two dozen most senior colleagues before launching them on Parliament and the public.

Douglas Hurd identifies as good generalists Mrs Thatcher 'no human subject was alien to her', Nigel Lawson 'fearless and highly intelligent', and Norman Tebbit (Hurd 1997). Enoch Powell recalled:

> My experience as a departmental minister in the Cabinet was that occasionally I had to take something to my colleagues in Cabinet. But before I took it to them I always used to feel 'This is a waste of time. Why on earth should I have to bother with putting this to these people. After all I've been through all this, I've worked through every aspect of it, I really understand the ins and outs of the subject, why should I talk to twenty people about it who really couldn't care and don't know about it.' And there was never a case when I'd taken anything to Cabinet but I wasn't grateful afterwards that I had had to do so, because they'd ask me questions which I hadn't asked myself. They'd ask the questions which are asked by people who aren't responsible, by people who have to meet questions from the public, the questions 'But what do we say when…?'
>
> (BBC 1990b)

As these 'non-involved' ministers gave their views and the ministers in conflict responded, a collective view slowly took shape: a combination of policy considerations, personality, instincts, outside pressures, the internal balance of forces of the Cabinet, the atmosphere of the meeting, a tangle of practical, political and personal factors which combined in a final decision that all ministers felt they could accept, albeit with varying degrees of enthusiasm, without feeling compelled to resign.

Ministerial discussions: balancing politics and logic

There is no objective yardstick for measuring the relative importance of the various factors involved: technical, financial, parliamentary, presentational; the balance of, say, national defence versus national industry. Often the Cabinet must choose between completely disparate priorities: should we spend more on roads or on agriculture? Should we negotiate with terrorists? To which countries do we refuse to sell weapons and at what cost to our armaments industry? For this instinctive judgement civil servants are dependent on ministers. In this sense officials are the technical or rational part of the machine, politicians the instinctive or irrational part.

Politics is as much about instinct and prejudice as about logic and analysis. Ministers exist to inject this element into the rational but colour-less decision-making of Whitehall. After six years in government Diamond judged:

> Logical argument does indeed play an important and persuasive part, but it does not suffice…personality, emotion, persuasiveness and the feeling of one human being for another all play their additional part.…A slip in the presentation of a case or an impatient comment may get a discussion going in a very different direction to the one intended; and one cannot recall the spoken word. The order of speaking may affect the issue: at a crucial stage in the argument when the issue is in the balance, a strong and authoritative intervention by A may succeed in pushing the argument in the desired direction. But if at that point B is called to speak and makes an equally strong and authoritative speech in the other direction, by the time A puts his view forward opinions may have hardened sufficiently to be unaffected by A's arguments. It is simply too exhausting to hold an open mind about issue after issue: at a certain stage the mind seeks relief in coming to a conclusion.
>
> (Diamond 1975)

The Cabinet at work: formulating a decision

Framing a decision from the disparate contributions was difficult. There was rarely a yes or no choice: there were ifs and buts and qualifications. Like as not, the eventual decision would be 'yes, as long as…' and tried to accommodate most of the stronger reservations expressed. This is the inevitable consequence of a collegiate, consensual system. The Crossman and Castle diaries abound in such outcomes. A typical one occurred in 1965 when the Minister for Technology asked for a three year preference for placing computer orders with British firms. The Department of Economic Affairs opposed this. Eventually the Cabinet agreed to a 25 per cent preference only, on condition – at the insistence of other ministers – that the government gained a share in the equity to prevent corruption; and on the Prime Minister's suggestion a Cabinet committee was set up to plan computer orders (Castle 1984). Douglas-Home's Cabinet decided to abolish retail price maintenance but wrote in a right of appeal for manu-facturers (Lawson and Bruce-Gardyne, 1976). The 1974 decision to produce only sixteen Concorde aircraft was a compromise between outright cancellation and the larger programme advocated by Tony Benn and the French government of Jacques Chirac (Castle 1980). And every round of Cabinet adjudications on departmental spending limits ended in some form of compromise.

The delicate task of framing the Cabinet's decision was up to the Prime Minister. The Cabinet did not vote, except on trivial procedural matters. First, there was rarely a straight yes or no choice. Second, a formal vote encouraged divisions and diluted the sense of collective responsibility, and the voting pattern might leak to the press. Finally, the Prime Minister had to take into account not only the numbers on either side but also the weight of opinion 'and by weight I mean the views expressed by some senior members of the Cabinet, carrying more weight than the views that are put forward by others' (Heath and Barker 1977). Wilson noted 'A Prime Minister's power when it comes to summing up a Cabinet discussion is enormous, provided that the chairman remains sufficiently detached and uncommitted' (Wilson 1971). It might be more accurate to say 'as long as he appeared detached' since by keeping his views to himself he could without reproach mould the discussion to a conclusion that suited him.

In many Cabinet debates few ministers spoke. Perhaps the issue was of crucial importance to the departmental ministers concerned but the rest of the Cabinet was indifferent. An issue might be so complex that few ministers had the time or inclination to get to grips with it – a notoriously incomprehensible instance being the EU's common agricultural policy. In such cases the ministers in contention would do almost all the talking, a few others might comment and the Prime Minister would suggest a formula for settling the matter.

However any Cabinet is a profoundly political gathering. If an issue stirred ministers' political instincts, it could lead to a serious debate. It might be a subject of great importance, or it might in objective terms seem trivial but be of doctrinal importance to ministers. Either way they could generate classic debates which genuinely exercised Cabinet control over a policy.

The reactive nature of the Cabinet 1945–79

For all this, there was a serious problem in the Cabinet system after the Second World War, deriving from a heavy workload and the growth of the committee system. The Cabinet was an entirely reactive body, and had been so long before 1945. To what extent the Cabinet ever took the initiative on policy issues, rather than responding to initiatives proposed by individual ministers, is open to question. However, in the nineteenth century when it was smaller, more cohesive, less burdened and its members met – formally and informally – more often, this must have allowed it some greater role in identifying problems requiring action and shaping policy as it evolved.

The growing workload and proliferation of committees as the twentieth

century progressed left the Cabinet only reacting to the proposals of ministers or committees. It rarely initiated action; at most, it might refer a
problem to a committee for study and report back. It did not generate
proposals, it responded to them. The Cabinet's power became essentially
negative: it could block, amend or qualify proposals but did not itself
initiate policy. The Cabinet was, and is, a brake, not a dynamo.

It was not inevitable that the Cabinet should evolve in this way. Certain
European Cabinets meet very frequently: the Dutch Cabinet spends
between 20 and 30 hours a month in session; so do Scandinavian
Cabinets, if informal sessions are taken into account, compared with 6 to 9
hours a month for their French and British counterparts (Andeweg 1993).
As it was, however, the framework and content of the Cabinet's discussions
were determined by inputs from its committees, and issues brought to it
often had been narrowed down to the point where only one facet of a
proposal might be discussed. Thus it might arbitrate between the Treasury
and the Home Office over the costs of reorganising county police forces
without ever discussing the fundamental question: should these forces be
merged or not? The discussion would probably be brief and partial.

In addition, by the time an issue had reached the Cabinet it might have
gained irreversible momentum. Lord Hailsham observed:

> On matters of importance the Cabinet as such is usually consulted
> fairly late in the day. The ground has usually carefully been prepared
> by discussions between civil servants, correspondence between minis-
> ters, informal meetings, Cabinet committee meetings…by the time the
> Cabinet is brought in as a whole, it may well be that only one decision
> is possible, even when, had it been consulted at the outset, the policy
> would have been wholly unacceptable.
>
> (Hailsham 1978)

So, the Cabinet became a more reactive body, confirming and
approving – and sometimes rejecting – decisions. There grew up a natural
reluctance amongst participants, having been through a subject once in
committee, to reopen it at Cabinet, especially if this challenged a policy
painstakingly agreed. Increasingly in the 1960s and 1970s, ministers came
to regard the Cabinet as a forum to be informed in general terms of what
was being done, but which should not necessarily question a decision
within the remit of one of its committees. In the Wilson government of
the 1970s colleagues 'not in the know' complained about committees
taking decisions without reference to Cabinet, particularly in the economic
and public expenditure spheres, but to no great avail (Elwyn Jones 1983).

Surprisingly some ministers would happily leave highly controversial matters to committee. In 1966 the government decided to buy F111 aircraft and to continue a role east of Suez – both subjects that divided the Labour party. When the Cabinet considered the White Paper prepared by the DOPC

> it soon became clear that all the details were now cut and dried...so the whole thing was fixed. All Cabinet could do was express opinions and influence to some extent the general tone of the white paper by drafting amendments. Of course there were some ministers like Barbara Castle who took up postures of protest. But the rest of us felt that there was nothing that we could do and that the procedure under which we had been excluded was not unreasonable. Fourteen of our twenty-three members of Cabinet are members of the Defence Committee. To the preparation of this white paper this fourteen had devoted nineteen meetings and two Chequers weekends. After all this, it was natural enough that they should expect Cabinet to give formal authorisation to the recommendations that they had worked out.
>
> (Crossman 1975)

Many ministers in many Cabinets would have agreed with that, considering that as long as the Prime Minister and the appropriate departmental ministers agreed, it was not for others to argue.

The Cabinet since 1979

The decline of the Cabinet as a decision-making body

In the 1980s the system changed further. Mrs Thatcher gradually but radically transformed the Cabinet's role. Initially she continued the system inherited from her predecessors: the Cabinet met weekly, with papers, and took decisions on key issues. However, it was deeply divided on economic and social policy. Mrs Thatcher was frequently in a minority amongst her colleagues. A skilful Prime Minister can dominate a large meeting more easily than a small one. He can also use meetings to educate colleagues to face what the premier sees as unshirkable realities: we must go into Europe, we must cut public spending. But Mrs Thatcher was less artful and more direct than her predecessors. Consequently, she found herself summing up against the mood of the meeting, and on occasion was overruled, for example on proposals for spending cuts in 1981.

Mrs Thatcher simply moved the fight to different battlefields. The Cabinet met less often and those meetings were briefer. Often major issues were kept away from it completely. If this proved impossible they were presented to Cabinet as matters decided by committee in which the Cabinet was invited to acquiesce, preferably without argument. Increasingly, she confined business to Cabinet committees or ad hoc meetings, the latter of which she could more easily turn in her favour by slanting their membership. As the dissident 'wets' left the Cabinet – most were gone by 1983 – she stuck with the new system, and if anything took it further; ministers with a tangential departmental interest in a subject could not always be certain of being involved in meetings that discussed it.

By the mid-1980s the presumption that committees and not Cabinet were the rightful bodies to take decisions was well established. The Home Affairs Committee in this epoch met weekly and operated virtually as a sub-Cabinet for domestic issues.* The Economic Affairs committee often met just before or just after meetings of the Cabinet, which was informed only in broad terms of what had been decided on its behalf. In February 1986, when the Cabinet was deeply divided over Ford's bid to take over Austin Rover (a bid supported by the Prime Minister), a Cabinet meeting in which the weight of opinion was strongly against the takeover was limited to one hour and was not allowed to come to a decision. The final word lay with a lengthy meeting of the Economic Affairs Committee, held in the Cabinet room as soon as the Cabinet dispersed, which in the event decided to block the sale (*The Times* 7 February 1986, Fowler 1991). One bizarre impact of the assumption that Cabinet committees were the proper locus for decision-making was that, when they considered issues affecting many departments, or of high political sensitivity, up to four-fifths of the Cabinet might attend.

The impact on the weekly Cabinet meeting was marked. The right of appeal to Cabinet by ministers defeated at committee was attenuated almost to the point of extinction. A discontented minister's recourse became instead appeal to the Prime Minister.* Very occasionally, the committee chairman might decide on his own authority to refer a sensitive matter to Cabinet for information and ratification. In the event of deadlock in a committee, it would be referred to the Prime Minister for resolution. Cabinet meetings became shorter and fewer issues were referred to it for decision. By the mid-1980s the number of papers submitted to the Cabinet for decision diminished to an average of sixty or seventy a year – a fifth of the annual number of papers thirty years earlier (Hennessy 1986). By the end of the 1980s scarcely any papers were put to Cabinet at all.*

The story is not one of uniform and muted decline. There were some classic, serious Cabinet debates but this happened less as the decade progressed. As early as 1984 Sir Geoffrey Howe acknowledged: 'There are very few discussions of government decisions by full Cabinet' (*Daily Mail* 6

February 1984). Lawson reckoned Cabinet meetings the least important aspect of his Cabinet membership (Lawson 1992). Those issues that featured at Cabinet did so because they were very significant, invariably had been discussed at length by committee beforehand, and were the subject of a usually brief discussion at Cabinet, usually without a paper.*

The re-emergence of the Cabinet as a focus for collegiate discussion

Yet while its decision-making role diminished, in another way the Cabinet's role expanded. The initial oral reports on foreign and parliamentary business became longer and were supplemented by two other standing items. Quite early in her premiership Mrs Thatcher revived Heath's practice of a regular slot for EU affairs, which now bulked much larger in Whitehall life than in the 1970s, under which ministers could report on business at the Council of Ministers, past and forthcoming. Second, and of great significance, in the mid-1980s home affairs was added as a further oral item to allow ministers in domestic departments to raise items of concern or interest. Significantly, home affairs is now taken as the second item of business, after parliamentary affairs (Young 1990, Seldon 1990). This is important because home affairs are usually the most politically lively issues the government faces, and an open-ended discussion of them strengthens the Cabinet's influence on current political developments.

In short, the Cabinet has become a different body. It now has few papers, usually none, and items are raised orally under one of four broad headings: parliamentary, domestic, European and foreign affairs. It is a stock-taking meeting. It is told of the most important decisions of committees and individual ministers, and may discuss them, but will not often go into detail. Even if a minister tries to reverse a decision of which he was previously unaware, he will usually fail (Fowler 1991).

Major deliberately ran his Cabinet in a very different style from Mrs Thatcher: relaxed, less formal, even discursive – although, significantly, meetings did not last longer. The Cabinet clearly discussed the great issues of the day; Seldon's well-informed study (1997) records discussion of the economy, the Gulf crisis, poll tax reform, local government reorganisation, the mines closure crisis, criminal justice, post office privatisation, the creation of the Committee on Standards in Public Life and senior salaries, not to mention many discussions of Europe – though Major, like his predecessor, tried to avoid collective debate on divisive issues like Europe (Seldon 1997). But these were discussions only. The decisions were taken at committee level. So the key issue of the replacement of the poll tax was agreed by GEN 8 and put to Cabinet for its blessing. EA decided to close thirty-one mines without reference to Cabinet, while the decision not to replace the royal yacht Britannia was taken by an ad hoc group of ministers. The known occasions on which the Cabinet became the point of decision were when a committee's decision had caused a crisis – notably the mines closure crisis – or (in the closing years of Major's premiership) on the divisive issue of Europe, where the European sub-committee prepared the ground, but the Cabinet seriously debated the overall stance, especially on European Monetary Union (Seldon 1997). Yet these were exceptions. Major's Cabinet meetings lasted between 45 and 60 minutes (longer if there was a Euro-crisis on) as opposed to the two or three hours typical as recently as the 1970s.*

Does this strengthen or weaken the Cabinet? To the extent that it now rarely takes decisions, its role is diminished. On the other hand, its role as a sounding board for developing policy and a political litmus test of a whole range of government decisions is widened. Previously ministers were heavily discouraged from raising matters not covered by specific items on the agenda, even under parliamentary affairs. In contrast, the current, more flexible format allows ministers to bring up matters that concern them under one of the four standing items, and allows them to express concern, something observable even under Mrs Thatcher (Seldon 1997).

While it is difficult to be sure, the new system may also allow ministers to voice concern about problems or developments earlier than they could do before the 1980s, when matters usually came to Cabinet at a late stage, with the main lines of the policy laid down and most of the details worked through. The system remains fundamentally collegiate in character and, given that it allows ministers to raise whatever bothers them in Cabinet, appears to bolster the collegiate responsibility of ministers for government decisions.

The practice has also developed since the 1970s of 'political sessions' of the cabinet to discuss party and electoral matters. These were occasionally held under Wilson, Callaghan and Thatcher, usually in the run-up to an election. Major made much greater use of them: they occurred almost weekly before the 1992 and 1997 elections. At such moments the Cabinet Office officials always withdraw and the Prime Minister's political secretary may take a note.

Conclusion

Post-1945 Cabinet government is a complex pyramid of decision-making, efficient, complex and over-burdened. Most decisions are taken by individual ministers or by bilateral agreements, or by clearing papers by correspondence. There is a strong emphasis on settling matters at as low a level as possible. But if ministers cannot agree, or if the policy's sensitivity or importance warrants it, issues are referred up to the extensive committee system that is the main clearing-house for policy decisions. While there is greater use of ad hoc committees and ad hoc meetings, these form part of the ordered framework of the committee system orchestrated by the Cabinet Office.

In the post-war period the Cabinet moved progressively (but not at a steady rate) from being a decisive body, considering and deciding on specific issues, to be being a court of appeal, adjudicating on issues referred up from committees. Then it went through a phase in the early 1980s when, like the Privy Council, it appeared to be almost residual; but the introduction of standing items on EU and home affairs changed it into a discursive body, exercising a general oversight, warning and commenting, but leaving decisions to be taken at other levels.

'Cabinet government' is no longer government by the Cabinet, if it ever was: it is now a more diffuse and complex mechanism. Inevitably there is a conflict between this tradition of decision-making and the traditional, collective ethos, but the sense of collegiate leadership remains strong. These trends all point in one direction: a heavy reliance on the Prime Minister if the Cabinet system is to be kept effective. He must ensure that, in its entirety, the system of Cabinet and its subordinate ministerial meetings is purposeful and efficient yet maintains a sense of collegiality. The paradox is that, if he fails to do so, the Cabinet's functions devolve onto him. The potential for a Prime Minister to concentrate power in his own hands at the Cabinet's expense is considerable. Just as the Prime Minister's role cannot be understood except in relation to his colleagues, so the Cabinet cannot properly be understood without an examination of its leading member.

4 The role of the Prime Minister

Observations in Chapter 1 about the Cabinet system in general apply also to the Prime Minister. His functions and powers are a matter of convention, not statute, and consequently are exceptionally flexible: the parameters of his role at any given moment depend on the circumstances of the moment and on the personalities and aptitudes of leading actors within the system. While any actor is constrained by the institutional restraints imposed by the role he fills, the constraints on the Prime Minister are looser than on most British politicians in elected office. It is only possible to set out the practices that seem to apply in most circumstances, and describe the repertoire of roles that a premier may undertake. Any explanation must be applicable to a variety of personalities from the relaxed post-war Churchill to the interventionist Mrs Thatcher, and to a spectrum of circumstances from the placid 1950s to the fraught 1970s.

The Prime Minister's fundamental tasks

Strangely, the Prime Minister arriving at No. 10 from a Whitehall department can find himself comparatively under-employed. A department provides a ready-made workload. In contrast, the Prime Minister has few duties that he must carry out. He is responsible for everything, yet obliged to do almost nothing. Callaghan observed in retrospect:

> To a large extent the Prime Minister makes his own pace. It is the Prime Minister himself who takes the initiatives, who pokes about where he chooses and creates his own waves. Ideally he should keep enough time to stand back a little from the Cabinet's day to day work, to keep in touch with Parliament and outside opinion, and to view the scene as a whole, knowing full well that periods of crisis will occur when this will be impossible.
>
> (Callaghan 1987)

These periods of crisis are the frequent and unpredictable storms that blow up out of nowhere and are of such importance that the Prime Minister must become involved: sterling crises, major strikes, trouble in Northern Ireland, international incidents...the possibilities are endless. After Macmillan retired from the premiership he was asked what had worried him most while at No. 10. He replied 'Events' (Redhead 1977). Yet while most of his preoccupations are dictated to him by external circumstances, the Prime Minister retains great latitude in choosing when and where to intervene. Asquith's seventy year old dictum still holds good: 'The office of Prime Minister is what its holder chooses and is able to make of it' (Asquith 1928).

The distinction between the political and administrative facets of the Cabinet system are reflected in the Prime Minister's role. In his work, as elsewhere in the Cabinet system, the two intermingle, but it is possible and helpful to distinguish between them. The political role derives from leadership of the dominant party in Parliament. He is the party's chief debater, propagandist and champion, in overall charge of its organisation, manifesto and tactics. In contrast his governmental role is 'to ensure that the Queen's government is carried on', that the government machine runs smoothly and that ministers produce competent decisions. His role as head of government can be divided into four broad categories: running the key functions of government; fostering collective responsibility; giving strategic leadership; and involving himself in individual policy issues.

The key functions of government

These consist of those basic tasks necessary to form a government and keep it running. The Prime Minister must appoint and dismiss ministers; chair the Cabinet; establish Cabinet committees and appoint their chairmen; and order the distribution of functions between ministers and departments. He is Minister for the Civil Service. He also has certain formal duties, including his accountability to the monarch for the running of the government and his responsibility for some patronage, fulfilled at an audience with the Queen every few weeks. These are the tasks which any Prime Minister, however passively inclined, must carry out.

Collective responsibility

Second, the Prime Minister must ensure the observance by ministers of collective responsibility, abiding by all government decisions and publicly defending them, whether at heart they support them or not. He should set colleagues an example in two ways. Most obviously he must himself observe the rules and forbear from communicating private misgivings to the public. (Wilson and Mrs Thatcher were prone to the vice of leaking, which encouraged their colleagues to do likewise.) But he must also foster actively amongst his ministers a sense of collegiality by ensuring that they are properly consulted on all major policy developments. Ministers cannot be a party to every one of the hundreds of ministerial decisions taken every year, but as Macmillan put it to Cabinet Secretary: the important thing is that ministers should 'feel reasonably in the picture' (PREM 11/3223).

Leadership and strategy

His third function is that of leader and chief strategist. He stands above parochial departmental concerns and takes an overall view of government policies. Just as in opposition he is greatly involved in drafting the manifesto, so in government he must oversee its implementation. He is the custodian of government strategy, ensuring that the efforts of different departments blend into a coherent whole. He must ensure that the governing party's programme is translated into action by all departments, and that ministers absorbed in detailed problems do not lose sight of their overall goals. Mrs Thatcher definitely had strategic vision; Wilson did not and allowed his government to drift aimlessly (see for example the criticisms in Healey 1989).

Leadership also involves bringing a sometimes reluctant Cabinet to terms with new situations which the Prime Minister believes require it to adjust its basic objectives. Notable instances have been the decisions, first of Macmillan and later Wilson, to guide their Cabinets round to applying for EU membership; the economic U-turn engineered by Heath; and Callaghan's persuasion of his colleagues to tackle inflation as their first priority. Leadership also requires concentration on means and ends: ministers may agree on what is to be done but not on how to do it. They may agree to nationalisation or privatisation but not on how fast to implement it, or on its financial arrangements, or on future regulation of the industry, or on how to acquire or sell the shares. In all this the Prime Minister must guide, lead, conciliate and inspire colleagues, drawing their individual efforts into a purposeful strategy. It is a task that requires the combined skills of prophet, conciliator, tactician and sheepdog.

Intervention by the Prime Minister in a policy area

These skills are most often exercised through the Prime Minister's fourth major function: intervening in any policy area where he feels his authority or judgement are needed. This takes up much of his working life, although where and how much he intervenes is largely a matter of discretion. The proliferation of international summits, particularly within the EU, draws him into foreign affairs, and he will want to devote time to economic matters, but in both areas he can only to a limited extent choose the depth of his involvement and the particular issues on which he wants to concentrate. Otherwise he intervenes pretty much when and where he chooses.

He may take up an issue because he thinks it politically important to the government; or because it is intrinsically important to the national interest; or because he thinks the minister in charge has got things out of proportion, or is pursuing a mistaken policy, or is simply getting it wrong. Whatever the reason, he can step in by inviting the minister in for a chat, sending a minute, or commissioning a paper for a committee. He decides on what he intervenes, in what depth, in what way and for how long. The only limits on this power are the departmental minister's forbearance, which perforce is usually considerable, and the premier's own interests and energy.

Primus inter pares, presidentialism and conflict with ministers

Having established the Prime Minister's functions, the next question is: what leverage does he exercise within the system? And here we have to clear out of the way three misconceptions that bedevil the study of British central government.

The first is the confusion caused to students by the familiar phrase *primus inter pares* (first among equals) – used, especially by politicians, to encapsulate their constitutional ideal of the Prime Minister as only the most senior of a collective of colleagues. It is neither an accurate nor adequate summary of the premier's position. The treacherous vagueness of this tag is illustrated by the fact that the minister who coined it, John Morley, who served in Liberal Cabinets from Gladstone to Asquith, used it to emphasise the predominance of the Prime Minister despite the theory of equality of ministers:

> Although in Cabinet all its members stand on an equal footing, speak with an equal voice, and, on the rare occasions when a division is taken, are counted on the fraternal principle of one man, one vote, yet the head of the Cabinet is *primus inter pares*, and occupies a position which, so long as it lasts, is one of exceptional and peculiar authority.
>
> (Morley 1889)

In other words, Morley put the stress on 'first' rather than on 'equals', whereas politicians today use it in the opposite sense: Michael Heseltine, for one, when he resigned from the Thatcher government over the Westland affair (*The Times* 9 January 1986).

A second misconception lies at the opposite end of the critical spectrum: that Britain now has quasi-presidential government, a thesis first advanced by John Mackintosh in the first edition of 'The British Cabinet' and popularised by Crossman, notably in his (greatly over-rated) introduction to Bagehot's *The English Constitution* (1964). The gist of the argument was that the Prime Minister had become the focal point of public attention and governmental power. He was effectively irremovable. He hired and fired ministers, dominated Cabinet by determining its agenda and formulating its decisions, created and dissolved committees and chose their chairmen. He controlled the civil service, patronage and publicity. Other ministers' desire for office was so great that they would be reluctant to stand up to him. Mackintosh's version of the thesis was more sophisticated than Crossman's, but in the end he too averred that the country was governed by the Prime Minister, taking decisions alone or in consultation with varying groupings of ministers and officials.

This theory reflected above all Crossman's own penchant for dramatic generalisation. It was never very subtle and, in the light of evidence now available, it appears remote from the truth. Indeed Mackintosh, in subsequent editions of his work on the Cabinet (for example, 1977) toned down his portrait of an omnipotent Prime Minister, due not least to the publication of Crossman's own voluminous diaries which provide day-to-day testimony of the power and impact of individual ministers and the constraints on the Prime Minister. But the damage was done: in the absence of much evidence to the contrary – sources were meagre at the time – the Prime Ministerial thesis had gained a powerful hold, although several academics demonstrated its exaggerations.[1] A simple distortion is easier to popularise than a complex truth. Besides, the flair with which Macmillan and Wilson exploited press, television and question time created a popular illusion of dominance, reinforced by Mrs Thatcher's personal ascendancy in the 1980s. Although as early as 1969 Professor George Jones methodically exposed the simplistic unreality of Crossman's claims, and despite the subsequent outpouring of ministerial writings which have discredited this thesis, it remains a widespread and potent perception. The myth becomes self-reinforcing because, if people believe that we have Prime Ministerial government, they will behave accordingly towards the Prime Minister.

A third, equally exaggerated thesis has been advanced in the aftermath of the Thatcher premiership by the academic Michael Foley, who argues that 'the new resources, strategies and motivations of British political leadership…have produced nothing less than the emergence of a British presidency' (1993). In essence, he contends that a party leader's relationship with the public is now central and decisive; that it is sustained and encouraged by the pattern of media coverage (which feeds an expectation of leadership); that political leaders have sought to develop their political authority by distancing themselves from their party and engaging in 'designer populism'; and that perceptions of the Prime Minister have been enhanced by his prominence in foreign and EU policy, which feeds the growing practice of seeing the Prime Minister as a national archetype. From this Foley concludes 'a British presidency has emerged…into the mainstream of Britain's political life'.

Much depends on what Foley means by 'presidency'. If he means that there is a greater emphasis on leadership generally and that this has enhanced the Prime Minister's public standing, and consequently his political standing, he is right. But he appears to claim more – although this aspect of his analysis is not terribly clear – for he deprecates those who define the Prime Minister's role in executive terms. He does not stipulate the factors according to which we should analyse the premiership: he simply exalts the importance of analysing public perceptions of Prime Ministers. But it is ludicrous – and a defiance of all available evidence – to pretend that the Prime Minister's executive function is a trivial consideration. (For that matter, Foley similarly treats Parliament, ministers and political parties as largely peripheral). As an analysis of the premiership, Foley's thesis does not hold a lot of water; although it is a pity that he exaggerates his case so severely because the central insight on which he based his analysis – the growing emphasis on leadership, which feeds on and is fed by the media – is of importance.

A further assumption underlying both the *primus inter pares* fallacy and the Prime Ministerial delusion is the analysis of the Prime Minister's relations with ministers largely in terms of conflict. Such perceptions are encouraged by the nature of political news coverage: 'PM clashes with Foreign Secretary' is news, 'PM agrees with Foreign Secretary' is not. This gives a distorted impression of the dynamics of decision-making. The Prime Minister is not forever embattled with ambitious colleagues, nor are ministers solely motivated by ambition. Undoubtedly, personal rivalry and conflict over policies are major factors in the internal politics of a Cabinet but they must be viewed in the wider context of national politics. After all, ministers are on the same side on fundamental issues and face a common enemy in a combative opposition.

Certainly, the Prime Minister will use his influence to steer the government in the direction he thinks best. But as often as not he and his ministers will think and work in the same direction. Indeed, if they were too often at loggerheads, the machine would seize up. Collaboration, not conflict, is the rule. This does not mean that when a disagreement occurs the Prime Minister can always impose his ideas, but it suggests that ministers are more receptive to Prime Ministerial involvement in their work than some writers have suggested.

Nor should we assume that there is a conflict between the Prime Minister's need to give leadership and his duty to maintain collegiality. There is a tension between the two, but they are not incompatible. The relationship for the years 1945–97 is shown in Figure 2.

This is very much a freehand exercise, dependent as it is on one author's historical assessment. It aggregates Prime Ministers' characteristics over time (except for Wilson, who clearly passed through three distinct phases) and over all policy spheres. Only broad conclusions can be drawn from it, but it does suggest quite strongly that the predominant characteristic of the post-war era has been a simultaneous combination of medium to high levels of both collegiality and Prime Ministerial leadership. It is worth noting that a survey of Cabinet ministers from twelve Western European countries came to a not dissimilar conclusion, finding that, while no automatic relationship existed between the forcefulness of a Prime Minister and the degree of collegiality in the Cabinet, the one does not preclude the other (Muller, Phillip and Gerlich 1993).

Strong leadership	Thatcher (11)	Eden (1) Wilson (1964–66) (3)	Macmillan (6) Heath (4) Callaghan (3)
Medium Leadership		Wilson (1967–70) (3) Major (7)	Churchill (4) Attlee (6) Wilson (1974–76) (2)
Weak Leadership			Douglas-Home (1)
	Weak Collegiality	**Medium Collegiality**	**Strong Collegiality**

Figure 2 The relationship between leadership and collegiality 1945–97
Note: Figures in parentheses show the number of years' tenure of each premier

The authority of the premiership

The deference of other ministers

Much ink has been spilt in measuring the Prime Minister's power in terms of the power he exercises over ministers: to hire and fire, to appoint committees, to intervene in colleagues' work and so on. All these are important up to a point, but his influence derives above all from the authority of his office which in itself guarantees the respect of colleagues and the obedience of Whitehall. Here, the single-party nature of the Cabinet system is significant: there is a strong contrast with some – but not all – Western European heads of coalition governments, the extreme example being the Italian premier who, at best, can expect a couple of years presiding with little authority over a rickety and infallibly short-lived government (Hine and Finocci 1991).

The British Prime Minister is both leader of his party and head of a single-party government. Ministers are both his colleagues and his subordinates. A few may be his rivals; some may dislike him; some will clash with him over policy; but all must accord him the respect due to his office. This attitude is reinforced by civil servants, who have a great respect for No. 10 and its utterances: they may not always agree with what the Prime Minister says, but they have a keen nose for where power lies.

Most post-war political developments have exalted the premier *vis-à-vis* other ministers. More than ever before, political coverage focuses on the clash between party leaders. Television, international summits and Prime Minister's question time have strengthened the public impression that in many ways the Prime Minister is the government. Other ministers still enjoy the prestige and the trappings of office: red boxes, chauffeur driven cars, the polite obedience of civil servants. Nonetheless, the authority attached to the Prime Minister's leadership role is far greater, and the apparatus surrounding him is more impressive. He chairs the Cabinet. He commands instant press attention. He advises the Queen. He meets presidents, monarchs, ambassadors and foreign ministers. He hires, fires and decides. A strong sense of the Prime Minister's authority comes out of most ministerial memoirs, even those of Barbara Castle who was long a favourite of the premier she served.

George Mallaby, an official who served under every premier from Chamberlain to Macmillan, observed:

> The deference accorded to every British Prime Minister by his Cabinet colleagues is very striking indeed...they will pay special attention to his views and his leadership, with a strong inclination to sink

their own opinions and defer to his. They will accept his reproofs. They will hurry, like schoolboys, to do his bidding.

(Mallaby 1965)

John Boyd-Carpenter confirms this from a minister's point of view:

Only those who have served in government fully realise the gulf between a Prime Minister and even the next senior and eminent of his colleagues. Even in casual conversation with them he ceases to be addressed as 'Anthony' or 'Harold' and except perhaps when there is no-one else present, becomes 'Prime Minister'.

(Boyd-Carpenter 1980)

Social relations have become a bit less formal in the four decades since Boyd-Carpenter was a minister, but the distance created by office is still there.* The degree of deference varies between ministers: the small fry of the Cabinet will be less assertive than the senior inner circle who have worked alongside the Prime Minister for years. Yet even they in the end are his subordinates, as all ministerial memoirs and diaries make very clear, even those of the powerful and successful Butler and Whitelaw.

Ministers expect the Prime Minister to give a lead on great issues in the way that, for instance, Attlee took charge of Indian independence (Burridge 1986), Wilson of the 1975 inflation crisis (Donoughue 1987) and Mrs Thatcher of the Falklands crisis (Hastings and Jenkins 1983). If the Prime Minister fails to lead, ministers are critical. In his brief premiership Douglas-Home was unwilling to tackle politically live problems such as profiteering by land speculators (Howard and West 1965). One observer noted of such indecision:

When ministers discovered that he really wouldn't do it, they began to huddle with each other, little groups of major figures. You would get from them enough agreement or accommodation to produce the main lines of a government position, something they could try to steer through Cabinet. Or if you couldn't get it, there was nothing to be done.

(Neustadt 1985)

Equally damaging was Callaghan's indecision during the 'winter of discontent' (Rodgers 1984, Morgan 1997). Similar criticisms were frequently made of Major over Europe in the last years of his premiership, although this fails to recognise that he was hobbled by a divided Cabinet (Seldon 1997).

Yet a Prime Minister's authority varies over time. He will ride high after an election victory and stay high if he seems successful, but a run of problems may erode his standing, and a serious setback – Suez, the Profumo affair, enforced devaluation – significantly weakens him. Conversely, a personal success boosts his authority: John Major started his premiership younger and with less experience than most of his predecessors, but his firm handling of the Gulf war against Iraq won respect.

Mrs Thatcher makes a good case study; her 1979 election victory was followed by a very short honeymoon, economic problems creating such unpopularity by 1981 that her authority within the Cabinet was seriously impaired. The Falklands conflict boosted her standing and the 1983 election confirmed it, but almost immediately afterwards a series of mishaps loosened her political command, culminating in the self-inflicted injury of Westland. However, the improving economy saved her and carried her through to a third election victory, only to see her authority weakened again as the economy faltered, the poll tax soured public opinion and the Cabinet split over European policy. A sign of her crumbling authority after Howe's resignation, but before Heseltine launched his challenge for the leadership, was the declaration by her new Education Secretary, Kenneth Clarke, that education vouchers were 'not on the agenda' even though she had voiced support for them in her conference speech a couple of months earlier (Commons debates 13 November 1990).

The reluctance of ministers to combine against the Prime Minister

Professor George Jones has suggested that ministers will combine to check the premier because they are his rivals (Jones 1969). There is not a great deal of evidence to support this, except the premiership of Wilson in the late 1960s when the argument was first advanced. Even then, when the Cabinet blocked Wilson's attempt to send the navy to the Gulf of Aqaba during the Six Day War, potential leadership rivals were to be found amongst both his supporters and his opponents. The same was true when the Cabinet split over the 'In place of strife' proposals which Wilson favoured (Castle 1984). Nor did his many rivals mount any real challenge to his handling of Vietnam, Rhodesia or devaluation.

Ministers tend to be moved primarily by departmental considerations. Few will place constitutional proprieties above their own policy interests. None will say 'The Prime Minister is asserting his authority to promote a policy that I support, but I will oppose it to prevent him from exceeding his proper role'. Politicians do not behave like that. They are policy-brokers, not guardians of the constitution.

A minister will only complain that the Prime Minister is exercising too much power if he disagrees with the policy that the premier is pushing. When Heseltine resigned in 1986, he denounced Mrs Thatcher for abusing the Cabinet's proceedings by cancelling committee meetings and manipulating the Cabinet agenda. But he had tolerated such behaviour from her for years – indeed on occasion he had benefited from it. He only complained now because she had used these to defeat him over the Westland affair. The same was broadly true of Brown's resignation from Wilson's Cabinet: ostensibly a protest against his style of government, it was prompted more by pique, emotional volatility and alcohol.

Nor is it easy to remove a serving Prime Minister. Party leaders today are elected by a much wider franchise than in former decades: Labour has an electoral college, the Conservatives election by the parliamentary party. A palace revolution without an appeal to these wider constituencies will succeed only in circumstances of high drama or emergency. A successful coup requires various unlikely preconditions. First, strong hostility must exist against the Prime Minister in his Cabinet and party. Second, there must be some focus of opposition: either a group of like-minded ministers or a powerful backbench focus for dissent, with some consensus on either alternative policies or a different style of leadership. Third, a coup must have the support of most of the Cabinet's heavyweights, and amongst these must be a 'Brutus', an honourable man willing to strike without personal ambition because, in Beaverbrook's dictum, 'he who wields the knife never wears the crown'.

This coincidence of political fortune, current of thought and personalities rarely occurs. In the absence of these factors, the mutterings against Attlee in 1947 and Wilson in the 1960s came to nothing. Mrs Thatcher's overthrow came about because she was unwise enough to alienate senior colleagues at the same time as a powerful centre of opposition coalesced on the backbenches around Michael Heseltine and opinion polls showed her to be an electoral liability. Even then she was safe until Howe resigned over European policy and cut the ground from under her in a lethal resignation speech. On this occasion Heseltine played Cassius to Howe's Brutus; neither gained the throne.

Prime Ministers' style and personality

A lot hinges on style and personality: ministers respond better to businesslike requests than to purposeless meddling, and to tact and humour rather than peremptory demands. There could be no greater contrast than between Attlee and Churchill: the former terse, efficient and direct; the latter a grandiloquent phrasemaker dispatching witty and memorable epistles to his colleagues. Yet both were effective managers in their different ways, knowing when to encourage a colleague, when to prod him and when to leave him to get on with it. In contrast Eden's 'chronic restlessness' (his Lord Chancellor's words – Kilmuir 1964), interference in detail and inability to delegate drove ministers almost to frenzy and seriously impaired his effectiveness. He had a vile temper, constantly dithered, had occasional bouts of paranoia and worried at ministers with constant unnecessary telephone calls. Even the impassive Cabinet Secretary, Norman Brook, was moved to sigh: 'Our Prime Minister is very difficult. He wants to be Foreign Secretary, Minister of Defence and Chancellor' (Clarke 1986, Lamb 1987).

Macmillan's 'unflappable' style was deliberately cultivated – he flapped often enough in private – but it was an effective antidote to Eden's jittery meddling. At one of Macmillan's first Cabinets each minister found at his place at the Cabinet table a packet of tranquillisers. The hint was well taken (Watkinson 1986). His purposeful authority, gentle tact and erudite wit was appreciated by colleagues, amongst them Macleod: 'Mr Macmillan set a new standard of competence in the business of forming, controlling and guiding a Cabinet. He knew how to delegate to ministers and to leave them alone' (*Spectator* 14 February 1964).

Of his successors Callaghan came closest to this gift for balancing judicious delegation against strong authority, rooted in an avuncular personality that varied from the genial to the grim (for example, Donoughue 1987). The mercurial Wilson, sometimes inspirational, sometimes interventionist, sometimes the absolute delegator, was respected for his brilliance but not trusted. Heath, austere and taciturn, was regarded with awe but personal relations were often stiff and uneasy.

Mrs Thatcher was at least straightforward. She told her ministers what she thought they ought to be doing. If they disagreed, she berated them. If they persisted, they argued it out in Cabinet or committee. If a minister argued too often, he was sacked. This 'Stalinist regime', as one former confidant described it (John Biffen in the *Sunday Telegraph* 5 July 1987) worked often but not always, and her peremptory missives could infuriate ministers. The resulting antagonism diluted the automatic respect due to a Prime Minister and departments complied grudgingly rather than rushing to oblige. John Major believed that the opposite approach was more productive.

> It is a matter of instinct that if you carry people with you rather than ride through people you will get a better outcome than otherwise…If, in the development of policy, I can reach a conclusion that I believe to be right with a minimum of noise rather than a maximum, I will do

so. If I can soothe wounds, I will do so. If I can avoid people feeling excluded, I will avoid people feeling excluded.

(*The Times* 27 November 1995)

His more courteous and thoughtful style went down well with his colleagues. As Heseltine famously put it: 'John sums up at the end of a meeting rather than at the beginning'. Ironically, though, when the going got rough some of his colleagues would ungratefully reminisce about his predecessor (Seldon 1997).

When intervening in a policy area, it pays for the premier to be circumspect; intervention can be taken as implicit criticism of the minister and can cause unnecessary friction. Besides, the Prime Minister's worry may be unjustified or his plan impracticable. Wise Prime Ministers do not order, they suggest: 'Perhaps we should look into this possibility or that implication before going ahead?' or 'I am a little concerned about this newspaper criticism: could you give me the background and supply the following figures?' Most ministers only receive this kind of enquiry from No. 10 occasionally and will be anxious to impress by helpfulness and efficiency, enabling the Prime Minister to flit in and out of the department's work with the minimum of fuss and the maximum effect.

Again, Macmillan had the gift of obtaining compliance without seeming to give direct orders. A fine example of firm instructions disguised as courteous suggestion was sent to Hailsham (whom Macmillan disliked) when he was made responsible for economic development in north east England:

> You will no doubt agree that your first act should be to visit the northeast in order to acquire first hand experience of the problems and to acquaint yourself with the personalities involved...I hope that you will prepare a definite plan for the whole area, which you can present to the Cabinet...I shall also welcome your advice on the best means of ensuring that the measures which we adopt may be promptly and effectively executed.
>
> (Macmillan 1973)

By such means he 'managed to interfere time and time again with ministries over the heads of various ministers' (Egremont 1973). For all this, however, there exists a mutual dependence between the Prime Minister and the departmental minister – a point explored later in this chapter.

The Prime Minister's formal powers

It is only once the authority of the Prime Minister's office is grasped that we can properly understand the Prime Minister's formal powers which, once examined, prove to be few in number and quite tightly circumscribed. Much time has been wasted in propounding and refuting exaggerated catalogues of Prime Ministerial powers. For instance, his ability to obtain a dissolution has been depicted as a threat to be used against colleagues, when it could easily be a suicidal misjudgement; his oversight of the Cabinet agenda has been portrayed as the ability to exclude any item from it indefinitely, which is untrue.

In fact the Prime Minister's powers are few and, although potent, hedged about by political restraints. They are: to select and dismiss ministers and – more important – to assign portfolios to them; to create Cabinet committees and choose their chairmen and members; to influence the outcome of important meetings through taking the chair; and some control over information, press relations and patronage.

The Prime Minister's power of appointment

In theory the Prime Minister has considerable freedom to choose his ministers. In particular, he is free of the restrictions that exist in many Western European Cabinet systems where the interests of the different sectors demand the representation of racial, regional, party, religious or linguistic interests – for instance, equal representation of Flemings and Walloons is required in the Belgian Cabinet – or coalition politics that restrain the Prime Minister's discretion – as in Italy and The Netherlands – to virtually nil (Jones 1991). And unlike the Australian and Canadian Prime Ministers, he does not have to worry about balancing representatives from different regions (Weller 1985a).

Nonetheless, the British premier faces many practical and political constraints. These include:

1   *The large number of appointments* – 110 in all – to be made, combined with the requirement that they sit in Parliament, unlike France or the United States, where ministers are barred from the legislature.[2] Most must come from the Commons, where most governments have around 350 MPs. Of these, many will be too young, too old, or for various reasons unsuitable. The mathematics constrain the premier's choice severely.

2   *The framework he inherits.* He must work to a large extent within the constraints of the front bench inherited from his predecessor. The new

leader taking charge in Opposition can make quite extensive changes – indeed this is expected of him – but too dramatic a remodelling may smack of panic and he cannot afford to lose too many able people at a stroke. He probably also needs to conciliate his leading rivals in the leadership election, as Mrs Thatcher did in 1975, offering posts to all her main rivals save Heath. The new leader who assumes the premiership when his party is already in government may have even less room for manoeuvre. In 1976 Callaghan inherited a team deeply involved in implementing departmental initiatives that severely inhibited his scope for changes, and John Major, taking over a Cabinet shuffled repeatedly by Mrs Thatcher in the previous year, could make only limited changes.

3   *Labour's Parliamentary Committee.* The Prime Minister does not face the restrictions imposed by the Australian Labor Party and New Zealand Labour party, where the parliamentary party elects the Cabinet (Weller 1985a). However, the British Labour Party imposes extra restrictions by electing a 'parliamentary committee' when in Opposition (but not when in government). Once the party returns to office, the party's standing orders require the committee's members to be included in the Cabinet (for details see King 1991). This requirement is constitutionally unenforceable, but politically a Prime Minister will ignore it at his peril, and may have to include in his Cabinet some figures who otherwise would have been left out. This happened to Wilson in 1964, and it took him some years to winnow out these unwelcome members.

4   *The claims of senior colleagues.* He must include most senior party colleagues in the Cabinet. He can get away with excluding a few he particularly dislikes: Mrs Thatcher refused office to Heath, and Callaghan left out Mrs Castle, but as Wilson sensibly points out 'forming a Cabinet is no time for settling old scores or bearing grudges' (Wilson 1976). Colleagues with any substantial following or those of high ability or great popularity could be troublesome if left on the backbenches. Even Heath, intolerant of dissidents, brought in the sharp-tongued independent John Peyton to keep him quiet (Bruce Gardyne 1986) and throughout the 1980s Mrs Thatcher accommodated the unrepentantly 'wet' Peter Walker. Almost anyone who made a reasonable showing in the last party leadership election will get a fairly senior post; John Major marked the beginning of his premiership by bringing in Michael Heseltine, his closest rival, from the backbenches, and kept in his Cabinet four Eurosceptics – Howard, Redwood, Lilley and Portillo – critical of his policies. These factors taken together will impose up to a dozen ministers who must go to

fairly important posts: Crossman estimated that Wilson was committed by circumstances to accept the majority of his first Cabinet (Crossman 1975).

5   *The balance of party factions.* The Prime Minister is further hampered by the need to balance various groupings and streams of opinion in the party. The need is less pressing than in some countries: the internal negotiations between the factions of the Japanese Liberal Democratic Party when it forms a government are more tortuous than the formation of inter-party coalitions in many countries. In Britain, this was historically a pressing need in the Labour party, more prone to factionalism than the Conservatives. In 1964, and in the many reshuffles that followed, Wilson scrupulously balanced left against right, old faces against new, intellectuals against trade unionists. One minister complained:

> The number of people who were in the government and even in the Cabinet solely on the basis that they were balancing someone else was alarming. Some of them would never have got there any other way.
>
> (Marsh 1978)

On the same principle Callaghan had to include left-wingers Stanley Orme and Albert Booth in the Cabinet against his will (Rees 1985) and for a long time kept the centre-right Joel Barnett out of the Cabinet because he lacked a left-winger with whom to balance him. Curiously, as the 1990s progressed, the position had been reversed: factional balance was not a pressing consideration in the Blair Cabinet, whereas Major had been compelled to balance Europhiles and Eurosceptics.

6   *The specific requirements of certain posts.* The Lord Chancellor must be a lawyer, and the Secretaries of State for Scotland and Wales ought to come from those countries – although Heath, Thatcher and Major, all lacking suitable candidates, all appointed English MPs to the latter post. A prolonged spell in Opposition can leave the party – like Labour in 1964 – with few frontbenchers of Cabinet experience, who then really have to be included.

7   *The need for capable committee chairmen.* Every Prime Minister needs safe pairs of hands to chair Cabinet committees and cope with sensitive problems, the trustworthy assistants described in the previous chapter. The names of Lord Addison, Harry Crookshank, Robert Carr or Edward Short may mean little to anyone but historians, but their quiet reliability underpinned the Cabinets in which they served.

8   *Cultivating younger talent.* The premier also has to think ahead. He must bring on younger ministers to ensure an adequate pool of experienced colleagues for the future. Conservative governments in the 1950s neglected this, leaving Macmillan embarrassingly short of middle rankers suitable for promotion (Evans 1981).

9   *The need for capable, 'ordinary' ministers.* Every government needs some stable, unambitious people who are competent administrators, or good in the House, or keep the Cabinet in touch with opinion in the country at large. Attlee describes it well:

> You've got to have a certain number of solid people whom no one would think particularly brilliant, but who between conflicting opinions can act as middle men, give you the ordinary man's point of view. I'll tell you who was an ordinary man and a very useful man. You'll remember little George Tomlinson. He was Minister of Education. A Lancashire man. I can remember a thing coming up which looked a good scheme, all worked out by the civil service. But I wasn't sure how it would go down with the ordinary people, so I said "Minister of Education, what do you think of this?" "Well," says George, "it sounds all right but I've been trying to persuade my wife of it for the last three weeks and I can't persuade her." A common-sense point of view like that is extremely valuable.
>
> (Attlee 1969)

Together, these factors severely limit the Prime Minister's freedom of action. Yet he retains a marginal discretion. He can make one or two dramatic promotions. Michael Foot, with no ministerial experience, was unexpectedly made Employment Secretary by Wilson. Callaghan moved David Owen at a stroke from junior minister to Foreign Secretary. Mrs Thatcher abruptly promoted two little-known junior ministers, Cecil Parkinson and Norman Tebbit, to the highly sensitive posts of Party Chairman and Employment Secretary, and later translated John Major suddenly from Chief Secretary to Foreign Secretary. But this power must be used sparingly, as Mrs Thatcher herself recalled: 'Too rapid promotion can jeopardise politicians' long-term future. It turns peers and colleagues against them; they become touchy and uncertain about their standing; and all this makes them vulnerable' (Thatcher 1993).

Prime Ministerial patronage can extend to bringing in the occasional complete outsider. Macmillan made Percy Mills, a businessman who had advised him on the 1950s housing drive, a life peer and Minister of Power at a stroke. David Young, the little known chairman of the Manpower

Services Commission, received from Mrs Thatcher a peerage and Cabinet responsibility for promoting economic enterprise. Wilson made Frank Cousins, general secretary of the transport union, Minister of Technology and engineered a by-election to get him into the Commons. However such discretion can only rarely be used, and is marginal compared to the overall constraints on the premier's powers of appointment. Significantly, none of the three ministers cited above, lacking a parliamentary base of support, made it to the top rank of the Cabinet.

The Prime Minister's power of dismissal

Nor can the Prime Minister dismiss ministers at will. Regular reshuffles are necessary to winnow out ministers who are ill or past it, and to bring in new blood. If this is not done regularly, the government's efficiency suffers. Prime Ministers generally dislike reshuffles: even robust characters like Mrs Thatcher and Callaghan found them an unpleasant necessity. However a Prime Minister must be, in Gladstone's phrase, a good butcher. Wilson was dangerously soft-hearted and debilitated his ministry by keeping on burned-out colleagues in secondary posts.

Nonetheless, a Prime Minister will find it difficult to remove an able colleague who does not want to go. Dismissal is a two-edged weapon. The Prime Minister can usually survive the acrimonious departure of a senior colleague, or even several, but the government suffers. Any sacked minister is a potential focus for backbench dissent. The governing party is made to look weak and unhappy. The Prime Minister, who instigated the trouble by the dismissal, attracts the odium of dividing his followers. This can weaken rather than strengthen him.

Consequently, any minister who has a reasonable party following, is popular at the dispatch box or seems successful in his department is hard to remove, as successive premiers have tacitly acknowledged by leaving strong colleagues in post. Sometimes there are just one or two senior figures who cannot be lost: Butler in the 1950s, Whitelaw in the 1980s. Sometimes there are a group of ministers any one of whom it is difficult to remove: Attlee was ruthless in dismissing junior and middle-ranking figures, but his half dozen most senior colleagues could effectively defy him to sack them and by the late 1960s Wilson's room for manoeuvre in Cabinet-making was seriously inhibited by a core of half a dozen senior figures, none of whom could easily be excluded. In particular, he dared not sack Callaghan, even at the nadir of their personal relations during the conflict over the 'In place of strife' trade union reform proposals. Mrs Thatcher was saddled with a number of 'wets' in her first Cabinet and could only dismiss them piecemeal over the years, while Major had to keep a group of Eurosceptic ministers in his Cabinet despite evident tensions.

There are other considerations. First, the Prime Minister may disagree with a colleague, even dislike him, but this is rarely strong enough to prompt a dismissal. If antipathy were enough, Mrs Thatcher would have sacked Michael Heseltine long before his resignation; in fact, the year before the Westland crisis provoked his resignation. She agreed to the placing of a shipbuilding order on Merseyside rather than Tyneside to avoid his resignation (Lawson 1992). Second, any party has a limited supply of able people: to ensure his government's competence the Prime Minister cannot lose many of them. Third, any dismissal entails a ministerial reshuffle, always a complex, far-reaching and disruptive exercise, especially if he is trying to balance competing factions in the Cabinet. Fourth, too many dismissals create the impression that the Prime Minister is nervous, or not in control, or heads a divided Cabinet. Macmillan's 'night of the long knives', the dismissal of half his Cabinet, made him appear panicky and weak (Alderman 1992).

Nevertheless, the power of dismissal remains a potent psychological threat for one reason: uncertainty. The Prime Minister may swing the axe only rarely, but all except the most powerful know that they could be the unlucky target.

> I am aware that I am there at the Prime Minister's discretion. The Prime Minister can withdraw that discretion any day he likes without stating a reason. And there is nothing much I can do about it – except succeed, and so build up my own strength.
>
> (Crossman 1972, see also King 1994)

The Prime Minister's power to allocate portfolios

Although the power to hire and fire is severely constrained, the discretion to decide who goes to which post is wide. A politician's standing and abilities suggest the seniority of his post but his actual portfolio is at the discretion of No. 10. Even Attlee, surrounded by powerful colleagues, could send Bevin to the Foreign Office and Dalton to the Exchequer, and not the reverse as they had expected. In 1964 Wilson sent Crossman to Housing and Local Government and Stewart to Education. They had held the reverse portfolios in opposition and asked Wilson to give them their old responsibilities back. He refused.

This bestows control over personality and policy. In personal terms, the Prime Minister can keep a colleague he mistrusts out of a sensitive or powerful post. Despite the claims of seniority and ability, Macmillan never made Butler Foreign Secretary, just as Wilson refused the Foreign Office to Brown in 1964 and to Jenkins a decade later. For a long time Macmillan kept Hailsham out of any senior post, finding him in Hailsham's words 'personally distasteful' (BBC 1986a). For policy reasons, Mrs Thatcher did the same to Peter Walker with whose politics she disagreed, while Major refused to appoint Eurosceptics to any economic post.

Conversely, he can also promote his favoured candidates further and faster than they might otherwise expect. The 'Heath-men' found places in the sun unusually rapidly in the 1970s while the Conservative right did poorly. This was reversed by Mrs Thatcher. Churchill over-indulged his taste for surrounding himself with old companions. Right-wing Conservatives were not favoured by Macmillan. In his first government Wilson deliberately promoted safe but uninspiring candidates to the senior offices. However, favouritism can be dangerous: Churchill's cronyism aroused resentment and Heath's swift promotion of his supporters contributed to his downfall.

As to influence over policy, the Prime Minister can influence a department greatly by installing a minister whose views agree with his own. Wilson replaced Benn with Varley at Industry in 1975 and Mrs Thatcher appointed Tebbit to replace Prior at Employment in 1982: in each case a minister at odds with No. 10 was moved to a less illustrious post and in each case the new man swung policy in a direction favoured by the premier. The swift elevation to the Foreign Office of John Major by Mrs Thatcher was intended to make that department more amenable to the Prime Minister's intentions. Baker replaced Joseph as Education Secretary in 1986 because Mrs Thatcher 'felt that something had to be done'.

Sometimes reshuffles can transform completely the government's approach to a question. When Callaghan entered No. 10, convinced that tighter control of public spending was needed (Donoughue 1987), he refused to move a tough Chancellor, Healey, to the Foreign Office and appointed unimpressive ministers to spending departments, weakening their defence of their budgets. In the early 1980s Mrs Thatcher kept economic departments in the hands of ministers of 'dry' views in spite of the scepticism or opposition of the majority of her colleagues to her economic policies. Admittedly there is no guarantee that a minister once appointed will do as Downing Street wants, but the freedom to choose a person of certain views for a certain job stacks the odds in the Prime Minister's favour.

The premier's discretion faces some practical restrictions. He must bear in mind colleagues' abilities: many politicians lack the intellectual grip to run the Treasury, the tact to be Foreign Secretary or the elusive gift of 'managing' the Commons. The Prime Minister may be trammelled by his own limitations: Douglas-Home, having no gift for economics, needed a strong Chancellor; Mrs Thatcher, initially ignorant of overseas matters, had to lean on an experienced Foreign Secretary. Even so, both had a choice of candidates.

A very few senior colleagues may dictate their office. Douglas-Home desperately needed Butler to add weight to his government and could not refuse him the Foreign Office. In 1964 Wilson felt that he could not refuse Callaghan the Exchequer, which meant that Brown, who could not be trusted at the Foreign Office, had to have Economic Affairs. In 1990 John Major could hardly move Douglas Hurd from the Foreign Office against his will, especially during the Kuwait crisis. Ministers may occasionally feel strong enough to impose conditions on their acceptance of a post. Macmillan reluctantly moved from the Foreign Office to the Treasury under Eden only after stipulating various insolent conditions, including blocking Butler's appointment as Deputy Prime Minister (Macmillan 1969). Clarke agreed to go to Education in 1990 only on the understanding that he would not introduce education vouchers, despite Mrs Thatcher's enthusiasm for them (Balen 1994). However, usually only senior colleagues can get away with this kind of bargaining. Most ministers would be foolhardy to attempt to dictate their post or impose conditions; they take what is offered for fear of getting nothing. Competition for the few popular portfolios is keen; as Baldwin remarked, every Cabinet minister thinks he should be Foreign Secretary, but few think they should be Minister of Labour (Eden 1962). Jenkins refused Education in 1965 in the expectation of higher things, and duly became Home Secretary the following year (Short 1989) while Heseltine in 1979 turned down Energy and got Environment instead (Young 1989). But not many can afford such confidence in their abilities.

The Prime Minister's control of collective ministerial discussions

The Prime Minister has absolute discretion to arrange the Cabinet committee system as he wishes. This is a remarkably wide discretion by international standards: most countries require legal sanction of changes to the system or impose *de facto* restrictions through the need to square coalition partners. The premier can exercise influence through the committee system in three ways:

1   *Control of the decision-making process.* The Prime Minister creates and dissolves Cabinet committees and decides which business goes through which channels, whether it will go to a committee or to a smaller ad hoc meeting. Every weekend the Cabinet Secretary puts to him a projection of Cabinet committee business for the coming three weeks,

and a less detailed projection for the three months after that. The Prime Minister holds a weekly Monday morning with the Cabinet Secretary, expanded under Blair to include the heads of the Cabinet Secretariats, his chief of staff and the head of the No. 10 Policy Unit (*The Times* 26 February 1998). This allows him to decide how a policy will be processed, to hasten or delay a decision, to use an existing committee or set up a new one, to give a steer to a committee chairman on how to handle an issue, or exercise a closer control by assuming the chair himself.* So, for instance, Wilson, at Crossman's behest, created an ad hoc committee to consider his Rent Bill, rather than put it to the Home Affairs Committee where opposition was anticipated (Crossman 1975).

This control of structure can be exploited in a number of ways. When in 1979 Chancellor Howe tried to resist a NATO commitment to increase defence expenditure annually by 3 per cent more than the rate of inflation, the Prime Minister ensured that he was defeated by choosing the Defence and Overseas Policy Committee as the forum for the discussion (Howe 1994). Alternatively, the premier can go out of his way to create a committee to get a grip on a policy area. For example, during the 1947 fuel crisis Gaitskell was made Minister for Fuel and Power at a comparatively early age, so Attlee prudently established a Power Committee to oversee him (Attlee 1960). And when the Chrysler motor corporation threatened to close its loss-making Linwood plant in 1975, it was by setting up a Cabinet committee under his own chairmanship that Wilson was able to manoeuvre a reluctant Cabinet round to accepting a rescue operation (Dell 1992). Alternatively, the Prime Minister can create a committee or ad hoc group as a tool for engineering change, for example those which oversaw the social security review of 1985 and the health service review of 1988–9 (Fowler 1991, Lawson 1992).

The Prime Minister can similarly use informal ad hoc meetings to circumvent the normal processes of decision by committee. This was done in particular by Mrs Thatcher who rigged memberships to suit her purposes and used them to take significant decisions (Lawson 1992). As her admirer Ridley put it:

> she was determined to avoid being faced with a decision or a policy from a small group with which she did not agree…I participated in many such small groups – from the miners' strike, through educa-tion policy, football hooliganism, to small matters like trying to attract a film studio to settle in Rainham Marshes.
>
> (Ridley 1991)

2   *Appointment of the chairman.* The Prime Minister lacks time to chair many committees: Wilson and Callaghan chaired only two a week (Donoughue 1988). However, taking the chair gives him a unique opportunity to influence the way the subject is presented, the conduct of discussion, and the eventual decision. By this means Wilson took charge of industrial policy in 1974 when Tony Benn's White Paper on industrial development proved not to be to the taste of the Cabinet (Castle 1980). Mrs Thatcher chaired ad hoc committees in fields as diverse as local government, Hong Kong, anti-radar missiles, and teachers' pay (Hennessy 1986). This discretion allows the Prime Minister to flit in and out of policy areas with great ease and effect.

However, as pointed out in the last chapter, the most important committees are chaired by non-departmental ministers appointed by the Prime Minister, who can hold the ring between those in contention and who will see the issue in a wider perspective than departmental colleagues. These committee chairmen are close to the Prime Minister, seeing him formally and informally several times a week; Major took the relationship to its logical conclusion and, after his regular Monday morning meeting with the Cabinet Secretary to go through Cabinet committee business, met the main committee chairmen to go over the same ground.* The premier can have a quiet word with them about business coming up before their committees, mention any worries he has or drop a hint about the way things might be handled. They are independent, politically acute people with minds of their own, who will give honest and if necessary unwelcome advice to their premier but who, in the last resort, owe their loyalty to him. Wilson and Callaghan exercised their influence with chairmen discreetly; Mrs Thatcher was less surreptitious and was wont to pass on to committees her views on subjects they were to discuss through their chairmen.

3   *Choosing committee members.* As mentioned in Chapter 3, Wilson's practice of adding a few uncommitted ministers to each committee allowed him a certain leeway in weighting committee memberships – a freedom also exploited by Callaghan and Mrs Thatcher. However, the practice in the 1990s of selecting committee memberships almost exclusively on functional grounds has reduced this discretion to the occasional addition of a single senior colleague (see Chapter 3 for examples). This underlines further the great importance of the Prime Minister's prerogative of deciding which minister gets which portfolio.

The Prime Minister's control of information

A corollary of the Prime Minister's position as lynch-pin of the government machine is his superior access to information. He can keep abreast of progress by studying Cabinet and committee papers – he alone amongst ministers gets the papers of all committees – and by selective reading of inter-departmental correspondence, the most important of which is copied to him. No other minister receives so much information about so many departments.

Whitehall is a huge network of lines of communication all of which ultimately converge on 10 Downing Street. The No. 10 Private Office maximises the effectiveness of this torrent of information by sifting and ordering it so that he receives only the most important items in the most easily assimilated form, and supplements it by its own intelligence network. There is a highly-developed bush telegraph between the ministerial private offices of Whitehall, amongst whom the No. 10 Private Office enjoys the same pre-eminence as the premier enjoys *vis-à-vis* his colleagues. The Cabinet Secretariat has a similar web of contacts, but wider and reaching further into the operational divisions of departments. Although neither is omniscient nor infallible, both keep the Prime Minister in touch with the germination of policy and inject his views at an early formative stage.

In contrast, other cabinet Ministers cannot always know what is being discussed, where or by whom. Practice seems to vary between governments, but in general ministers usually only receive the minutes of the committees they serve on, and while they can ask for the minutes of other committees – whose existence is, of course, public – the use of ad hoc meetings can make it difficult for ministers to know what to ask for. A minister interviewed by Burch and Halliday (1996) found this a hindrance to participation in collective decision-making. Some of this is unintentional – how many managers in large organisations know exactly what their colleagues are up to? – but there is ample evidence that certain Prime Ministers, notably Wilson and Mrs Thatcher, deliberately prevented colleagues from receiving information, particularly in the two areas of greatest interest to No. 10, foreign and economic affairs.

Wilson concealed much information from colleagues before devaluation, including the worsening trade deficit in 1966, and ordered the destruction of a paper from economic advisers advocating devaluation (Callaghan 1987, Contemporary Record 1988a). Castle and Crossman were refused access to diplomatic telegrams on Rhodesia and the EU (Castle 1984, Crossman 1976) and Callaghan three times refused Benn a copy of the Chancellor's paper on the European Monetary System (Sedgemore 1980). Under Mrs Thatcher many ministers knew nothing of many policy announcements until they read of them in their newspapers (Hennessy 1986). On occasion Prime Ministers have set up totally secret committees, known only to those who serve on them. Callaghan's 'economic seminar', its successor under Mrs Thatcher, the 1978 committee on Polaris replacement and the 1984 committee on chemical weapons were known only to their small membership; there was no way for other ministers to discover their existence (Donoughue 1987, Hennessy 1986, Page 1985).

The Prime Minister's influence over the press

As emphasised in Chapter 2, presentation is now an integral part of policy-making and media coverage is of intense interest to all politicians. The Prime Minister enjoys greater coverage than any other politician and this is a potent factor in projecting his leadership to the world at large (Foley 1993). This influence extends to control over statements made by colleagues: virtually any important ministerial announcement must be cleared by No. 10, giving the Prime Minister considerable opportunity to influence its timing and content. Something of a fuss was caused when the Blair government's 'Code for Ministers' was published, for in addition to the unsurprising requirement for ministers to clear with the No. 10 Private Office the policy content of all major policy speeches, press releases and new policy initiatives, it also required the clearance with the No. 10 Press Office of all major announcements and media interviews, press and broadcast. Also – and most controversially – it required the keeping of 'a record of media contacts by both Ministers and officials' (Cabinet Office 1997a). However, similar rules have operated under previous governments: in the 1980s Francis Pym complained: 'Increasingly, ministerial and inter-departmental press releases are channelled through Downing Street and suppressed or modified as necessary' (Pym 1984). But such rules are often honoured in the breach: William Rodgers, a cabinet minister in the 1970s, recalled happily that he would send his speech for clearance to No. 10 just as he left to catch the train and – in those happy days before mobile telephones – would be unavailable until it was delivered (Lords debates 28 October 1997, Col. 1037).

The lobby system of unattributable briefings has also encouraged some Prime Ministers to use No. 10 to denigrate colleagues out of favour with the Prime Minister. In particular under Wilson and Mrs Thatcher, 'Downing Street sources' used the lobby – in Lord Hailsham's words – to 'create an atmosphere of real or imaginary Cabinet rifts and to undermine the confidence of Cabinet ministers' (*Evening Standard* 30 October 1989).

The Prime Minister's control of patronage and the machinery of government

The Prime Minister also has considerable powers of patronage. Here we must distinguish between honours – life peerages, knighthoods and the like – which are useful in terms of political management, and appointments to public office, which generally have policy overtones. By preferring a candidate of certain opinions to head a Royal Commission or a public body the Prime Minister can indirectly influence an area of policy. Appointments can also be used more crudely as bargaining counters, like the offer in 1976 of an EU commissionership to Roy Jenkins that lessened his appetite for contesting the Labour leadership. The Prime Minister must be consulted on the appointment of Royal Commissions, independent inquiries, chairmen of public corporations, nationalised industry boards, the more important departmental committees, heads of non-ministerial departments, and all politically significant appointments – and 'Ministers should take a wide view of what constitutes political significance', although political discretion in such appointments is now restricted to some degree by the requirements for fairness, openness and independent scrutiny policed by the Commissioner for Public Appointments (Cabinet Office 1997a).

The Prime Minister also has sole responsibility for the machinery of government. Here, for once, his powers are codified in the Ministers of the Crown Act 1975, but these powers are near absolute. He may – subject to the formality of an Order in Council – create, abolish, merge or split departments and shuffle functions between ministers. Some changes are inspired by a genuine desire to improve the workings of government, such as recreating the Department of Energy after the 1973 oil crisis.* Others are used to influence the development of a policy: the absorption of the Commonwealth Relations Office into the Foreign Office in 1968 removed an obstacle to EU membership, and Mrs Thatcher abolished the Civil Service Department because she saw it as an impediment to civil service reform. But just as often, decisions are driven by personalities. On three occasions Mrs Thatcher rejigged the responsibility for enterprise policy to keep it under the control of Lord Young as he moved from one post to another; and when a crisis in health service funding undermined her faith in the Health and Social Security Secretary John Moore, she hived off health into a separate department under Kenneth Clarke. In the same spirit Wilson split the Department of Trade and Industry into three to fit his pattern of ministerial appointments (Part 1990) and Callaghan split Transport away from Environment to bring the right-winger William Rodgers into his Cabinet (Pollitt 1984).

The Prime Minister's relations with individual departmental ministers

All participants in the political system expect the Prime Minister to intervene extensively in departmental policy matters. This is no mere statement of the obvious: the autonomy of individual ministers is stronger in the UK than in most countries, and in certain countries – notably Italy and The Netherlands – the premier's authority for such interventions is minimal (Hine and Finocci 1991; Andeweg 1988).

It is necessary to consider separately a Prime Minister's bilateral relations with individual Cabinet colleagues, and his relationship with his colleagues as a group. The dynamics of the bilateral relationship will depend on the Prime Minister's interest, the departmental minister's abilities and the political and intrinsic importance of the area for which the minister is responsible.

It is useful to distinguish between four possible roles a Prime Minister may play when intervening in a policy area. He may act as:

1   *Coordinator*, making sure that the initiatives of different departments do not conflict with each other and that issues are brought for discussion by colleagues at the right time.
2   *Arbitrator*, sorting out disputes between colleagues on an issue on which he has no particular view and wishes only to reach an acceptable solution.
3   *Protagonist*, becoming involved in the issue and pressing a particular policy line.
4   *Strategist*, ensuring that individual ministers and their departments contribute actively to the key goals of the government.

These categories overlap: for instance, a Prime Minister may first intervene in a subject as an arbitrator, but then develop strong views; or he may find that he must become a protagonist on a particular question in order to achieve the government's overall goals. The inclinations of different premiers vary: Douglas-Home tended towards a coordinating and arbitration role; Mrs Thatcher was very often a protagonist; Callaghan a mixture of the two.

There are many ways in which the Prime Minister can be alerted to a problem and involve himself in its handling. These include:

1   *Involvement at the initiative of the departmental minister.* Often departments go out of their way to keep Downing Street in touch with their work. Douglas Wass, Permanent Secretary to the Treasury in the 1970s,

recalled: 'the Prime Minister has come to expect to be consulted, personally and outside the Cabinet, by departmental ministers when they are contemplating important steps within their own competence' (Wass 1983). But this is nothing new, and is an efficient way of doing business: a century ago Gladstone commented of the Prime Minister: 'Nothing of great importance is matured or would even be projected in any department without his cognizance, and any weighty business would commonly go to him before being submitted to the Cabinet (Gladstone 1878).

So, Maudling abandoned abolition of retail price maintenance as soon as Macmillan announced his opposition; equally, Douglas-Home's support was crucial to Heath's later success in pushing abolition through (Lawson and Bruce-Gardyne 1976). Rees cleared with the premier his plan for a Northern Ireland constitutional convention (Rees 1985) and Baker got Mrs Thatcher on side for his plans to create a national curriculum (Baker 1993).

This suits the minister. The premier's approval is a strong card that he can play if colleagues obstruct him. It also improves his chances of getting a slot in the legislative programme: Boyle used Douglas-Home's backing to get a legislative slot for introducing middle schools (Kogan 1971) and Crossman used Wilson's support to get a large housing programme through Cabinet and protect it against cuts (Ponting 1989, Crossman 1975). On the other hand, if the Prime Minister opposes a departmental minister despite all persuasion, that minister will face an uphill struggle. Intriguingly, most interventions of this kind from No. 10 in the Labour governments of the 1970s sought to dissuade a minister from taking too narrowly departmental a view and made him think in terms of a broader governmental interest (Donoughue 1987).

2 *Through the conduct of Cabinet business.* Many questions come to the Prime Minister's notice by emerging through the usual channels of the Cabinet and its committees, especially through the voluminous inter-ministerial correspondence, all of which is copied to the No. 10 Private Office. An issue may surface as a disagreement between ministers in which, even if it does not go to committee, the Prime Minister must arbitrate before things get out of hand. Hence Callaghan had to step in when his Chancellor and Energy Secretary clashed over the future use of North Sea oil revenues (Donoughue 1987) and Mrs Thatcher was initially brought into the Westland affair to calm the row between Brittan and Heseltine. Alternatively the Cabinet Office, which has a close working relationship with the No. 10 Private Office, will flag up an issue that, although not yet in flames, has incendiary potential.

It should be noted, however, that the growth of large departments with disparate responsibilities means that some decisions are now taken by a minister within his department that previously might have been discussed with ministers. For instance the remit of the Department of the Environment, Transport and the Regions is so wide that its secretary of state will take decisions between such competing priorities as the protection of the green belt versus the encouragement of private development, or the regeneration of inner cities versus restraint of local councils' spending, or environmental protection versus regional economic development. The Prime Minister ought to be alert to such internalising of decisions within departments and if necessary bring the argument into a wider forum.

3   *From outside representations.* All manner of personal contacts – chats with backbenchers, meetings with industrialists, complaints from constituents, ideas from personal advisers – may set the Prime Minister in motion. For example, privy councillors exercise their right to write directly to him: when the leader of the Scottish Nationalists wrote asking for customs coverage for a Scottish airport, Mrs Thatcher summoned a Treasury minister to justify his refusal (Bruce-Gardyne 1986).

4   *From Parliamentary developments.* Many premiers pick up points from parliamentary debates: Callaghan was a devotee of Hansard, and Churchill once upbraided senior colleagues when a Lords debate revealed their failure to reduce the numbers of official 'snoopers' empowered to enter private property without warrants (PREM 11/100). Parliamentary questions in particular provoke many inquiries from No. 10. Heath's political secretary, Douglas Hurd, recalled:

> In briefing himself for PQs the Prime Minister has a marvellous opportunity to poke his nose into details of the work of government which would not normally come his way. Departments have to arm him with facts and figures to deal with any supplementaries…Often these facts and figures would show clearly that a particular policy was progressing slowly or that some hitherto unreported danger was emerging. When this happened a brisk telephone call or minute would be authorised to urge things on.
>
> (Hurd 1979)

Although in 1997 Blair altered the format from two 15-minute sessions a week to one 30-minute session, the preparations beforehand have not changed (they are usefully described in Seldon 1997). The Prime Minister's private secretary for parliamentary affairs gathers information from departments on topics likely to come up, briefs the Prime Minister and, on his orders, commissions extra briefing from departments. This array of briefing on up to fifty issues often provides early warning of a new issue, exposes an unexpected problem or reveals departmental failings. For instance, a Commons question provoked Mrs Thatcher's interest in commercial surrogate motherhood and led to legislation banning it,* while after questions on housing benefit in 1981 caught her on the hop, she made sure that by the next Prime Minister's Questions on Thursday she knew the policy rather better than the departmental ministers did (Fowler 1991).

5 *From the news media.* Newspaper reports provoke queries. For example, they moved Eden to urge his Home Secretary to take stronger action against drunken drivers (PREM/830). Mrs Thatcher had a notorious habit of listening to BBC Radio 4's early morning Today programme and taxing her ministers with issues that had come up (Armstrong 1994).

By all of these means the Prime Minister can discover when civil servants are dragging their feet; when a minister is failing to pursue a policy with sufficient energy; when two departments are developing policies at odds with one another; when the Treasury is being unreasonably mean or a department unnecessarily profligate; when a policy is being developed that, although making sense in the eyes of the department, overlooks political realities; when a policy ignores the general thrust of government strategy; when the views of an important interest group have been given insufficient consideration or too much weight. Thus forewarned, the Prime Minister can have a quiet word with the responsible minister, or more officially send a minute giving his views or asking for more information, or invite the minister to a meeting at No. 10. If matters seem to be going seriously wrong he can use the Cabinet Office to engineer a working group of officials to ginger up the department or bring the matter to a Cabinet committee to 'encourage' the minister.

In a 1994 seminar, Nigel Lawson made two pertinent observations about the relationship between the Prime Minister and departmental ministers. First, he pointed to the danger of 'creeping bilateralism', in which departmental ministers find it convenient not just to consult the Prime Minister beforehand about a proposal, but to use the Prime Minister's agreement as a substitute for collective approval by colleagues. It is an arrangement full of temptation for the Prime Minister but potentially damaging to the cohesiveness of the government – a problem analysed in Chapter 6.

Second, Lawson percipiently observed:

> there is a large area of government where what might be called a mutual blackball system exists. By that I mean that if a Minister wishes to do something within his own field which the Prime Minister profoundly disapproves of, then the Prime Minister has a blackball which he or she can cast.... [Equally]...if the Prime Minister wants something done in a particular area, and the Minister responsible disagrees with it, then it will not happen because he will effectively veto that idea: he has a blackball, too.
>
> (Lawson 1994)

Mrs Thatcher provided ample evidence to support this analysis: she variously refused to abolish the National Economic Development Council, to grant the Bank of England its independence, to remove the funding and control of schools from local authorities, and to abolish the Dock Labour Scheme in 1985, though she changed her mind in 1988 (Lawson 1992). Conversely, though, her Education Secretaries were able to block her wish to allow state schools to charge fees (Baker 1993), her Home Secretary blocked the privatisation of Channel 4 (Thatcher 1993) and Howe pushed through abolition of exchange controls in the teeth of her reluctance (Howe 1994). On tax relief for mortgages she reached an uneasy stalemate with Lawson: he as Chancellor blocked her wish to extend it, while she prevented him from restricting it (Lawson 1992). The mutual blackball does not operate in all circumstances – Mrs Thatcher forced Lawson to accept tax relief for private health insurance and compelled the Home Secretary to create a Broadcasting Standards Council (Lawson 1992) – but it is valid as a general rule operating for most of the time.

Counterweights to Prime Ministerial influence

The combination of Prime Ministerial authority, the powers of his office and his opportunities for intervention may suggest a formidable total of power, an impression heightened by the image of purposefulness and control that Prime Ministers and their publicity aides like to project. Yet there are two strong restraints on the Prime Minister: his own lack of time to intervene in more than a handful of subjects at once, and the political weight of other ministers both individually and collectively which balances his influence.

Time constraints on the Prime Minister

The Prime Minister lives in a constant rush. He must chair the Cabinet and its leading committees, meet colleagues, make speeches, pay visits abroad, receive foreign dignitaries, answer parliamentary questions, attend a regular audience with the Queen, make visits throughout the country, keep up-to-date with news stories, attend the Commons to keep in touch with his troops, go to party meetings, keep an eye on his constituency and a host of other duties. Before meetings he must study his papers and before public engagements he must spend time briefing himself on what he is to see and who he will meet (Donoughue 1988).

This hectic pace is well captured in Wilson's record of his preoccupations during the Whit recess of 1967: a dozen speeches on assorted subjects around the country; day and night meetings on international tariff reduction negotiations; riots and strikes in Hong Kong; the collapse of negotiations in Aden leading to replacement of the High Commissioner; renewed conflict with Spain over Gibraltar; talks with King Faisal of Saudi Arabia; a series of trade union conferences decrying the government's pay policy; trouble over the third London airport; problems with de Gaulle over Britain's EC application; and a campaign against the clampdown on pirate radio stations (Wilson 1971). Life has become no quieter since then. As Macmillan said, 'Events'.

Restraint of the Prime Minister by other ministers

The Prime Minister's influence is also checked by the independence of mind of departmental ministers. People who have served in Downing Street do not seem to have felt any great sense of power; rather they recall frustration at having to influence policy through the medium of departments.* In part this mirrors the difference of perspective between centre and periphery in most organisations: the centre complains 'don't they realise how important this is?' and people on the periphery complain 'do they think we don't know how important this is?' But a Prime Minister is in a very real sense at the mercy of departments. He cannot take a policy out of the hands of a minister, at least not for any sustained period: he has few staff; they lack the detailed knowledge, experience or time to run the policy; and over time that policy would develop out of kilter with the rest of that department's policies. The premier can ask questions, insist that other options be considered, or strongly urge or discourage a course of action, yet in the end he depends on the minister on the spot to do the work. This puts the minister in a strong position if he disagrees with No. 10.

The varying influence of individual ministers

The clout of individual Cabinet ministers varies: there is a definite hierarchy. This bears little relation to the formal list of precedence published by the Prime Minister's office (most easily found in Hansard) which reflects length of service as much as anything. Nor is there a formal tier of 'superior' ministers like the four Ministres d'Etat in the French Council of Ministers. The truly significant hierarchy is informal. Those in junior posts recently appointed to the Cabinet see themselves, and are seen, as being on trial, and show a certain diffidence at large meetings of senior colleagues. Even the redoubtable Mrs Thatcher, when Education Secretary under Heath, felt insufficiently senior to ask questions at Cabinet and would ask a more senior neighbour to raise points so that she could follow with supplementaries.

Slightly more exalted in status but a more diffuse grouping is the middle order of the Cabinet. Ascent to this level is a subtle mixture of length of service, importance of office and political reputation. Into this category fall ministers like the Defence and Environment Secretaries, whose departmental responsibilities are wide and important, and who usually have previous Cabinet experience but who have not attained the 'inner circle' of the Cabinet.

Finally, the top tranche of most Cabinets is an identifiable group of half a dozen usually including the Foreign Secretary, the Chancellor of the Exchequer, the Home Secretary and the more senior non-departmental ministers. They frequently see their senior colleagues, including the Prime Minister. They bear a greater share of the burden of ensuring the government's success. They are generally not shy to express views across the spectrum of policies, to contradict powerful colleagues and to speak their minds. (For a slightly different view of what he terms the 'big beasts', see King 1994.)

From time to time one senior minister enjoys the title of Deputy Prime Minister, as Butler, Whitelaw, Howe, Heseltine and Prescott have done (for a history of such appointments see Hennessy 1996). This is a courtesy title carrying no executive function beyond deputising for the Prime Minister in his absence, notably by chairing the Cabinet and answering Prime Minister's questions. Butler and Howe combined the post with the Leadership of the Commons, but in neither case was this a comfortable arrangement because it was clear that they had been made Deputy Prime Minister only because the premier wanted to exclude them from the Foreign Office. Heseltine held no other government post; his responsibilities were rather unconvincingly padded out with responsibility for competition issues and overall charge of government presentation.

Generally, Deputy Prime Ministers have looked more comfortable and substantial when they have combined the title with a departmental post: Whitelaw as Home Secretary and Prescott as Secretary of State for the Environment, Transport and the Regions.

This three-fold typology is necessarily arbitrary. The standing of an individual is influenced by other more personal factors: the seniority of his post, his standing in the eyes of colleagues, personality, ability, party rank and political success. All are difficult to quantify and are always changing. Some ministers by strength of personality carry great weight. One such was Denis Healey whose heavyweight frame and blunt speaking made him highly effective in posts – first Defence, then the Treasury – where the instincts of Labour colleagues were against him. Some carry authority through experience: the enormous influence of William Whitelaw in the first eight years of the Thatcher governments has been mentioned above: the then Cabinet Secretary reckoned that Whitelaw effectively wielded a veto within the government, although he used this influence sparingly (Armstrong 1994).

Lord Hailsham, who served for over thirty years in Conservative Cabinets, imprinted his character on all facets of government discussions, in earlier years through his ebullient personality, later by forceful use of his unrivalled experience. A vignette of his later years is provided by the Treasury minister who advanced a plan to replace student grants with loans.

> A submission duly went forward to the Cabinet, finely honed by all of the Whitehall inputs. Only to encounter the unyielding opposition of the Lord Chancellor. He was not open to negotiation or persuasion. Up with student loans he would not put. Not for the first time, or the last, his stance proved decisive.
>
> (Bruce-Gardyne 1986)

Another colourful character was Ernest Bevin, who on one occasion silenced a bumptious official by leaning across the table, 'roaring like a full-grown lion' and telling the man he would not accept his advice (Jay 1980).

However, for every such character there will be a dozen less colourful figures. Some will be personally uninspiring but will compensate by an efficient mastery of their departmental case – the trait that made David Eccles so effective at Education under Macmillan, or Michael Stewart an effective advocate at Wilson's Cabinet table. Some, like Aneurin Bevan and Richard Crossman, bluster. Some may be obvious failures, such as Fraser and Soskice who were rapidly ejected from Wilson's first government. Tony Benn in the 1970s showed that a minister's unpopularity may be counter-balanced by brilliance in argument; conversely, Michael Foot in the same epoch proved that personal popularity may compensate for lack of forensic gifts.

Some ministers have the gift of seeing things in the round. One such was Antony Crosland of whom Barnett judged: 'This quality of objectivity, combined with his knowledge, experience and considerable ability, made him the minister who had the greatest impact on Cabinet decisions on most issues' (Barnett 1982). Others can offer experience: Lord Addison, over four decades, served under Asquith, Lloyd George, MacDonald and Attlee. This last respected him highly and encouraged him to intervene in Cabinet on issues as diverse as housing, agriculture, health and defence (Morgan 1981). Douglas-Home, Hailsham, Carrington, Callaghan and Jenkins developed in time only slightly less authority.

Paradoxically, success within his own department also gives a minister greater weight when speaking on matters outside his departmental remit. If he appears to be dealing competently with his own work, shows flair dealing with the press and performs well at the dispatch box, he will steadily accumulate political credit and colleagues will pay attention to his views on other areas of policy. Conversely, if he is lacklustre in the Commons or on television or seems to lack control over his department, colleagues will think less of his pronouncements on other subjects.

In short the influence of ministers will vary according to a host of personal factors – which is why, in 'collecting the voices' at the end of a discussion, the Prime Minister gives differing weight to different ministers' contributions. There will generally be enough ministers of sufficient standing to provide some counter-weight to the considerable influence of the Prime Minister.

Relations between the Prime Minister and individual departmental ministers

The balance of forces between Prime Minister and departmental minister is delicate and complicated, varying subtly according to their respective political standing and popularity. But given a competent and able Prime Minister – and no other kind will last long – there are three possible models for their relationship:

1   a Prime Minister with a weak minister;
2   a Prime Minister with a strong minister with whom he is at odds; or
3   a Prime Minister with a strong minister with whom he generally agrees.

Prime Ministers and weak ministers

Superficially, a weak minister might seem a boon to No. 10: he can be manipulated, bullied and used as an agent rather than a colleague. In practice the opposite is true: a weak minister is a burden. The Prime Minister lacks the time or resources to take over a department full-time. A minister who mishandles problems, fails to tackle crises, lacks political flair, cannot handle his officials or puts up politically insensitive proposals only generates trouble. A notable example was Emmanuel Shinwell. Despite clear signals in late 1946, he refused to take advance precautions to avoid a fuel shortage or to give priority to power stations. Consequently when blizzards struck in early 1947 the government had to cut off electricity from industry in much of Britain and from all domestic consumers for 5 hours every day. The junior fuel minister, Gaitskell, and officials took charge, rationing and redistributing stocks under the supervision of a Cabinet committee chaired by a furious Attlee. Later that year Shinwell was demoted from the Cabinet and Gaitskell promoted to his place (Williams 1979).

Macmillan faced similar problems when his Chancellor Selwyn Lloyd failed to tackle the pay problem (Macmillan 1973), as did Wilson when Fraser at Transport and Soskice at the Home Office proved inept. Each Prime Minister found this a wretched burden, wasting time meeting departmental officials or chairing committees to manage matters the minister ought to have managed himself. In each case the weak minister was removed as soon as decently possible and replaced with someone capable.

Strong ministers at odds with the Prime Minister

When possible, Prime Ministers avoid putting into sensitive departments ministers with whom they will have trouble. This applies particularly to foreign and economic policy – explored in the next chapter – and any department particularly sensitive at the time. Still, given the number of people they are obliged to appoint to the Cabinet, often with claims to senior posts, Prime Ministers are usually obliged to appoint an uncongenial minister or two. It often spells trouble.

Chapter 2 records the process by which Benn's radical industrial policy was undermined by his Prime Minister, who exploited Benn's lack of support in Cabinet to brief the press against him, orchestrate protests from industry and engineered a Cabinet committee that rewrote the White Paper.

The contrast with James Prior, who was able to enlist the help of colleagues against Mrs Thatcher, is instructive. Prior favoured a gradual approach to trade union reform, Mrs Thatcher a radical approach. However, he had held the Employment portfolio in Opposition and, since in 1979 she had allocated all economic posts to her own allies who were in a minority in the Cabinet, she felt unable to refuse him the Employment Department. For two years they differed sharply over the pace and scale of reform, but Mrs Thatcher failed to force him into more precipitate action. In Cabinet committee he successfully appealed to other ministers to resist her attempts to restrict union powers and immunities more tightly in the 1980 Employment Act, or to rush through an emergency bill to ban secondary picketing (Young 1989, Stephenson 1980).

By 1981 Mrs Thatcher felt strong enough to replace him with the more radical Norman Tebbit, and to move Prior to Northern Ireland. But even there he proved a thorn, pushing through a plan for a local Assembly in the teeth of her determined opposition in committee and Cabinet. Prior records that when the Cabinet was asked to 'guillotine' the bill to curtail parliamentary debate

> she made her views absolutely clear, saying that she thought it was a rotten bill, and in any case she would not be voting for it because she was off to the USA. But the guillotine went through.
>
> (Prior 1986)

Strong ministers in tune with the Prime Minister

As Barnes has put it, the relationship between Prime Minister and departmental minister is symbiotic (Barnes 1999). The minister needs Downing Street's consent, support and trust to make a success of his policies and his career, while the Prime Minister needs an able, energetic minister he can trust to make a success of an area, give him good advice, accommodate his wishes if possible, stand up to him if necessary, and generally not make a mess of it. Dud appointments will only weaken the government and the premier. The Prime Minister intervening in a particular issue is influential; the departmental minister on his own ground is strong. They need each other to be capable and reliable.

A minister may be glad of the Prime Minister's intervention if it helps to mobilise opinion behind a policy. In the 1970s Callaghan began to share the mood of unease in the country about the quality of education in schools and, knowing that the world of education was not keen to open up the issue, he delivered a famous speech at Ruskin College calling for a 'great national debate' on education, now perceived as the starting point for the upheavals of the 1990s. His Education Secretary, initially resistant, came to accept the value of his intervention (Donoughue 1987, Williams 1996). When in the 1990s Education Secretary Kenneth Clarke was trying to impose radical reforms on a reluctant teaching profession, he can only have welcomed his Prime Minister's public calls for a tightening of examination standards, reform of the schools inspectorate, the overhaul of further education and the introduction of training credits. The Prime Minister's profile in initiating policy was raised, Clarke was strengthened in his struggle with the teachers and, paradoxically, Major's interest made it easier for Clarke to obtain a substantial pay rise for teachers (Seldon 1997). As the *Times Education Supplement* put it: 'The Education Secretary has decided that education is too important to be left to the educationalists...The Prime Minister has decided that education is too important to be left to the Education Secretary' (16 July 1991).

They are bound to disagree sometimes. A sensible premier recognises that any decisive minister will have an independent viewpoint. If the departmental minister digs in his heels the Prime Minister, who always has other fish to fry, will weigh up the drawbacks of a row – he cannot afford to undermine good colleagues – against the importance he attaches to getting his way in this instance. Even the formidable Mrs Thatcher was obliged by her Home Secretary to abandon immigration quotas and a register of immigrants' dependants, and by her Foreign Secretary to abandon support for the Muzorewa regime in Rhodesia (Stephenson 1980).

Threats of resignation by ministers

Prime Ministers will be particularly wary because, although ministers are reluctant to stick their necks out on matters outside their own departments, the possibility of defeat on their own ground may well be countered with a threat of resignation. Any resignation damages both the government and the premier; Robert Armstrong, after 8 years as Cabinet Secretary, judged the threat of resignation still to be 'a powerful check on the Prime Minister' (Armstrong 1994).

Resignations are difficult to classify: ministerial motives are often mixed, sometimes secret. But given ministers' preoccupation with their departments, we might expect most ministerial resignations to be over matters touching their own departmental policies, rather than wider government policies outside their concerns. Surprisingly, the reverse is true. An analysis of the resignations catalogued in Butler and Butler's *British Political Facts* (1994) show that in the period 1957–97, twenty-three ministers resigned on policy grounds (as opposed to personal reasons or misdemeanour). Of these, sixteen resigned on matters outside their departmental responsibilities (eight Cabinet ministers, eight junior ministers) as opposed to seven (three Cabinet, four junior) who resigned over matters within their departmental responsibilities.

On the other hand, ministers who have successfully got their way by threatening resignation have done so almost exclusively over matters within their departmental responsibilities. Such a list is difficult to compile, since threats are often privately made, but the better known of the same period 1957–97 are:

Lennox-Boyd, Eden's Colonial Secretary, to prevent immigration controls (Lamb 1987)

Macmillan when Chancellor to obtain abolition of milk and bread subsidies (Lamb 1987)

Macleod several times when Colonial Secretary over African policy (Horne 1989)

Heath when President of the Board of Trade to compel the Cabinet to abolish retail price maintenance (Bruce-Gardyne and Lawson 1976)

Healey when Defence Secretary to stop defence cuts (Healey 1989)

Roy Jenkins when Home Secretary, to secure parliamentary time for legislation to reform the censorship laws (Campbell 1983)

William Ross when Scottish Secretary to save Chrysler's Linwood plant in Scotland from closure (Dell 1992, Donoughue 1994)

Pym when Defence Secretary to protect the defence budget (Howe 1994)

Heseltine when Defence Secretary to ensure shipping orders were placed with a Merseyside yard (Tebbit 1988)

Fowler when Health and Social Services Secretary to prevent the sale of BL to General Motors (Fowler 1991)

Lawson and Howe's joint resignation threat in 1989 to force Mrs Thatcher to accept the long-term principle of European monetary union (Howe 1994, Lawson 1992)

Rifkind in 1990, when Scottish Secretary, to secure financial concessions for poll tax payers in Scotland (Seldon 1997)

Most of these threats observe five rules. First, the minister must be in the Cabinet: junior ministers rarely have the clout to pull off such a trick, unless their Secretary of State is willing to threaten resignation too. Second, the issue must affect the minister's own department (true of all the above except Fowler, for whom it was a constituency issue). Presumably it is more difficult for the Prime Minister to engineer a concession in another minister's bailiwick, which could spark a rival resignation threat. Third, the minister must be senior or popular enough to cause considerable embarrassment by his resignation. Fourth, the Prime Minister must be able to

meet without inordinate difficulty the concessions needed to avoid resignation. Finally, threats of resignation must be used only rarely; the more
frequent they become, the less effective they are. If these rules are
observed, a shrewd minister can win his point and enhance his reputation
into the bargain.

The minister who threatens resignation must be willing to see it
through. The Ross threat catalogued above was countered by a counter-
threat of resignation by Varley, the Industry Secretary; Varley lost but
stayed in post. Similarly John Moore, Social Security Secretary under Mrs
Thatcher, threatened resignation over the rate of child benefit, but then
backed down. Both, who had been regarded as possible leaders of their
parties, found that their careers were stopped in their tracks.

The Prime Minister's relations with his Cabinet

This mutual dependence between Prime Minister and departmental
minister also exists between the Prime Minister and his colleagues collectively. As pointed out previously, ministers expect their premier to be a
leader, to give purpose and direction to their collective efforts. They rely on
him to be a fixer, to oil the wheels of government, to solve problems and
act as honest broker between ministers in dispute. And they look to him to
encourage a sense of common purpose between them, to provide the
cement that holds the Cabinet together.

In return the Prime Minister depends on his colleagues collectively for
something less easily defined but nevertheless important: a spirit of joint
political purpose, a willingness to share in the overall burden of government, to sink their differences for their common good. He needs them to
close ranks against outside critics, to give and take in policy disagreements,
and to raise their eyes from the problems of their own departments to the
government's wider political horizons.

Consequently, at any gathering of ministers – full Cabinet, committee
or impromptu conference – the Prime Minister performs several contradictory roles. He must conciliate colleagues and work to keep them thinking
jointly rather than selfishly, which implies a submergence of his own views.
On the other hand, colleagues look to him for guidance and leadership,
which impels him towards taking a decisive stance in any choice facing the
government. Given that Prime Ministers are people of clear opinions, they
are most likely to take a view on the policy issue and then try to guide
colleagues round to agreement with it.

Contrary to Richard Crossman's wilder claims, the Prime Minister does
not exercise unfettered control over the agenda of Cabinet or its committees. The pressure of business and departmental timetables largely

determine this for him; the problem is keeping the flow of business down to a manageable volume. Keeping an item off the agenda is difficult if the responsible minister wants it on. The Prime Minister can try to persuade him not to press the issue as far as Cabinet. Even very senior ministers may give way to such pressure: in 1971 Maudling withdrew a paper arguing for an incomes policy at Heath's request (Maudling 1978). However, if the minister insists, the Prime Minister can delay but not refuse.

It is true, nonetheless, that the framework for the discussion will have been set by the forum chosen by the Prime Minister; by the previous discussions between the Prime Minister and the departmental minister which may, for instance, have ruled out some options; and by any other previous discussion with colleagues that the Prime Minister may have held.

In addition, at the meeting itself there are three useful tactics to which the Prime Minister may resort: the arts of chairmanship, rushing colleagues into decisions, and circumventing the Cabinet.

1   *Control through chairmanship.* Once the Cabinet, or a committee chaired by the Prime Minister, is under way, he largely determines its tone and progress. Much hinges on his style of chairmanship. Wilson said of this difficult task:

> The Prime Minister must be ever alert to issues which raise fundamental, doctrinal or almost theological passions on the part of one or more ministers, and do all he can to avoid an unnecessary clash without sacrificing principle, and without fudging an issue on which a clear decision has been reached…Above all, the Prime Minister must be ever-watchful of the political implications and dangers of a given course of action, particularly when a departmental minister might be tempted to under-emphasise them, because of his immersion in administrative technicalities or his proneness to accord too much weight to outside pressure groups on his department.
>
> (Wilson 1976)

Alas, Wilson often failed to practice what he preached.

Cabinets seem to appreciate two contradictory qualities in their chairmen: dispatch in the conduct of business, and cultivation of discussion on controversial issues. Post-war premiers illustrate a spectrum of behaviour. At one extreme Churchill, who liked a late lunch, would let debate drag on; on one occasion, wanting to avoid discussion of Britain's military presence in Egypt, he engaged the Home Secretary in a pointless argument about Lord Derby's footman, who had shot his butler (Horne 1988). At the other extreme Mrs Thatcher would invite the responsible minister to introduce the subject, then state her own view and argue with anyone who disagreed with her (Prior 1986; various ministers quoted in the *Guardian* 4 January 1988). Whitelaw wearily recalled: 'Her unquenchable appetite for argument is rather trying...She must lead from the front, provoke everybody, challenge them and stir them up. It can be very wearing' (*The Sunday Times* 23 April 1989). Mrs Thatcher was actually a better listener than she was given credit for being, but once she had made up her mind was tenacious and not above summing up against the mood of the meeting.* The occasion on which Mrs Thatcher rejected membership of the EU exchange rate mechanism against the collective advice of her Deputy Prime Minister, Chancellor, Foreign Secretary, Trade and Industry Secretary, Party Chairman and the Governor of the Bank of England was not an isolated instance.

Those Prime Ministers who came closest to the happy medium in the dispatch of business were Attlee, brisk and to the point; Eden, less terse but effective; Douglas-Home, whose businesslike manner was a relief to some after Macmillan's prolixity; and Major, whose style was deliberately more collegiate than Mrs Thatcher's. Rather a difficult Prime Minister to classify was Heath, whose summing up tended to the cryptic:

> one could not always be sure about Ted's position even by the end of Cabinet: he would quite often go his own way afterwards ... Ministers were never quite sure in Ted's day what Cabinet had decided until we saw the Cabinet minutes the next day.
>
> (Prior 1986)

Chapter 3 described the way in which the Prime Minister can set the framework for a ministerial discussion, especially by deciding the forum for debate – Cabinet, committee or an ad hoc meeting – and the timing. At the meeting itself, the easiest way for the Prime Minister to sway the outcome is to state his opinion. This carries great weight with colleagues: not only do individual ministers often follow his lead but in every Cabinet there is a 'king's party' of lesser ministers who usually provide a core of support that he can rely on. Michael Heseltine, only days after resigning from Mrs Thatcher's Cabinet accusing her of abusing her power, acknowledged: 'The fact that a Prime Minister has a decisive influence over many ministers' support in Cabinet is a perfectly legitimate, perhaps even desirable feature' ('Weekend World', London Weekend Television 12 January 1986). Of course, such willingness to follow the premier's lead can occasionally go to extremes. During Callaghan's premiership the Agriculture Secretary asked the Cabinet to raise the price of milk. The Prices Secretary was opposed. Callaghan, himself a weekend farmer, pronounced the increase desirable to help farmers, since the price of calves was rising. In fact this was nonsense: those farmers who would profit from higher calf prices would also profit from higher milk prices, but the Prime Minister had spoken and undecided ministers followed his lead.*

Much hinges on the timing of the Prime Minister's intervention. Wilson was a dissimulator who if possible kept his views secret to avoid open defeat, only stating his view if he thought it would be decisive. Callaghan, during the IMF crisis, kept his own counsel while his opponents wore themselves down by lengthy debate, and finally threw his own opinion into the scales to tip them in his favour. Heath listened to the arguments in silence, then abruptly made a pronouncement that was often decisive.

The order in which the Prime Minister calls ministers to speak can affect the debate. Lawson recalled of Mrs Thatcher's carefully orchestrated Cabinet discussions of public expenditure: 'George Younger…was always a reliable opening batsman, and Willie Whitelaw was ideal at the end. (After Willie's retirement, Geoffrey Howe was an ideal substitute in this role.) The one colleague who could be guaranteed to be unsound was Peter Walker: it was useful to have his contribution immediately followed by one from Norman Tebbit' (Lawson 1992).

For sheer artistry, Macmillan was probably the supreme manipulator of his Cabinet. By repute, his most memorable performance was given when he persuaded the Cabinet to accept the Concorde project. The first meeting was evenly split. Macmillan was non-committal and adjourned a decision. He then privately reassured ministers worried about the implications for their budgets and talked round the Chancellor. At the next meeting

> The Prime Minister was in reminiscent mood. He told his colleagues about his great aunt's Daimler, which had travelled at 'the sensible speed of thirty miles an hour' and was sufficiently spacious to enable one to descend from it without removing one's top hat. Nowadays, alas! people had a mania for dashing around. But that being so Britain ought to 'cater for this profitable modern eccentricity'.
>
> (Bruce-Gardyne and Lawson 1976)

One participant recalled:

> Macmillan was at his subtlest. Only late in the day did he play the French card. With great solemnity he then stressed its historic importance. Concorde, and the expense involved, were made to seem relative trivialities. The Cabinet, in a state of elevated emotion, acquiesced.
>
> (Boyd-Carpenter 1980)

It should be noted that this tactic of adjourning the meeting and twisting arms in the meanwhile, a ruse beloved of Churchill and Macmillan (Mallaby 1965, Macmillan 1972) is today rendered impossible by increasing pressure on the Cabinet's time.

Such examples are highly personal and may seem trivial, but can be highly significant at moments of decision. Nonetheless, such ploys have to be exercised within the framework of the need to bring the Cabinet to a conclusion acceptable to all: in Denis Healey's phrase 'to steer a very unruly rabble of ministers who may disagree profoundly and have totally different interests...towards a common conclusion' (BBC 1990b). Of themselves the arts of chairmanship will not win the argument for the Prime Minister, but they are a useful addition to his armament.

2 *Rushing a decision*. Prime Ministers also occasionally 'bounce' their colleagues into decisions by allowing an issue to be raised at the last moment and insisting on an immediate decision. From the 1950s to the 1970s, when economic crises frequently required a round of spending cuts, this stratagem was much favoured by Prime Ministers and Chancellors acting in tandem. There are several descriptions of this happening under Wilson, such as the July 1965 emergency spending cuts described by Crossman as being

> as near to central dictatorship as one is likely to get in a British Cabinet. At Cabinet we were not given the time either to discuss the underlying strategy or even to consider the document as a whole. We were told to 'take it or leave it as it stands'....Most of the Cabinet did not agree. They objected with varying degrees of strength to the whole package...The discussion drifted on till nearly twelve thirty when it became obvious that we wouldn't have time to go through the draft in great detail. It would have to be bulldozed through. And that's what happened.
>
> (Crossman 1975. Other episodes are described in Castle, 1980 and Crossman 1976)

However the more disciplined approach to public spending since the 1970s has made this tactic largely redundant, and it rarely seems to be used in other areas.

3   *Avoiding a discussion.* Alternatively, if the Prime Minister and the responsible departmental minister are worried about being overruled by colleagues, they may succeed in keeping a policy away from Cabinet or committee entirely. This seems mainly to happen in economic and overseas affairs for, as described in Chapter 5, collegiate concerns dominate in the domestic arena. Wilson and his economic ministers prevented discussion of devaluation for three years despite the misgivings of many colleagues (Lawson and Bruce-Gardyne 1976, Crossman 1975 and 1976, Castle 1980) just as Mrs Thatcher avoided any Cabinet discussion of economic policy throughout 1979 (Young 1989) and refused to put the question of the ERM to Cabinet (Lawson 1992). Ministers who disagreed lacked the cohesion or determination to demand a discussion – in the case of the ERM, because the Prime Minister threatened resignation. Wilson refused to allow discussion of a nuclear warhead test in 1974 (Castle 1980) and prevented serious discussion of Britain's role east of Suez for years, despite the opposition of many ministers to it (Walker 1972, Crossman 1975 and 1976, Castle 1984). No Prime Minister since Macmillan has allowed Cabinet any substantial discussion of nuclear weapons policy (Hennessy 1986).

The Cabinet's self-assertion against the Prime Minister

For all this, the Prime Minister cannot automatically bend the Cabinet to his will. First, the more the Prime Minister uses these devices, the more he risks antagonising his colleagues; and the sharper the trick, the less often it can be used. Second, for all the devices open to the Prime Minister, there is plentiful evidence of premiers being overruled in Cabinet or committee, although often this is not apparent because, as pointed out earlier, a wise Prime Minister will conceal his own views until late in the debate when he will speak his mind only if he thinks he can do so without being overruled. In this way much of the Cabinet's restraint on the Prime Minister is covert.

So, for instance, Macmillan was outvoted on several occasions, such as on the Japanese trade treaty and defence reorganisation (Barnes 1987), but he wisely accepted defeat with humour and good grace. Several times Wilson came to grief trying to force a line on his Cabinet. In 1965 he tried to restore cuts in the overseas aid budget and was defeated after a 90-minute row with the Chancellor and Economic Affairs Secretary: 'the worst Cabinet we've ever had, and the worst for Harold Wilson' (Crossman 1975). A similar row accompanied the Cabinet's refusal to send ships to the Gulf of Aqaba during the Six Day War (Castle 1980). In 1975 Wilson and his Chancellor were not allowed to announce reserve powers in the White Paper on pay policy (Benn 1989, Castle 1980).

Mrs Thatcher's very different style of 'leading from the front' in Cabinet and committee, although often successful in pre-empting dissent, on occasion rebounded disastrously on her. The Cabinet ruled out drastic anti-union legislation in the early 1980s; in 1980 they insisted on accepting a settlement of the EU budget dispute; in 1981 they blocked proposals for £5 billion of cuts in public spending. The following year Mrs Thatcher failed to prevent a £500 million package to alleviate unemployment and was later defeated over a radical programme of privatisation and spending cuts in the welfare field. On later occasions the Cabinet or committees under her chairmanship rejected the abolition of private rent control, overruled her reluctance to ratify the European Convention on Human Rights, overrode her objections to plans for a Northern Ireland assembly and refused to sell Austin Rover to Ford Motors (Howe 1994, Young 1989, Stephenson 1980, Keegan 1984). This is a remarkable catalogue of defeats to be imposed on one of the century's most dominant Prime Ministers.

Inner Cabinets and 'inner circles'

It is helpful to distinguish between an inner Cabinet and an 'inner circle'. An inner Cabinet is a formal body, properly established and recognised, with some degree of authority for taking decisions on behalf of other ministers. On that reckoning, there have been only two, possibly three, inner Cabinets set up since the war, all by Wilson in the 1960s, all at moments when he was politically weak. The first, the Economic Strategy Policy Committee, was created in 1966 when Crossman led a faction in Cabinet to try and force devaluation, but side-tracked himself into demanding an inner Cabinet instead. Wilson debilitated it by stealth: it 'was duly constituted, packed with such luminaries as the Secretaries of State for Scotland and Wales, and disappeared from sight' (Lawson and Bruce-Gardyne 1976).

Later Wilson voluntarily set up, with some fanfare, a Parliamentary Committee that a year later was re-christened the Management Committee. Both met regularly but, while they discussed some substantive issues – pay settlements, race relations, the finance bill – they did so in a desultory way, with little in the way of clear decisions. Often the agenda was dictated by that day's headlines. Those ministers who were excluded were jealous, and those included were bored when the same ground had to be retrodden at Cabinet. It was no more than a Wilsonian exercise in gimmickry (Crossman 1977, Castle 1984, Benn 1988).

Formal inner Cabinets are equally uncommon overseas. A rare exception was the 'consiglio di gabinetto' which operated in Italy in the 1980s, and was even given a statutory basis in 1988; it sought to improve decision-making by concentrating power in a small group of people but was undermined by the insistence that all coalition parties be represented on it (Cotta 1988, Criscitiello 1994). The Priorities and Planning Committee of the Canadian Cabinet fulfilled something like an inner Cabinet function for some years and to some extent New Zealand's Cabinet Expenditure Committee did the same (Campbell 1985, Weller 1985). More often, Western European Cabinets will have a coalition committee to manage relations between the parties which make up the government, but these tend to perform a conciliatory rather than strategic task (Laver and Shepsle 1994).

More common and less formal is what can be termed an 'inner circle' in which a Prime Minister meets regularly with a small cadre of senior colleagues who act as informal counsellors, discussing issues of the day, shaping the main lines of policy, giving coherence to the government's activities (Phillips 1977, James 1994). It is never easy to discern when the Prime Minister is merely consulting senior colleagues on their departments' work and when he is discussing a much wider range of business with them, but when the latter happens, an inner circle is developing.

Although such meetings are frequent, records of them are rare: the best documented are from the premiership of Macmillan, who had a flexible grouping – generally including the indispensable Rab Butler and the current Chancellor – to discuss major issues before they came to Cabinet. He used such meetings variously to prepare for a discussion of defence and the American offer of Thor missiles in February 1957, and another that July to discuss the situation in Iraq and Cyprus (Barnes 1987 and 1998).

Similar groups have been discernible at certain times under later premiers: the troika of Wilson, Brown and Callaghan in the early years of the Labour governments of the 1960s; Callaghan's less cohesive inner circle consisting of himself, Foot and Healey, although he also consulted Merlyn Rees. Major had no inner cabinet as such, but in the run-up to the 1992 election the group working on the manifesto, including Hurd, Lamont, Clarke, Patten and Heseltine, discussed some general policy issues as well (Seldon 1997).

Other Prime Ministers rely mainly on one colleague. Attlee's government pivoted around his partnership with Ernest Bevin; Wilson in his last government had a weekly chat with Callaghan (Callaghan 1987). Sometimes Prime Ministers have no colleague senior enough to share the burden: Heath had a recognisable group of trusties in Carrington, Prior and Whitelaw (Armstrong 1994) but none was senior enough to take the place of Macleod or Maudling, who were both lost to the government early on. Consequently Heath leaned more on advice from top officials.

In the end, whether or not an inner circle exists depends on the Prime Minister's own self-sufficiency, the personalities in the Cabinet and the political circumstances of the moment. These factors change rapidly over time, as Mrs Thatcher showed. Her first two administrations were dominated by the axis between her and the veteran Whitelaw, but separately she consulted with more radical colleagues: first a group of junior economic ministers including Joseph, Nott, Biffen and Lawson; later, when that group dispersed, she relied first on Parkinson and, after his resignation, Tebbit. Briefly, after the Westland crisis in 1986, she contemplated the formation of a semi-formal inner circle, but never followed the idea through (Lawson 1992, 1994). Once Tebbit and Whitelaw left, no colleague of sufficient seniority remained and she tended instead to rely on officials or external advisers like Alan Walters.

In short, there is no fixed pattern, and it is all very personal and informal. But more often than not a government will contain an inner circle of ministers, varying from two or three to half a dozen in number, which does some of the fixing and dealing necessary to keep any government working and, in some cases, may give some vague strategic steer by receiving papers and thinking ahead. Even so, when this happens, experience suggests that it is haphazard, only partially successful and strategic only in the loosest sense of the term.

The danger of 'folie de grandeur'

One personal danger that stalks every Prime Minister is the 'folie de grandeur' of high office. The machinery and mystique surrounding his office reinforces his self-importance. Security precautions isolate him physically. His private staff are the best and brightest in the civil service and have as their sole function to serve and advise him. He mixes with monarchs, presidents and ambassadors. Powerful interests entreat his help. He may appear in the press and on television almost as he wishes. He can summon ministers at will; senior officials will rush to do his bidding.

All this can go to his head: without realising it he can by degrees become remote from his colleagues, intolerant of disagreement, authoritarian in tone, disdainful of opponents. It is an insidious trap: colleagues become resentful, officials wary, the government less happy. If the Prime Minister is heedless of warnings and dissent, he may lose touch with political reality. When big trouble breaks – perhaps over a trivial issue – an irate premier forms his wagons into a circle against the outside world. The press turns hostile, backbenchers mutter, the Prime Minister stands at bay at the despatch box and serious political damage follows.

Eden was temperamentally prone to this kind of behaviour and it contributed to his fall. Much the same happened to Heath and Mrs Thatcher, who in their final months in Downing Street seemed remote from their party and the rest of the country. Of the latter, one adviser describes 'trouble [arising] largely from within, from the concentration of power, from the isolation it imposed, and from the character deformation it imposed' (Cradock 1997). Other Prime Ministers have succumbed to it in a milder form: Macmillan developed a perceptible autocratic streak in his last years in office and the mercurial Wilson had phases of suspicion and intolerance. At such times their governments were at their weakest.

There are countervailing pressures. A few colleagues senior enough to argue with the Prime Minister as friendly near-equals will help him to keep a sense of proportion. Roy Jenkins reckoned:

> All the best governments are governments in which you have two or three people who have an independent constituency of their own, whom the Prime Minister needs as much, or maybe more sometimes, than they need the Prime Minister…and therefore their advice can be given…as people with an independent political position of their own.
>
> (BBC 1990b)

Absence of such colleagues was a great handicap to Macmillan and to Mrs Thatcher, who towards the end relied heavily on official advisers with no electoral or parliamentary experience.

Perceptive private secretaries and a wise Cabinet Secretary will tactfully seek to check the early symptoms. The regular audience with the monarch is a potent reminder to the premier that he too is a subordinate. The weekly Prime Minister's question time, unconstructive in itself, serves to take him down a peg or two occasionally. A strong chief whip and the more eminent backbenchers will sound discreet danger signals. Yet ultimately all depends on the Prime Minister possessing a sense of proportion. Attlee, Douglas-Home and Callaghan were modest about themselves and tactful with their colleagues. Consequently, they ran fairly happy Cabinets (all under adverse conditions) enhancing their reputations and that of their office.

Conclusion

The picture of the premiership that emerges is one of considerable authority and influence, circumscribed by many practical and political restrictions. The inherent authority of the Prime Minister's office is not invincible but remains great. His freedom to hire and fire is hedged about with many restraints, but he still has much room for manoeuvre, especially in the allocation of portfolios. His control over the Cabinet committee system, official information, the machinery of government, civil service appointments and patronage are not immense if considered individually, but taken collectively are a notable addition to the other levers under his hand. Overall his scope for imprinting his views on policy is considerable. Nonetheless, his departmental colleagues are powerful and expert on their own ground; individually and collectively they are a potent check on an over-zealous premier.

That said, relations between No. 10 and departments cannot be founded on permanent conflict; indeed the norm is a simultaneous combination of Cabinet collegiality and Prime Ministerial leadership. The Prime Minister leads, guides and supports his team but relies on their energies and expertise, just as they in turn rely on his leadership. The dynamics of the system are variable and the forces within it occasionally push at tangents to each other, but generally all ministers are trying to move in the same direction. The relationship is essentially one of mutual reliance. A strong Prime Minister needs strong ministers.

5 The dynamics of collective decision-making

In examining the respective roles of the Prime Minister, departmental ministers, the Cabinet and its committees in making policy, it is important to re-emphasise the great flexibility within the system. A single pattern of relations will not suit all circumstances or all personalities: there are too many variables, human and political, to permit that. Consequently it is possible only to describe the bounds within which the various actors usually operate and identify working rules which hold true in most cases. Given these limitations, six principles seem generally to hold true:

1   The decision-making process is segmented: that is, different patterns of policy-making operate in different policy areas. The Prime Minister is deeply and continuously involved in foreign and economic policy, less deeply and more sporadically in other areas. [1]
2   The Prime Minister's relationship with the lead minister in each sphere varies accordingly: he must work particularly closely with the Chancellor of the Exchequer and the Foreign Secretary, while in other fields he deals with ministers on a less regular basis.
3   Given a capable departmental minister, the depth of collective ministerial involvement tends to be the inverse of the Prime Minister's involvement: shallow in foreign and economic policy, deeper in other domestic areas. This has held true both before 1979 and under the rather different system that has since evolved.
4   The Prime Minister needs strong ministers. A weak minister is a drain on the energies of his colleagues and the Prime Minister.
5   In public expenditure a completely different set of dynamics applies, with each minister fighting his corner and an arbitration role played by a committee of senior ministers, with an occasional appeal to the Prime Minister or Cabinet.

6   As argued in the previous chapter, the Prime Minister has a relationship of mutual dependence with each departmental minister; and to a
large extent each can veto a proposal advanced by the other.

A study of each sphere of policy reveals much about the roles of all
these actors and the relations between them.

Foreign policy

The growth of Prime Ministerial involvement in diplomacy

Diplomacy has always been a preoccupation at No. 10: in past centuries,
since government intervention in everyday life was very limited, foreign
affairs loomed very large in the concerns of the Prime Minister and his
Cabinet. Although in this century government involvement in economic
and domestic life has grown immensely, and ought logically to be taking up
proportionately more of the premier's time, Prime Ministers remain
heavily involved in diplomatic affairs; indeed, in the last three decades
their involvement has deepened. There are three main reasons for this:

1   A revolution in communications allows politicians to travel faster and
more frequently, permitting more personal and regular contact
between world leaders. In the 1930s Chamberlain used to receive
news during weekends at Chequers of Hitler's acts of aggression on
an upright telephone with a rotary handle in what used to be the
butler's pantry; and Chamberlain's subsequent journey by air to
Munich was considered a novel and dangerous enterprise. Today,
communications are instant and world travel routine: as Robin Cook
put it:

I can travel to the United States supersonic, arrive before I left, as it
were, and give a speech which immediately becomes available on the
web all round the world.

(BBC 1998)

2   Membership of the EU has made a vast number of domestic policy
issues the subject of international action and so brought them under
the Prime Minister's eye, not least through his involvement in international summit meetings. No important step in EU policy is taken
without his involvement.

3   Outside the EU the nature of international relations has similarly widened to encompass such issues as trade, economic cooperation, joint defence projects, overseas aid, cultural relations, fishing rights, fiscal harmonisation, environmental pollution, industrial collaboration and the prevention of terrorism. As Mrs Thatcher put it after a visit to Moscow: 'Foreign affairs aren't foreign affairs any more. They cover everything' (BBC 1987). The fusion of these concerns, domestic as much as diplomatic, cannot be left to the Foreign Secretary alone. The Prime Minister is the only minister who can synthesise them into a coherent, balanced policy.

Partly to accommodate this 'new diplomacy', there has been a great increase in summit meetings. Meetings of heads of government are frequent and add substantially to a Prime Minister's workload. Commonwealth Prime Ministers meet every other year. The 'G8' heads of government of the leading economic nations meet to discuss economic issues on average twice a year, and meetings of NATO heads of government are held rather less often. In addition, there are many bilateral meetings with other heads of government, notably the German Chancellor and French President once or twice a year, in addition to frequent telephone conversations with them and other European leaders.

The most onerous area of summitry, however, is the development of the European Council as a focal point for decision-making within the EU. It convenes twice a year and lasts several days. Its meetings are usually informal, partly because they are kept relatively small: officials are firmly excluded and only heads of government and foreign ministers are present. A lot of business is transacted in lunch breaks and adjournments. The 1992 Treaty on European Union defines its functions as providing the necessary impetus and policy guidelines for the EU's development. In particular this means taking the major decisions about the EU's development and to some degree providing strategic impulse for the Community. For instance, the 1982 Copenhagen meeting was a decisive step on the road to the single internal market, the 1989 Madrid summit was a turning point in the development of monetary union, and the Maastricht summit was a milestone on the way towards economic and political union.

Second, it resolves problems which the Council of Ministers has failed to solve, like the 1984 Fontainebleau meeting that at last resolved a long-running wrangle over the Community's budget with which the Council of Ministers had long wrestled in vain. While the European Council has to operate as a consensual body, making it more discursive than decisive, it has increasingly become the forum in which major decisions about the EU are made.

In his first 4 years as premier John Major paid sixty-three overseas visits, two-thirds of them on EU business (*The Economist* 10 September 1994, quoted in Hennessy 1996). Wilson (1976) estimated that between 1974 and 1976 he had three or four foreign affairs-related meetings per week and, while no more recent estimate has been made public, the burden has not reduced in the 1980s and 1990s (for example, Thatcher 1993, Seldon 1997).

The Prime Minister's diplomatic involvement is not confined to visits abroad. Back at home he plays host to heads of government, foreign ministers, and the economic ministers and trade ministers of more important countries. In Wilson's final 9 months in office he was visited by two presidents, ten prime ministers and twenty-four senior ministers. On top of this come senior officials of international organisations, trade missions and parliamentary delegations. The Prime Minister will usually see any British ambassador posted to an important country when in London (Wilson 1976).

Why does a Prime Minister get involved in foreign affairs? As political leader of the nation he feels a certain responsibility for its international reputation and the electorate, while not much bothered about foreign policy as such, holds his government responsible for the country's standing in the world. If under a Prime Minister's leadership Britain distinguishes itself in world affairs he may hope to gain credit at home. During the 1959 election Macmillan exploited his involvement in diplomacy between the United States and the USSR to advantage. Mrs Thatcher played the same card very successfully in a highly-publicised visit to Moscow in the run-up to the 1987 election. Conversely, the Prime Minister may be blamed however unfairly for any disaster in the international sphere. A dramatic example was the invasion of the Falkland Islands when ministers predicted that unless the government took military action it would fall (Hastings and Jenkins 1983). In contrast, the success of the military campaign that followed greatly increased the government's popularity, and that of Mrs Thatcher above all other.

Prime Ministers generally have a further, personal motive. Visits abroad and summit meetings have glamour. Every Prime Minister has devoted decades to seemingly intractable domestic problems. The world stage offers a different kind of politics where he automatically enjoys dignity and prestige and is treated with a respect rarely found at the Commons despatch box. At home, he is a politician. Abroad, he is a statesman.

The degree of premiers' detailed involvement in overseas questions varies according to their interests and personality. Some intervene constantly, as Churchill and Eden did, to the annoyance of their Foreign Secretaries. Some are preoccupied only with certain areas: Heath had a powerful ambition to take Britain into Europe but limited interest in other areas of diplomacy. Some premiers' interest changes over time. There is a strikingly similar pattern between the two longest-serving post-war premiers, Wilson and Mrs Thatcher. Both first came to office concerned primarily with domestic and economic matters, restricting their diplomatic involvement to such unavoidable issues as Rhodesia, the EU and relations with the United States. However, as time wore on and particularly after they won their second elections, both showed more interest and devoted more time to overseas visits and summit meetings. But these are really just variations on a basic theme: that no Prime Minister can avoid involvement in foreign policy. As Macmillan told the Commons three decades ago, the Prime Minister's involvement in foreign affairs 'is no longer a matter of choice but a matter of fact' (Commons debates 29 July 1960).

Three consequences of the growth of summitry are worth noting. First, it gives the Prime Minister scope for personal initiative. The Castle and Benn diaries show the difficulty that the Cabinet had in restraining Wilson and Callaghan at EU summits; Mrs Thatcher clearly approached such meetings in the assumption that she could change her stance and commit her government just as the German Chancellor and French President did (Thatcher 1993). This is not limited to EU meetings: when Mrs Thatcher met President Ershad of Bangladesh in 1983, she agreed beforehand with the Foreign Office to reject his request for extra aid, yet at the meeting promised him an extra £20 million (Jenkins and Sloman 1985).

Second, it absorbs a lot of time. Every meeting requires extensive briefing: even a courtesy call or short, single subject meeting requires a written brief in the overnight box, while a European Council or major conference runs to several volumes of notes, and several full-dress briefings beforehand at No. 10 (Wilson 1976).

Third, the more the Prime Minister is involved in overseas affairs, the more other governments expect him to be involved. Foreign heads of government, particularly presidents, including the US President, tend to by-pass the Foreign Office and go straight to No. 10 (Young and Sloman 1986).

Relations between the Prime Minister and the Foreign Secretary

The Prime Minister and Foreign Secretary need to have a close working relationship, not least because they spend so much time travelling together. In key areas the Prime Minister will seek command. Even Attlee, who allowed Bevin a very free hand – 'You don't keep a dog and bark yourself, and Ernie was a very good dog' (Harris 1982) – kept a close eye on imperial and colonial matters, especially India (Bullock 1983). And because he is the subordinate, the Foreign Secretary must either enjoy the Prime Minister's trust or be treated as his subordinate. If the two are constantly at loggerheads, either in temperament or over policy, the Foreign Secretary will have to go.

Only four times since 1945 has a Prime Minister been saddled with an uncongenial Foreign Secretary. None lasted long. Eden and Macmillan rapidly fell out, and a reluctant Macmillan was soon transferred to the Exchequer. Wilson appointed George Brown because there was no other post senior enough for him, but Brown, with justification, resented Wilson's high-handed behaviour, such as his despatch of personal envoys on missions to Vietnam and Rhodesia. After innumerable rows, the mercurial Brown resigned. When Carrington resigned after the Falklands invasion, Mrs Thatcher had no sufficiently senior replacement except Francis Pym. They had long been at odds over domestic policy, and Pym's more conciliatory attitude towards foreign negotiations – over the Falklands, the EU, Palestine and arms control – put them so utterly out of step that by late 1983 the Home Secretary had to act as go-between (*Sunday Times* 9 January 1983; *The Economist* 27 November 1982). Pym was dismissed after the 1983 election. Before many more years elapsed, she had similarly fallen out with his successor Howe – by that late, imperious stage of her premiership, she would probably have fallen out with any holder of the office – and he was demoted after falling out with her over Europe (Howe 1994).

In contrast, when the Prime Minister and Foreign Secretary work in tandem they can more or less run foreign policy between them. Heath, a rather autocratic premier, worked well with Douglas-Home, a uniquely experienced Foreign Secretary. In 1971 they initiated talks with the French, about which even the Cabinet knew little, that paved the way for the successful British application to join the EU. In these Douglas-Home accepted without jealousy Heath's leading role. Heath in turn acknowledged his Foreign Secretary's authority in other areas, notably Africa.

Similarly Dr David Owen, not a born subordinate, worked well with Callaghan who had confidence in his appointee but gently kept Owen in line:

> He had a remarkable gift for letting me know his views privately. He didn't have to send memos, he didn't have to write letters. Jim Callaghan could let you know just in a couple of sentences if he thought you were slightly going off the rails, or warned you about an attitude that he was going to adopt.
>
> (Young and Sloman 1986)

The longer a Prime Minister holds office, the more likely he is to lord it over his Foreign Secretary. Surprisingly Churchill, who boasted fifty years of international experience to his Foreign Secretary's mere twenty, nonetheless treated Eden with circumspection. But Selwyn Lloyd recalled of Macmillan:

> He would send us a draft. My officials would examine it with me. Our hair would occasionally stand on end. We would alter the draft. My job was then to convince him that our amendments flowed from his own ideas.
>
> (Thorpe 1989)

And while Mrs Thatcher came to power with little experience of foreign affairs, she developed strong views over 11 years. As Geoffrey Howe, her Foreign Secretary from 1983 to 1989 put it: 'Tensions are bound to develop as time passes and the Prime Minister develops his own view' (BBC 1998). Hurd explains his relationship with Mrs Thatcher in terms near-identical to Lawson's 'mutual blackball' described in the previous chapter:

> Both sides of Downing Street had a veto: the Prime Minister could block a decision by the Foreign Secretary but equally if the Prime Minister wanted something done by the Foreign Secretary he could say 'No'.
>
> (Dickie 1992)

Certainly Major, despite his meteoric promotion to the Foreign Office by Mrs Thatcher, found her difficult to work with and resented her high-handed behaviour – for example, in re-writing a communiqué on sanctions against South Africa that he had negotiated at a Commonwealth summit (Seldon 1997).

It is often said that the toughest negotiations that any Foreign Secretary faces are with his own Prime Minister (BBC 1998). But if the two agree the frontiers of their respective roles, a close working relationship can be turned to the Foreign Secretary's advantage. The Prime Minister may be called in in order to overrule the opposition of a senior colleague. His authority can be brought to bear on a foreign leader: when President Reagan began talks with the USSR on arms control, Mrs Thatcher, at the Foreign Office's behest, made him adjust his policies to accommodate the interests of European allies. Similarly, the advent of Major to the premiership and his close relationship with his Foreign Secretary Douglas Hurd allowed the Foreign Office to take a more pragmatic and conciliatory line towards Europe in which the Prime Minister's personal summitry played an important part.

Foreign affairs: the involvement of other ministers

Other ministers do not get much of a look-in on foreign affairs. At Cabinet, as noted in the previous chapter, the regular 'tour d'horizon' by the Foreign Secretary does not lead to much substantial discussion. The Prime Minister wants to minimise debate to prevent disruption of the policy agreed by the No. 10–Foreign Office axis. Even Churchill, who had an elaborate respect for Cabinet discussion, discouraged questions and only the most independent minded – Salisbury, Crookshank and Macmillan – dared risk a comment (Seldon 1981). As Foreign Secretary, Gordon Walker used to have before Cabinet 'a previous word with the Prime Minister about what to disclose or to keep quiet about for the moment' (Walker 1972).

Major issues will appear on the agenda and be seriously debated if the Prime Minister and Foreign Secretary want them to or feel that the issue is too important for the Cabinet to be circumvented. Barnes (1999) observes that this was a feature of Cabinet life well into the 1960s, discussing variously diplomatic overtures to the USSR (Colville 1985), Suez – although misled by Prime Minister Eden – and committing troops to the Western European Union. In the Labour governments of Wilson and Callaghan such discussion seems to have been more perfunctory (for example, Castle 1984), doubtless because the key overseas issues – EU membership, Vietnam and Rhodesia – split the Cabinet. Unexpectedly, there seems to have been more substantial discussion under Mrs Thatcher in the 1980s: issues such as the Hong Kong settlement, the EU budget, the Anglo-Irish agreement and the Rhodesian settlement all appeared and were seriously discussed because of their political sensitivity and intrinsic importance. But the Cabinet's true influence depends largely on the stage at which the Cabinet is involved. Because Mrs Thatcher consulted her Cabinet late in the day, its scope for altering what was proposed may have been very limited – the Anglo-Irish Agreement of 1986, for instance, was presented 'almost as a fait accompli' (Lawson 1992). The Cabinet's leverage was considerably greater when internal divisions over the EU compelled Major to consult his Cabinet colleagues earlier in the formulation of policy – an episode described below (Seldon 1997).

Cabinet committees in foreign affairs exercise little collective control. The Defence and Overseas Policy Committee, whose creation was announced by Macmillan in 1963 (Cmnd 2097), seems consistently to have been 'a purely reactive body, in general confirming the line already agreed by its senior members' (Barnes 1998). Protests by other members at support for the US bombing of Libya in 1986 were a rare instance of dissent (Cradock 1997). By the 1980s it was meeting quite infrequently (Howe 1994) not least because its leading members were spending (and still have to spend) a lot of time out of the country. Major used it more than most – convening an emergency meeting to discuss the 1991 coup in Russia and holding a 6-hour meeting in 1992 to discuss Bosnia and Iraq (Seldon 1997) – but such efforts at collegiality were exceptions. When DOP (Defence and Overseas Policy Committee) meets it is dominated by the quadrilateral relationship of Prime Minister, Foreign Secretary, Defence Secretary and Chancellor of the Exchequer. Its sub-committee on European questions deals mainly with casework, although Major and his Foreign Secretaries made it an important forum for deciding the UK stance in advance of European Councils (for example, Seldon 1997). Under Major a battery of small sub-committees existed to deal with Hong Kong, East European security, the former USSR, nuclear defence and terrorism, but it is unlikely that these met much, since Blair was able to sweep them all away and handle the business through the DOP net.

The signs are that it is more common for the Prime Minister to attempt – and succeed – to keep an issue away from collective discussion in foreign affairs (and indeed in economic matters – see pp. 155–60) than in domestic matters. If pressed in Cabinet he can vaguely offer a future debate that may well never materialise – like the debates on Vietnam and Europe that Wilson occasionally promised – or which does happen but is allowed to lead nowhere. Alternatively, the Cabinet may be kept completely in the dark. Wilson had a notorious penchant for conducting policy in secret. Before he became Prime Minister he struck a deal with the US to maintain Britain's world-wide commitments, especially East of Suez, and to avoid reflation or devaluation in exchange for American support for sterling. Seemingly only the Chancellor knew of this and it remained a secret from the rest of the world – although suspected by many – until revealed in the 1980s (Ponting 1989). Similarly, although many ministers held strong views on Vietnam and Rhodesia, Wilson's Cabinet rarely held informed debates on either and they were dealt with privately by the Prime Minister and Foreign Secretary. In mid-1965 he launched peace initiatives in Vietnam of which his colleagues only learned when he announced them in the Commons (Crossman 1975).

Obviously this is more difficult for the Prime Minister to achieve if the issue excites the political instincts of ministers. Three case studies illustrate different degrees to which the Prime Minister's discretion may be circumscribed by his colleagues' political interest.

1 The 1961 EU application

This was very much Macmillan's initiative. He had failed to rekindle the special relationship with the US, and his personal summitry had collapsed at the 1960 Moscow conference. He was still looking for a central theme for British foreign policy and his mind moved gradually towards EU membership. Opinion in the press and the Foreign Office was coming round to the idea. However, Conservatives were divided, and the implications for agriculture and the Commonwealth particularly sensitive. Macmillan had to move cautiously.

The decisive act was to redraw the map of Whitehall in Europe's favour in 1960. First, Sir Frank Lee, an enthusiast for Europe, became Permanent Secretary to the Treasury, and Macmillan immediately asked him to head a working group of officials to examine the implications of EU membership. Naturally, it came out in favour, as it was meant to. Second, Macmillan reshuffled his Cabinet, sending the pro-European Sandys to the Commonwealth Relations Office and Soames to Agriculture. Selwyn Lloyd, always amenable to intervention by his premier, was made Chancellor. Edward Heath, a staunch supporter of EU membership, became number two at the Foreign Office with Cabinet rank (since the new Foreign Secretary, Home, sat in the Lords). The balance of the Cabinet was tilted decisively towards Europe.

Thereafter it was much easier, but still Macmillan proceeded with great circumspection. He cautiously sounded out Commonwealth leaders and the US President. Reaction was favourable. Business and farming opinion began to swing round. Increasingly ministers talked of EU membership as a real possibility. The last major hurdle was the ambivalent 'Rab' Butler, Deputy Prime Minister. Cunningly, Macmillan asked him, in his capacity as Party Chairman, to tour the country paying particular attention to farming opinion. Butler returned convinced. There followed over four months of Cabinet and committee meetings discussing every aspect of the issue, culminating in a meeting in July 1961 in which, Macmillan recalled, all ministers with his encouragement spoke and unanimously agreed to apply for EU membership.

The lesson is two-edged. By use of his prerogative of assigning portfolios Macmillan set a pro-EU framework for debate. Yet, with the playing field tilted in his favour, he felt obliged to proceed with immense caution and carry his colleagues with him at every stage (Macmillan 1973, Lawson and Bruce-Gardyne 1976).

2   Rhodesia policy 1974–79

Rhodesia had been a running sore throughout the 1960s Labour governments. When Labour returned to government in 1974 the urgency had
slackened but Prime Minister Wilson renewed attempts to reach a settlement in tandem with his Foreign Secretary Callaghan. However, other
ministers were not minded to negotiate with the Rhodesian regime and
overruled a plan for a constitutional conference in 1975 and, in 1977, a
proposal that Britain commit armed forces to a Commonwealth force in
Rhodesia. On the other hand, in 1976, in defiance of a Cabinet discussion
that showed clearly that colleagues opposed any such move, Wilson and
Callaghan sent envoys to hold discussions with the Rhodesian government.
The first the Cabinet heard of this was from press reports, and it was then
too late to stop it (Castle 1980, Benn 1989 and 1990).

The conclusion suggested by this rather mixed episode is that the
Cabinet can exercise considerable restraint when a major, long-term exercise is being proposed – a peace conference, sending troops – but the
Prime Minister and Foreign Secretary may get away with overriding their
colleagues if the issue is of the 'hit and run' variety.

3   The 1991 Maastricht EU summit

This gathering was to agree a wide-ranging treaty on a political union that
deeply divided the Major government, with some ministers particularly
hostile to the Social Chapter, European Monetary Union and EU responsibility for border controls. While technical preparations for Maastricht
were made by a Cabinet committee chaired by Foreign Secretary Douglas
Hurd, Major went to elaborate lengths to consult colleagues, secure their
agreement to negotiating positions and bind colleagues into the agreement. Major himself chaired an important series of Defence and Overseas
Policy Committee meetings in the months before Maastricht, and held
several meetings with the Eurosceptic Home Secretary and Social Security
Secretary, culminating in a harmonious Cabinet the week before the
summit. He simultaneously staged a Commons debate on the subject,
forcing Eurosceptic colleagues to close ranks. Even from Maastricht he
rang home to consult the Employment Secretary on possible concessions
on the Social Chapter and, receiving a dusty answer, gave no ground in the
negotiations (Seldon 1997).

The implications from these few case studies are that the policy initiative lies with the Prime Minister and Foreign Secretary, the former having
great influence over the framework for debate. If the issue excites political
instincts it may be impossible to avoid consulting colleagues: much then

depends on the tactical approach. Macmillan and Major achieved their aims by patience and guile, but must have found the process of squaring colleagues deeply frustrating. Wilson's frontal attack ran a much higher risk of defeat and of antagonising colleagues. No hard and fast rule can be promulgated, except that the Cabinet cannot easily be overridden if an issue sets political pulses racing.

Defence policy

As with diplomacy, so with defence. The recession of British power has entailed greater cooperation with NATO allies. More than ever, defence is a specialised off-shoot of foreign policy, entwined with the other skeins that make up the more complex contemporary conception of diplomacy. Therefore any major development is heavily influenced by the No. 10–Foreign Office axis and the Cabinet is rarely involved despite the huge implications for public spending. This is encouraged by Prime Ministers' vague sense of responsibility for 'national security' and by the secrecy that perforce surrounds many issues, discouraging collective discussion, sometimes unnecessarily.

Defence: the involvement of the Prime Minister

Prime Ministerial involvement seems to have been high in the 1940s and 1950s (Eden 1960, Horne 1988) but to have slackened in recent decades, partly because of the shrinking of overseas military commitments; partly because Macmillan's successful reorganisation of the Ministry of Defence resolved many conflicts; and partly because defence decisions generally turn on technical details, which deters those outside the department from taking an interest in them. Muller, Phillip and Gerlich (1993) demonstrate from a survey of ministers that the British premier is seen by his cabinet colleagues as much less involved in defence than in foreign or economic matters, and not much more involved than in social questions.

Nonetheless, premiers retain control of the great issues, particularly nuclear weapons policy which they have kept firmly in their own grip, directly supervising the Defence Secretary's work or – like Macmillan and Callaghan – negotiating personally with US presidents. Nuclear policy has largely been determined by No. 10: Attlee forced through the decision to build an atomic bomb, Churchill the construction of the hydrogen bomb. Macmillan negotiated with the Americans over Skybolt and Polaris and energetically pursued a nuclear test ban treaty. Wilson forced his colleagues to keep Polaris and later foisted the expensive Chevaline project on them. Callaghan and Mrs Thatcher kept the Trident project firmly under their own control (Hennessy 1986, Callaghan 1987 and Zuckermann 1988).

Outside the nuclear field, what little is known suggests that the Prime Minister can make or break a defence project – for expenditure reasons, if nothing else. Wilson was clearly deeply embroiled in the 1960s defence reviews and his attitude clinched the cancellation of an aircraft carrier and the F-111 aircraft. The decision whether or not to stay east of Suez pivoted around his change of mind (Castle 1984). Mrs Thatcher took great interest in defence economics and involved herself in arguments over frigate design and the cancellation of the Nimrod radar system.* Certainly the Prime Minister must be involved if British troops are deployed overseas – which as Hennessy points out (1996) has happened fifty times since 1945.

Defence: the involvement of other ministers

In matters of defence, ministers' collegiate role appears minimal. All Prime Ministers except Churchill and Macmillan have refused to allow Cabinet discussion of nuclear weapons (Barnes 1998, Hennessy 1986). Wilson used either a small Nuclear Policy Committee including those ministers departmentally concerned, or simply ad hoc conversations with senior colleagues (Benn 1988, Ponting 1989). He once dropped a vague reference to Chevaline in Cabinet, but so obliquely that ministers never realised the import of what had been reported (Whitehead 1987). One suspects that many Labour politicians, unhappy in principle about nuclear weapons, did not really want to be told. Attlee thought some ministers 'not fit to be trusted with secrets of this kind' (Mackintosh 1977); Wilson, Callaghan and Mrs Thatcher simply feared being overruled. So far Blair has appointed no nuclear committee.

Even outside the nuclear sphere the Cabinet has little impact. The Cabinet will always be strongly influenced by any recommendation of the Defence and Overseas Policy Committee, and it would take a mighty Cabinet rebellion to overturn the combined advice of the Prime Minister, Foreign Secretary, Chancellor and Defence Secretary, especially since – as the Wilson Cabinet's discussions of defence cuts showed – the papers were usually circulated late and rarely contained much hard data (Castle 1984, Crossman 1975). There are signs that the Cabinet has got more of a look-in when jobs in the British defence industry have been at stake – there were long debates on the Nimrod radar system and the Challenger tank in the 1980s – but the Cabinet still would be heavily influenced by any previous committee discussion.

Economic affairs

Relations between the Prime Minister and the Chancellor of the Exchequer

The Prime Minister's involvement in economic problems, as in foreign affairs, is now unavoidable. Callaghan as Prime Minister had not intended to get deeply involved but 'economic problems obtruded at every street corner' (Callaghan 1987). Economic management remains an unquestioned key function of government, dominating the news and determining elections. The Prime Minister must be involved; his additional title of First Lord of the Treasury carries no formal functions, but embodies a significant truth. At the same time, the Chancellor is a remarkably powerful minister: he combines responsibility for taxation, monetary policy and public expenditure – a span of control unrivalled in any major developed country except France.

Consequently, relations between the two are of great importance, not least because the Chancellor – despite his power – is an exceptionally vulnerable member of the Cabinet. The Chancellor attracts more criticism than most ministers. The economy affects the public intimately and directly; when troubles arise – and the past thirty years have been fraught with difficulty – the Chancellor is violently criticised and needs all the help he can get. In the Cabinet he can easily be isolated by colleagues, most of whom will have some pretensions to economic knowledge and all are highly sensitive to constituents' complaints and backbench discontent. There is inevitable antagonism between spending ministers and the Chancellor: he is always surrounded by potential critics.

Yet a policy defeat for him is infinitely more damaging than for the Foreign Secretary. Defeat in Cabinet on the Falklands or the EU or relations with China leaves the Foreign Secretary discomfited but he can carry on because his department is a gathering of compartmentalised responsibilities; a defeat over one does not necessarily undermine his overall policy. In contrast economic policy is a seamless robe: defeat on one aspect can destroy the whole edifice. If the Chancellor is outvoted on, say, tax or interest rates, his whole strategy unravels. Only the Prime Minister can outface the whole Cabinet, so the Chancellor needs him as an ally. Hence, for example, Selwyn Lloyd's reliance on Macmillan's support to get approval at a stormy Cabinet meeting for creating the National Economic Development Council (Thorpe 1989), and Howe's dependence on Mrs Thatcher in her first government: he knew that unless he could overcome her reluctance to raise VAT to 15 per cent and abolish exchange controls, he would get nowhere (Howe 1994).

The bargain with the Prime Minister is as Callaghan described it to his Chancellor, Healey:

> I asked him to bring to me any major initiative he might wish to take before it went to the Cabinet, and if he and I could then agree, I would back him when such matters came before our colleagues.
>
> (Callaghan 1987)

Wass, at the top of the Treasury for many years, confirms 'every Chancellor I have known has obtained the Prime Minister's agreement to changes, even quite trivial ones, in the way the economy is run' (Wass 1983). In short, the 'mutual blackball' described in the previous chapter applies as much if not more to the Prime Minister's relations with the Chancellor, as demonstrated by Lawson's ability to refuse Mrs Thatcher's desire to increase mortgage relief, and her ability to stop him from reducing it (Lawson 1992).

As in the case of the Foreign Secretary, if the Chancellor does not see eye to eye with the Prime Minister life will be difficult and the Chancellor may have to go. Selwyn Lloyd's biographer has chronicled in detail the unhappy process by which, as Chancellor, he lost Macmillan's confidence and was eventually dismissed (Thorpe 1989). Relations between Nigel Lawson and Mrs Thatcher were bound to end in tears, for he was able, opinionated and not inclined by temperament to kow-tow to her increasingly inflexible views; since friction set in at an early stage, it is amazing in retrospect that they worked together for 6 years (Lawson 1992). The last few years crackled with tension, and Lawson declared in his resignation letter 'The successful conduct of economic policy is possible only when there is, and is seen to be, full agreement between the Prime Minister and the Chancellor of the Exchequer', in the absence of which he could not continue (national newspapers 27 October 1989). The relationship between Major and his Chancellor Lamont seems to have gone sour from an early stage, with Lamont reluctant to cut interest rates as fast as the Prime Minister wanted, failing to discuss his budget with him and reluctant to take action to lance the boil of the poll tax. After the debacle of sterling's ejection from the Exchange Rate Mechanism, Major refused Lamont's resignation, then sacked him after a further 8 months of deteriorating relations. Although politically maladroit, Lamont clearly felt that Major had used him as a shield (Seldon 1997).

Economic policy: the depth of Prime Ministers' involvement

Given the Chancellor's vulnerability, if the Prime Minister neglects economic policy damaging paralysis can follow. This was shown in 1974 when Wilson, for reasons of party management, was reluctant to bring economic problems to his Cabinet despite spiralling inflation; he saw little of his Chancellor and distracted himself with the EU referendum and devolution. Without his help Healey could not get the Cabinet to face the mounting crisis. Only when sterling slid in June 1975 did Wilson give a lead and guide his Cabinet into accepting an incomes policy (Donoughue 1987). However, political realities are such that it is very rare – and usually disastrous – for Prime Ministers to wash their hands of economic management.

Usually, Chancellors face the opposite problem: premiers are apt to press their own ideas on the Chancellor. Macmillan made the Treasury cut income tax in 1959, refused to deflate in 1960 and in 1962 imposed a prices and incomes policy (Barnes 1987, Macmillan 1972 and 1973). Wilson's involvement fluctuated but on the central issue of the 1970s – pay policy – imposed a policy on the Treasury. Heath, not Barber, drove the U-turn from free market policy to expansionist intervention, over-riding objections that inflation would increase (MacDougall 1987, Campbell 1993). Mrs Thatcher left her imprint on every aspect of economic policy throughout her government (Young 1989, Keegan 1984 and 1989, Lawson 1992). Usually this influence is exercised in the course of the Chancellor's routine consultations with the premier. But there are two rarer modes of intervention which, although infrequent, show the potential extent of the Prime Minister's influence: a long-term refusal to contemplate a policy option; and the short-term assumption of responsibility for some aspect of economic policy.

The 1960s devaluation saga

The long-term refusal to contemplate an option is illustrated by Wilson's refusal to devalue between 1964 and 1967 (Lawson and Bruce-Gardyne 1976, Contemporary Record 1988). Within hours of Labour's election victory, Brown (Secretary of State for Economic Affairs, a short-lived post) and Callaghan, then Chancellor, met privately and, fulfilling a secret deal struck by Wilson in Opposition with the US Treasury, vetoed devaluation. The Cabinet was never consulted, and although this entailed repeated and unpopular retrenchment measures, Wilson used every trick in the book to prevent discussion of devaluation as an alternative. To Healey's mind,

Wilson saw sterling 'as a sort of virility symbol; if sterling went, somehow you had failed the exam'. Shore judged 'his own credibility was involved, so that he wouldn't bring himself really even to discuss the matter after a certain time' (Whitehead 1985). In 1965 some economic advisers proposed devaluation: their suggestion never went to Cabinet or committee and their papers were suppressed on Wilson's orders. When the Chancellor once wavered the premier whipped him back into line (Wilson 1971) and when the Economic Affairs Secretary came round to favour devaluation Wilson ordered DEA officials to keep as much sensitive information as possible from their minister.

Eventually in 1966 the prospect of further spending cuts caused a pro-devaluation faction that included Brown, Jenkins, Crosland and Castle to coalesce in the Cabinet. Wilson outfaced Brown's resignation threat, argued down his critics and pushed through a deflationary package at the cost only of creating a Cabinet committee on economic affairs which he ensured had a weak membership and rarely met – a remarkable example of a determined and skilful premier imposing his will on the Cabinet (Castle 1984, Healey 1989). When in November 1967 it became obvious that devaluation could no longer be avoided, the crucial decision was again Wilson's. Once he agreed to devalue there was no question of preventing it. It is ironic that, Wilson having blocked devaluation for years, the Chancellor was made the scapegoat and was moved to the Home Office.

The 1976 IMF crisis

The Prime Minister's ability to take over an area of policy temporarily was demonstrated by Callaghan's handling of the 1976 IMF crisis. He was angered by what he saw as Treasury mishandling of sterling's depreciation leading to a run on the pound, and was infuriated when, after the Treasury raised interest rates to a politically damaging 15 per cent, sterling still fell. The government applied to the International Monetary Fund for a loan. The Chancellor asked for spending cuts of £3 billion to meet IMF conditions but Callaghan would not back him and the Cabinet refused. At this point Callaghan took over, personally negotiating with IMF representatives, discussing with the United States President and the German Chancellor ways of mitigating the damage to the economy and despatching as his personal envoys the Cabinet Secretary to Bonn and the Chancellor of the Duchy of Lancaster, Harold Lever, to Washington. He succeeded in restraining the IMF to some degree, arranged through personal contacts a safety net for sterling and vetted the detailed undertakings given eventually to the IMF. Only then was he prepared to back his

Chancellor in putting the IMF package to Cabinet (Callaghan 1987, Healey 1989, Donoughue 1987).

Obviously no Prime Minister can take charge of economic policy from the Chancellor for long, but the power to do so for a short while in a crisis is crucial. Although after the IMF affair Callaghan was never as deeply involved again, he still exercised strong authority whenever he wished it for the rest of his premiership over the exchange rate, prices and incomes policy and the European Monetary System, and he used summits with other world leaders to promote a plan for international recovery (Donoughue 1987, Barnett 1982, Keegan and Pennant-Rea 1979).

The Chancellor may resent the Prime Minister's frequent incursions into his territory but he undoubtedly benefits from the closeness of the relationship. He can occasionally use the authority of No. 10 to achieve something beyond his own influence. A memorable public example was Callaghan's 1976 Labour party conference speech renouncing neo-Keynesian economics, greatly strengthening his Chancellor's strategy against inflation. Less publicly, Mrs Thatcher came to the Treasury's rescue in 1985 by intervening with President Reagan to act to restrain the rise in the dollar (Lawson 1992).

On the other hand, if the Chancellor is dead set on a course the premier may be hard put to restrain him. The resignation of a Chancellor can seriously injure a government. Healey insisted on asking the Cabinet to raise the minimum lending rate to 15 per cent in 1976 even when Callaghan threatened to oppose him: at the last moment Callaghan had to give in and back him (Healey 1989). The joint resignation threat of Lawson from the Treasury and Howe from the Foreign Office over European monetary union was a pistol levelled at Mrs Thatcher's head to which she surrendered, and for all the friction with Lawson, his eventual departure was a milestone in the disintegration of her government.

Economic policy: the lack of involvement of the Cabinet

This mutual reliance between premier and Chancellor excludes other Cabinet colleagues from having any significant influence over economic policy – a practice of Mrs Thatcher's much remarked on, but which was similarly true of her predecessors and, reputedly, her successor.* This is demonstrated particularly in two areas: the budget, and the exchange rate and interest rates.

The Cabinet and the budget

Traditionally the Chancellor prepares his budget on his own, only consulting colleagues individually on a need to know basis. The Cabinet learns of its contents at a special meeting on the morning of budget day (or sometimes the previous day). Changes were made by the Cabinet to budgets in 1947 and 1962 (Wilson 1971, Boyd Carpenter 1980) but today the chance of making any last minute alteration is minimal, especially since the 'financial statement and budget report' (the 'red book') setting out the budget details goes to print several days previously (Young and Sloman 1984). Wilson's Cabinet disliked the Selective Employment Tax in 1966, and before the mini-budget in July 1974 it criticised the regional employment premium, urging instead direct investment in the construction industry (Castle 1980) but on neither occasion did ministers seriously imagine that the Chancellor would change his proposals at that late stage. Before Howe's first three budgets there was 'no significant prior discussion' by Cabinet, and when in 1981 the Chancellor sprang tax increases of £4 billion on his colleagues they complained bitterly but could not stop them (Howe 1994).

In 1977 Callaghan instituted an annual pre-budget strategy discussion a month or two beforehand but its influence was minimal: at the 1978 meeting ministers pressed for reflation but the Prime Minister and Chancellor ignored them (Callaghan 1987, Barnett 1982). After 1981 Mrs Thatcher appeased colleagues by re-instituting these meetings. Many ministers spoke at them but, in the words of a junior Treasury minister:

> From outside the Cabinet this exercise appeared to be conducted largely for the sake of form. If the Chancellor offered a comprehensive draft for discussion, his colleagues might complain that he was pre-empting their options. Besides, there was 'budget secrecy' to think about (not to mention the risk that one or other of his proposals might encounter insurmountable resistance). So it always seemed that he listened rather more than he spoke. Truth to tell, the colleagues rather like it that way as well. It enables those with 'alternative strategies' (Antony Crosland in the 1970s, Peter Walker in the 1980s) to get them off their chests. The Chancellor receives their counsel much as Mr Gladstone used to receive a Message from Windsor: respectfully, if impatiently.
>
> (Bruce-Gardyne 1986)

Other considerations apart, the gestation period of any budget is 3 to 6 months and certain indirect tax decisions must be taken 3 months before the budget speech is delivered, foreclosing some options before these Cabinet discussions occurred. This does not stop the Chancellor from discussing his budget ideas in advance with senior colleagues – Howe did so – but the Cabinet as such is frozen out.

The Prime Minister may not object to the Chancellor springing unpalatable proposals on an unprepared Cabinet but will hardly allow the Chancellor to do the same to him, and will insist on being involved as budget plans develop. Macmillan was involved in budget making to the extent of actually amending the Chancellor's budget speech (Macmillan 1972). Wilson and Callaghan either decided or heavily influenced budget policy and if either set his face against a tax proposal, the Chancellor had to drop it (Barnett 1982). The depth of Mrs Thatcher's involvement has been well advertised, including her imposition on her Chancellor of an immediate cut in top rate income tax from 83 per cent to 60 per cent and vetoing the abolition of tax relief on mortgages and pensions (Keegan 1989).

The Cabinet and interest rates

The arguments for excluding the Cabinet from discussing interest rates are undeniable – although largely superseded by the Blair government's 1997 decision to transfer day-to-day control of interest rates to the Bank of England. Market confidence is essential and crucial decisions must often be taken with speed and secrecy, neither of which are characteristics of Cabinet discussion. Even Heseltine, who initially protested at the failure to consult the Cabinet on the abolition of exchange controls, reluctantly accepted this necessity (Howe 1994). Occasionally a small group of senior colleagues will be involved in a decision: Major deliberately drew the Foreign Secretary, Home Secretary and President of the Board of Trade (Hurd, Clarke and Heseltine) into the crisis decisions when Britain was forced out of the Exchange Rate Mechanism, as a way of locking them into the decisions (Seldon 1997). When Blair and his Chancellor transferred responsibility for setting rates to the Bank of England in 1997, they consulted the Deputy Prime Minister and Foreign Secretary (Robin Cook quoted on Channel 4 1998). But if in most cases colleagues are shut out of decisions, the reverse of the coin is, again, that the Chancellor cannot act without No. 10's agreement. It is one thing to push up rates abruptly and present the Cabinet with a *fait accompli* with the Prime Minister standing at his elbow confirming it was unavoidable. To do this without getting the Prime Minister's agreement first would be suicidal. Furthermore 'Prime Ministers have an inbuilt tendency to interfere in interest rate policy, and political considerations ensure that their bias is to see them lower' (Barnes

1998) – as witness Mrs Thatcher's interventions in 1986, twice to prevent rate rises and once to force a cut (Lawson 1992). Lawson's failure to consult Mrs Thatcher before floating the idea of returning to fixed exchange rates was one cause of their eventual estrangement (Keegan 1989).

The Cabinet and other areas of economic policy

Even in other areas of economic policy-making Cabinet involvement is limited. To some extent this is because economic policy-making is a contin- uous process, with few milestone decisions, and such decisions as there are must be taken in haste, like those on the exchange rate. An exception is regional development policy that has been discussed, in a rather piecemeal fashion, by successive Cabinets – for example the Merseyside initiative in the mid-1980s. However, this is a conspicuous exception to the general rule. In Wilson's governments the Cabinet had little idea of what economic ministers were up to. Mrs Thatcher made sure the same was true of her government. Heath and Callaghan encouraged some discussion but had strong ideas about what the outcome should be.

The exception to this is when an economic decision vital to the govern- ment's survival cuts deep into the interests of many departments. Recent decades offer two instances of this. The first was the (now unfashionable) field of incomes policy, which posed great problems of implementation: Macmillan, Wilson and Heath all took their Cabinets carefully through proposals for pay control and Wilson was once overruled on the subject (Castle 1984). The second was the single European currency, which proved a fraught issue for Conservative governments from the late 1980s to 1997. Mrs Thatcher discouraged full Cabinet discussion of this, as of most issues, but it was the subject of a number of tense discussions under Major, notably a 90-minute debate on 19 December 1996 in which every Cabinet minister was reported to have spoken (*The Times* 20 December 1996).

Part of the reason for Prime Ministers' reluctance to allow serious discussion of economic policy must be because it jeopardises the line agreed with the Chancellor; but it must also owe something to premiers' awareness that a serious challenge can seriously weaken the Chancellor's position. Consequently, the Cabinet's influence on economic policy is at best that of a warning bell.

Nor do Cabinet committees in the economic field give much leadership. Wilson resisted creating a strategic economic committee in the 1960s and, when one was forced on him, deliberately made it ineffective (Lawson and Bruce-Gardyne 1976). In the 1970s he created a tangle of weak, rival committees (Donoughue 1987). Callaghan and Mrs Thatcher each created one principal economic committee but used it mainly for casework, setting the main strategy in private conversation with the Chancellor and officials.

The Cabinet and economic policy: the exceptional case of the IMF crisis

In the economic crises of 1976, Callaghan temporarily employed an effective alternative. Faced with a Cabinet opposed to the spending cuts he thought necessary he encouraged debate almost to a fault. He asked dissidents like Shore and Benn to put their ideas to Cabinet (Benn 1989). He kept the Cabinet informed of all developments and encouraged exhaustive discussion of the alternatives. He left the Chancellor to argue for cuts, keeping his own views to himself although stressing the gravity of the situation. He shadowed the debates with personal conversations with leading colleagues to ensure that when it came to the crunch and he came out in the Chancellor's favour, he could carry the Cabinet with him.

He did this twice in 1976. In the summer, £1 billion of cuts were agreed after seven meetings. At the end of the year came the famed IMF crisis when, as described above, Callaghan became deeply involved in international negotiations. Having satisfied himself that the terms were as good as could be obtained, he then patiently led his Cabinet through twenty-six meetings to discuss the necessary spending cuts (Barnett 1982, Callaghan 1987, Dell 1991). On each occasion alternative options were exhaustively debated and rejected; finally, only the Chancellor's option was left. Callaghan's first aim throughout was to avoid resignations and he succeeded brilliantly. As he said towards the end of the second crisis: 'Ministers have discussed the cuts so often, they come to think they have agreed them' (Donoughue 1987).

However, such exhaustive debates were produced by wholly exceptional circumstances. Once these crises were over Callaghan reverted to his predecessors' more private mode of government: when in October 1977 the pound was allowed to rise the Industry Secretary, whose interests were vitally affected, was not even a party to the decision (*Listener* 2 February 1984).

The Cabinet and economic policy: the reluctance of ministers to assert control

The Cabinet's attitude towards economic affairs is strangely passive (see for example Francis Pym and Peter Shore in the *Listener* 2 February 1984). Douglas Wass, former Permanent Secretary of the Treasury, judged that the Cabinet was excluded from some of the most important decisions of the 1970s (Wass 1983) and was astonished that they did not insist on a greater say. Yet the *Financial Times* will yield most of what you need to know about current economic problems, and the Treasury sends ministers a weekly economic bulletin, largely to help them to deal with media questions and constituency queries, but containing many of the statistics and information a minister needs to ask intelligent questions of the Chancellor.*

Still, ministers are strangely reticent at Cabinet; even at the main economic committees they rarely seek to widen the usual discussion of specific items to broader questions of economic strategy. Wilson's Cabinet never discussed the economy from February to December 1974, despite ominous portents; Healey made a report to an economic committee in July but it led to little discussion (Donoughue 1987). It is a recognition of the Chancellor's vulnerability that most colleagues prefer to influence him by personal contacts, perhaps a chat at the Commons or a quiet word after a committee meeting; certainly, Chancellors are very sensitive to this kind of approach. All told, the Cabinet's influence on economic management is not great and there is little pressure from ministers to increase it.

Public Expenditure

Ministerial parochialism and Prime Ministerial impartiality

The allocation of public spending between departments is dominated by the tendency of spending ministers to gang up against Treasury ministers. The Prime Minister's attitude is crucial: with his support the Chancellor will usually win; without it he will almost certainly lose.

In the less stringent 1950s Prime Ministers tried to stay neutral, balancing the need to contain spending against the political sensitivity of holding back spending in a particular area. By no means did they always back the Treasury. Churchill opposed Butler's attempt to reduce spending on defence and agriculture. Eden vetoed Macmillan's attempt to cut RAF spending and only agreed to scrap milk subsidies when Macmillan threatened resignation (Lamb 1987). A year later, Macmillan, now in No. 10, accepted the resignation of all three Treasury Ministers over the refusal of the Cabinet, at Macmillan's instigation, to cut public spending.

In the 1960s and 1970s priorities changed. Inflation and recurring sterling crises forced repeated spending cuts and Prime Ministers found themselves increasingly compelled to back their Chancellors. At the same time, premiers had to keep sufficiently detached from the Treasury line to appear a fair umpire to spending Ministers. While reluctantly acquiescing to overall cuts in principle, spending ministers still fight their corners fiercely. The affinity that rapidly develops between ministers and their departments soon converts them into warriors for their spending programmes.

The Heath government was elected on a programme of spending cuts, but within a year Mrs Thatcher, then Education Secretary, was proclaiming:

> I have done everything possible to show my confidence in the future of higher education. In my monthly battles with the Treasury, I managed to get another £76 million for student grants and last week announced the biggest ever development programme for further education and polytechnics.
>
> (Heclo and Wildalsky 1981)

When she became Prime Minister her ministers, after a few months' enthusiasm for retrenchment, reverted to fighting their corners, including, most embarrassingly, her trusted former Parliamentary Private Secretary, Ian Gow, who threatened to resign as Housing Minister if his budget were reduced, and Sir Geoffrey Howe who, after 4 years as Chancellor imposing unprecedented cuts, fought fiercely from the Foreign Office to protect overseas aid (*The Times* 9 and 15 October 1984). Against such attitudes the Chancellor does not stand a chance without the Prime Minister's help.

Allocating public spending : fixing the total and bilateral negotiations

Spending battles come in two forms. The first is the annual expenditure review, which reaches a climax in the Chancellor's annual statement on the government's spending plans. The second is the occasional package of emergency cuts to stem a fall in the pound. Either way the process comes in three stages. First, the Chancellor asks Cabinet to agree an overall spending total for the coming year – or, if it is an emergency package, to cut the total by so much. The Cabinet either agrees, refuses or reaches a compromise figure. The Chief Secretary then undertakes 'bilaterals' – lengthy discussions with each Minister on his departmental budget. Finally, any case in which the Chancellor and the departmental minister cannot agree is resolved collectively. Up to the mid-1980s this was done by the Cabinet; since then by a Cabinet committee, whose role throughout the 1990s has expanded to give it an increasingly active role in directing the overall spending allocation process. The Prime Minister gets involved at two stages: fixing the total, and settling any disputes that the committee fails to resolve.

At the first stage, once the Chancellor has chosen his overall spending target, he must persuade the Prime Minister in private discussions to accept it. If the Prime Minister wants modifications, the Chancellor almost certainly has to accept them, since without No. 10 backing his chances of carrying the Cabinet are slim. The agreed figure is then put to the Cabinet. Other ministers may disagree, but they are poorly placed to mount a challenge. They have no alternative advice on which to question the Treasury's arguments. The debate is often in terms of abstract figures; at this stage, there is no breakdown of the impact on individual departmental programmes. If the Chancellor is forced to modify his proposal, it will normally only be a small alteration to the sum agreed with the Prime Minister. In other words, these two and the Chief Secretary set the framework for discussion and any compromise in Cabinet is merely a variation on their basic target (Heclo and Wildalsky 1981).

There are many tactics by which the Prime Minister can discreetly help his Chancellor. He may lobby a few senior colleagues before the meeting. He may let the Chancellor evoke an atmosphere of crisis, a tactic recalled with feeling by Lord Hailsham:

> The Prime Minister, with a face clouded like that of Jupiter Pluvius would ask the Chancellor of the Exchequer to report on the serious financial situation which had apparently burst on an astonished administration with the unpredictability of an earthquake....the only acceptable proposal to emerge would be the wholly irrational imposition of a fixed percentage cut all round, with only a few and very limited exceptions.
>
> (Hailsham, 1978)

The Prime Minister will certainly use the arts of chairmanship described in the previous chapter to guide the meeting in the Chancellor's favour. He can cast his authority into the balance and state bluntly that for the good of the economy, the Chancellor must be supported – although this is a last resort, for the premier's authority is the more impressive if infrequently deployed. Normally, a combination of Treasury muscle and No. 10 stealth will carry the meeting. Cabinets can refuse cuts – Mrs Thatcher's did in 1981 – but the Prime Minister usually prevails, as Mrs Thatcher usually did (Keegan 1989). A former Chancellor judged in the early 1970s, 'The one thing that matters is the Queen because she counts for all the pawns. If the Prime Minister supports him then the Chancellor will certainly win' (Heclo and Wildalsky 1981).

Allocating public spending: collective resolution by the Cabinet and Prime Minister

Up to the mid-1980s the Cabinet arbitrated in any case in which the Chief Secretary and a departmental minister remained at loggerheads. The Prime Minister would confer with Treasury ministers and agree privately with them where the Cabinet will be urged to take a strong line and where the Chancellor might give some ground. Usually the Chancellor would have cultivated allies by agreeing early on in his bilaterals a generous allocation for one or two colleagues in the exchange for their support in Cabinet. Such bargains were repeatedly struck with the Defence Secretary, Healey, in Wilson's early governments.

There are complaints and occasional histrionics, but few resignations. The process has the advantage of committing the Cabinet collectively to the outcome and a defeated minister can feel that he had been allowed to argue his case at the highest tribunal. However, the process was long and wearisome and sometimes (thanks to press leaks from spending departments) publicly embarrassing.

Allocating public spending: the Star Chamber, EDX and PX

Because of the right of appeal to Cabinet, occasional attempts in the past to relegate spending disputes to Cabinet committees generally failed: the defeated party insisted on an appeal to full Cabinet. However, in the difficult years of retrenchment of the early 1980s Mrs Thatcher wrought a notable innovation. In line with her policy of delegating as much as possible to committees, she instituted for several years a "Star Chamber" of non-departmental ministers to decide unresolved disputes. This met intensively, sometimes as often as four days a week, in the late summer (Lawson 1992). This settled about half the disagreements, but in the remainder the departmental Ministers still appealed further. Mrs Thatcher then held meetings with these recalcitrant Ministers, sometimes with the Chancellor also present, which solved most remaining problems. However, Ministers could still insist on their final right of appeal to Cabinet although only two – one successfully – took this drastic step in the period 1983–89 (Whitelaw 1989, Lawson 1992, *The Times* 9 November 1984).

This system was further entrenched under the Major government when the Star Chamber was given permanent existence as EDX, given a remit every year to oversee the public expenditure round, including resolving disputes. But this too appears to have been subject to ratification by Cabinet – this happened in November 1992 – and the Prime Minister was still called in as necessary to broker agreement with the most recalcitrant spending ministers, as happened in 1995 (Seldon 1997). Under the Blair government, this committee (now PX) reverted to a membership of non-departmental ministers. However, following the comprehensive spending review announced in 1998, the committee was given a wider remit of over-seeing a 'continuous scrutiny and audit' of spending departments which, in exchange for a 3-year allocation of expenditure, had to meet objectives and targets before funding would be released (Commons debates 14 July 1998, col. 189).

Domestic policy

The involvement of the Prime Minister

Although the Prime Minister cannot avoid entanglements in economics or diplomacy, non-economic domestic policy offers a vast and varied field where he is freer to pick and choose his interests. But not totally free: he will be drawn into any serious problem occupying the headlines on which the public expects government action. Major strikes are a case in point. Both Macmillan and Wilson found themselves, in Wilson's words 'dealing with these problems on a day-to-day and almost an hour-to-hour basis' (King 1985). Callaghan chaired a succession of ministerial meetings throughout the 1979 'winter of discontent' (Rodgers 1984). Heath and Mrs Thatcher were originally determined to keep their governments out of industrial disputes. Yet he ended up inviting union leaders to Downing Street for beer and sandwiches, while she chaired the Cabinet committees that oversaw two miners' strikes – personally approving the terms settling the first – and a steel strike, and was much involved in negotiations in other industries.

Governments' preoccupation with industrial policy also draws Prime Ministers into contacts, formal and informal, with both sides of industry; sometimes very public, like Heath's tripartite talks with the CBI and TUC, or Labour's links with the unions in the 1970s; sometimes behind closed doors, as witness Heath's secret meeting with the miners' leader in 1973 to try to avert a coal strike and Callaghan's close relationship with the chairman of the CBI (Gormley 1982, MacDougall 1987).

There are also political issues that are so explosive that the Prime Minister has to take charge. A notable recent example was how to defuse the crisis over the poll tax after Mrs Thatcher's fall: Major had no choice but to take the leading role, and indeed was criticised for not acting faster to replace it; he pressed the Chancellor to raise VAT to 17.5 per cent to raise funds to reduce the poll tax, and he chaired GEN 8, the ad hoc committee that oversaw the development of the replacement council tax (Seldon 1997, Butler, Adonis and Travers 1994).

However, in addition to these issues that force themselves on him, the Prime Minister can also intervene in areas without prompting. Wilson observed that 'a Prime Minister governs by curiosity and range of interest' (*Observer* magazine 24 October 1965). As described in Chapter 4, one of his greatest powers is the ability to intervene in any department's affairs if he is unhappy with a department's handling of a policy or feels that he must put his authority behind it. This can have great impact. Major in 1990 deliberately ended the freezing of child benefit and agreed to compensation for haemophiliacs accidentally infected with the HIV virus as an ostentatious way of distinguishing himself from Mrs Thatcher's inflexible stance on both issues (Seldon 1997). Blair very publicly took charge of the Northern Ireland peace talks as they reached their climax in 1998.

Yet it is essential to remember the constraints on the Prime Minister discussed in chapter 4. He has little time to go looking for extra work: one reason that Major had such difficulty getting a grip on domestic policy was that his first 6 months in office were dominated by the Gulf crisis (Junor 1996). When he dips into a department he will find himself questioning a colleague who devotes much of his working life to this subject, supported by junior ministers and officials. Nor is it enough for the Prime Minister merely to launch an initiative; he must also find the time to follow it up, or it will run into the sand. Once Callaghan had launched his 'great national debate' on education he had to prod and chide an unenthusiastic education department for months to carry it through (Donoughue 1987, Callaghan 1987). Wilson originally showed enthusiasm about an imaginative 'life-lease' plan for council tenants, but when he lost interest, it collapsed (Donoughue 1987, Haines 1977).

There is a counter-balancing factor. The Prime Minister can, in a brief conversation or a short written minute, alter a policy on which a minister has been working for months. Ironically, the Secretary of State then finds himself in the same position as the official who, after months of preparation, puts a policy submission to his minister only to see the minister reject it or ask for changes, perhaps radical, after 10 minutes' consideration, often for reasons which, although politically sensible when seen in a wider framework, may not appear the best course to the departmental specialist. A minister's proposal, although excellent sense in the context of his department's concerns, may be queried or changed by No. 10 because it conflicts with other considerations the Prime Minister judges more important. The Prime Minister, after skimming through the papers, may ask that this option be considered in greater depth; or warn that if the Treasury opposes the proposal he will back the Chancellor; or that the proposals must be put on ice until after the next general election; or that back-benchers will not stand for this aspect of it; or raise one of a multitude of objections or criticisms which send the department back to the drawing board for months.

Chapter 4 dwelt at length on the mutual reliance between the Prime Minister and the departmental minister: Barnes' symbiotic relationship. For all the authority of the premier's office, a minister is strongest on his home ground, while a Prime Minister will be reluctant to risk a threat of resignation or a damaging row. For most practical purposes, each maintains the power of veto over the other's proposals: Lawson's 'mutual blackball'.

Domestic policy: the involvement of other ministers

It is in home affairs that the Cabinet and its committees are at their most energetic. Between 1945 and 1979 over half of Cabinet debates were on non-economic domestic subjects as a comparison of three sample years, as illustrated in Table 1, will show.

The diaries of Mrs Castle, Crossman and Benn also suggest that discussion of domestic issues was fuller and more purposeful than discussion of foreign and economic matters, which squares with the limited role of Cabinet and its committees in these two latter fields, observed earlier in this chapter. Far more ministers influenced decisions on the home front than on economic or foreign affairs, and it was in this field that the sense of collegiate government between ministers was at its strongest.

There are several reasons for this focusing of collegiality on domestic issues. It is easier for ministers as a group to be marginalised on overseas and economic questions, which are continuous processes, whose moments

Table 1 The subject matter of Cabinet debates

	1955	1965	1975
Foreign affairs and defence	129	116	10
Economic and incomes policy	23	29	6
Public spending	9	14	10
Non-economic domestic issues	222	106	41
	383	265	67

Note: The 1955 and 1965 figures are drawn from the Cabinet papers in the Public Records Office. The 1975 figures are drawn from diary entries by Castle and Benn; although incomplete, the 1975 figures give an idea of the balance of subjects. The 1965 foreign affairs figures are influenced by Rhodesian UDI that year.

of decision are fewer and unpredictable. The Prime Minister's continual involvement makes it easier for him and the Foreign Secretary or Chancellor to cut the Cabinet out of the loop. In contrast, domestic policy is a succession of discrete issues whose resolution requires definite decisions and often legislation. The Prime Minister's sporadic involvement in particular issues makes a conspiracy to sideline the Cabinet less likely. Second, it is a normative assumption of the Whitehall machine that things are done in this way. The Treasury and Foreign Office instinctively channel business primarily through bilateral relations with No. 10 while other departments unquestioningly feed their business into the Cabinet and committee system, because that is the way things have been done for years.

Third, domestic policies are most likely to excite public interest and criticism. Few voters care about the future of Belize; many care about the closure of a car plant in the West Midlands. It can occasionally happen that a minister launches a major domestic initiative without consulting colleagues, if it does not affect other departmental interests: Kenneth Baker, with the connivance of Mrs Thatcher, was able simply to announce that he was introducing a national curriculum into English schools without consulting colleagues (*Times Education Supplement* 31 May 1996).

Half a dozen case studies illustrate the variable geometry of policy influence between the ministers in charge of home departments, the Prime Minister and ministers collectively.

1 North Sea Gas

This was at the time – the late 1960s – a minor issue: the government's share of the profits from North Sea gas. Wilson had limited faith in the ability of the Minister of Power, Ray Gunter, to negotiate the best deal with the oil companies exploiting the gas. He established an ad hoc Cabinet committee to supervise Gunter's efforts, licensed his economic adviser, Balogh, to watch progress and appointed Mrs Castle, then Employment Secretary, to the Committee to support Wilson if necessary (she personally disliked Gunter). At the first two committee meetings Wilson and Mrs Castle prompted by Balogh urged Gunter to be tougher (Castle 1984). Subsequently Wilson appeared half convinced that Gunter was right, then changed his mind and at the last meeting asked Mrs Castle to support his proposal against Gunter's opposition to establish a corporation to manage Irish Sea development (Castle 1984). This rather muddled episode reveals both the Prime Minister's ability to influence a policy through manipulating the decision-making framework, and the wariness with which he approaches the domain of even a weak minister.

2 'In place of strife'

A major political crisis blew up over the industrial relations proposals in this White Paper. Wilson enthusiastically read Mrs Castle's proposals, based on the report of a committee of inquiry, but extended to include legal sanctions against unofficial strikes. The Prime Minister scrapped the Cabinet committee he had planned, partly for fear of leaks and partly because he wanted to present the Cabinet with a package agreed by the key ministers which he could push through with a minimum of discussion. He therefore set up a small ad hoc committee packed with 'safe' colleagues. Its recommendations went down well in Cabinet which, however, resisted legal sanctions. Wilson backtracked and referred it back to an expanded committee, which nonetheless still excluded several critics. This revised the proposals but the Cabinet, led by Callaghan, still resisted the sanctions. Eventually strong external opposition from trade unions and Labour backbenchers scuppered the proposals (Callaghan 1987, Castle 1984). In contrast to the North Sea Gas discussions, this episode shows the limits of the Prime Minister's power to shape policy by manipulating the institutional framework.

3 The funding of BL

The memoirs of Michael Edwardes, former chairman of the car manufacturer British Leyland, describe at length his dealings with government. He recalls that Callaghan left most decisions to his Industry Secretary and only once intervened directly, when BL closed its Speke plant, at which Callaghan called Edwardes in to question him for half an hour. Mrs Thatcher was the exact opposite.

> Anything of any conceivable political consequence was referred to No. 10 – not only the strategic decisions on funding, but even matters such as the chairman's remuneration. Moreover this was no rubber-stamping process. Recommendations on other matters were frequently overturned.
>
> (Edwardes 1983)

A good example came when the high exchange rate prompted BL to ask for £1 million extra government funding. The Prime Minister insisted on a lengthy meeting with Edwardes and her Industry Secretary, Sir Keith Joseph, before reluctantly commending it to a Cabinet committee which approved it. She then, seemingly on her own authority, amended Joseph's parliamentary statement extensively to commit the government to BL's early privatisation. The entire episode illustrates Joseph's subservient attitude towards his Prime Minister, and Mrs Thatcher's perfunctory attitude towards the role of Cabinet committees.

4 The proposed sale of BL

In early 1986 the Trade and Industry Secretary, Paul Channon, with the agreement of the Prime Minister, conducted secret negotiations to sell British Leyland to the American General Motors. The story leaked to the press, provoking not only a revolt by Conservative backbenchers, led by the former premier Edward Heath, but dissent from two Cabinet ministers, Norman Fowler and Peter Walker, neither in charge of economic departments but both MPs for West Midlands industrial constituencies. Fowler, normally a Thatcher loyalist, protested vehemently at Cabinet and a hastily convened meeting of the Economic Affairs Committee overruled the Prime Minister and Channon to call off the plan (Fowler 1991, James 1997).

5 Broadcasting

In 1987 a committee of inquiry under Alan Peacock recommended moving towards a market system in broadcasting with greater access for independent programme makers to terrestrial television through a quota system and by moving in the long term to 'pay as you view'. This came against the background of the slow growth of cable television and the anticipated arrival of satellite channels. Mrs Thatcher held strong – not easily compatible – views on the need for a freer market and tighter controls on sex and violence. In the former she was backed by Chancellor Lawson and the Trade and Industry Secretary David Young, but the Home Secretary Douglas Hurd was less keen.

The upshot of a long tussle was the creation – against Home Office opposition – of a Broadcasting Standards Council. Mrs Thatcher failed to privatise Channel 4 or to phase out the BBC license fee, but succeeded in creating a system of auctioning franchises which, when implemented in 1991, produced farcical results including the loss of the popular TV-AM franchise which caused Mrs Thatcher to disown her own legislation – an episode smudged over in her memoirs (Lawson 1992, Thatcher 1993). The episode is not untypical of Prime Ministerial interventions in that the premier often has to settle for half a loaf, and his policies are as vulnerable to the vicissitudes of implementation as any departmental minister's, possibly more so.

6   *The mines closure crisis*

In 1992 the market for coal was shrinking because the newly-privatised electricity generating system was switching to gas power. British Coal wished to close thirty-one pits, making 30,000 of Britain's 55,000 miners redundant. The President of the Board of Trade, Michael Heseltine, agreed, sold the idea to the Prime Minister and cleared it with the Cabinet's Economic Affairs Committee in the summer. But when the decision was announced in October, the policy was made unsustainable by a tidal wave of press and public criticism, not least from normally loyal Conservative supporters, with some backbenchers threatening rebellion (James 1997).

The handling of the crisis was made more difficult in its early stages by the earlier failure to consult the Cabinet in the summer – apparently because Heseltine feared leaks.* Disquiet erupted at a Cabinet meeting two days after the announcement, scheduled to take 30 minutes but which lasted two hours (*Daily Telegraph* and *Financial Times* 16 October 1992). Ministers complained that the Economic Affairs Committee decision had never been referred to full Cabinet, whose members were now being blamed for decisions to which they had not been party (Seldon 1997). The Welsh Secretary had been unaware that the Point of Ayr colliery in Wales was closing and the Employment Secretary reportedly claimed that she, too, had not been consulted despite the obvious impact on her responsibilities (*Sunday Telegraph* 18 October 1992). Heseltine admitted the former, but denied the latter (BBC 1992). Much of this leaked to the press, and No. 10 took care to invite the Employment Secretary to an emergency Sunday evening meeting that agreed concessions, and to call an extraordinary Cabinet to confirm the package the following morning (Seldon 1997). These and further concessions, together with a deal with the Ulster Unionists, allowed the government to scrape home in a Commons vote.

Conclusion

In summary, there are three patterns of policy control. In economic and diplomatic affairs the Prime Minister and Chancellor or Foreign Secretary jointly run the policy more or less on equal terms, and the involvement of other ministers collectively is occasional and sporadic. In other domestic matters the axis between the Prime Minister and a departmental minister can be highly influential if the Prime Minister takes an interest, but this varies from issue to issue. The Cabinet (or more recently its committees) are more energetic and effective in this sphere. In public expenditure the Prime Minister and Cabinet share an unusual arbitration role. In all spheres, though, the relationship between the Prime Minister and the minister is one of mutual dependence. The Prime Minister relies on each minister's competence and expertise, the minister on his premier's help and support. In any crucial policy area the two must concur and – especially in the cases of the Chancellor and Foreign Secretary – enjoy mutual trust.

6 Problems of the Cabinet system

The survey of the Cabinet system in the preceding chapters reveals a complicated, uneven, sometimes inconsistent picture but three underlying characteristics are clear.

First, the main component units of the system are individual departments and, particularly, their Secretaries of State: the dynamics of the system are dominated by this predominance of individual ministerial authority.

Second and simultaneously, the system retains a fundamentally collegiate character and ministers still take the most important decisions and share responsibility collectively.

Third, this collegiality is nonetheless attenuated by the diffusion of power and responsibility from the Cabinet to smaller decision-making fora – committees, ad hoc groups and bilateral discussions. The closely-knit pre-war Cabinet machine has become more diffused and, as collegiality has weakened, there is an even greater emphasis on the personal relations between each minister and the Prime Minister. The system is similar to an exploding galaxy: as the central gravitational force weakens, different elements of the system begin to drift out of synchronisation with each other, disjointing the coordination of the system but still strongly influenced by, and influencing, the central force.

This system has serious weaknesses, all interlinked, eight of which are examined in this chapter:

1   The immersion of ministers in the work of their departments, distracting them from their responsibilities as Cabinet ministers.
2   The fragmentation of collective decision-making into three separate spheres, with consequences for the Prime Minister's role.
3   Pressure in recent decades on ministerial collective responsibility.
4   The adequacy of briefing and advice for the Prime Minister.

5   The lack of any mechanism to brief ministers on matters outside their departments.
6   The tendency of departments to coordinate policy at the lowest common denominator, which can debilitate cross-departmental initiatives.
7   The lack of a strong strategic impulse in the entire system.
8   The arrangements for reaching decisions on the allocation of public expenditure between departments.

Departmentalism and the briefing gap

Ministers' absorption in their departments

Outsiders might expect Cabinet ministers to consider participation in Cabinet their most important duty. In fact the reverse is true. Most Cabinet ministers think of themselves first and foremost as departmental heads; participation in Cabinet discussion is a secondary role. A rare systematic study of ministers' attitudes in the 1970s interviewed fifty former ministers of whom thirty had served in the Cabinet. When asked 'What are the most important tasks a minister has to perform?' only five mentioned taking part in Cabinet as a collective decision-making body. Only nineteen mentioned their role as a Cabinet 'battle-axe' representing their departments' interests in Cabinet. Most answers instead stressed the departmental and parliamentary roles of ministers (Headey 1974). Most ministerial memoirs and diaries anecdotally confirm this finding. Although most ministers seem to have some interest in general policy discussions in Cabinet, each is mainly preoccupied with his own department and, in Cabinet, primarily concerned to defend its interests.

Chapter 2 sets out the main reasons for this. First amongst them is each minister's massive departmental workload: a problem highlighted by successive studies, notably one by Mrs Thatcher's Efficiency Unit (Jenkins, Caines and Jackson 1988). This is aggravated by the fact that ministers are moved from one post to another every two or three years, and by the behaviour of departmental officials who monopolise their time and attention with departmental problems at the expense of broader issues. The problem was candidly recognised by Blair 6 months after becoming Prime Minister:

> One of the things we have lost from Opposition is that shared sense of purpose and strategy. Ministers have become preoccupied by their departmental brief and we need to draw them back more.
>
> (*Observer* 23 November 1997)

Nor is ministerial parochialism entirely involuntary. A minister's political success is gauged mainly by his impact on his own sphere of policy. This is particularly true in the lower reaches of the Cabinet where the Minster has been given his first big chance to prove himself. In the eyes of the public and his colleagues, a minister is Secretary of State for Education or Transport and will be judged mainly by his impact on his home ground. Barbara Castle, for instance, knew little of pay policy and may even have opposed it before she became Employment Secretary in 1968. However 'once she was responsible for making a policy work, she became its greatest enthusiast and it became the essential ingredient in the success and survival of the whole government' (Hattersley 1995).

An ambitious politician will therefore see Cabinet and its committees mainly as a battlefield where he must fight his own corner and defend his budget. Excursions into other areas are a luxury of effort for little reward. The Agriculture Secretary gains little credit for showing interest in electric cars or North Sea oil, nor the Employment Secretary for demonstrating his mastery of immigration law or export credit guarantees.

The impact of departmentalism on collective discussion

This can debilitate ministers' contributions to Cabinet and its committee. Many do not have time to study their documents in any detail before attending meetings, let alone prepare their own interventions. They may be so preoccupied or exhausted that they are unable to make a proper contribution. Some ministers take a frankly minimalist view of their Cabinet responsibilities. Anthony Crosland recalls: 'One minister I knew simply read his departmental brief out to the Cabinet. The whole thing was underlined in red ink and he simply read it out. Absolutely extraordinary' (Kogan 1971). On occasion this can have laughable consequences. Joel Barnett recalls:

> on one occasion I had been told by officials that I could be confident that one senior Cabinet colleague would support me…As it happened, when I read the papers that evening, I decided to take the exact opposite line to the one recommended by officials. Next morning I duly argued as I had decided, and my friendly colleague studiously read out one line from his brief: 'I agree with the Chief Secretary'.
>
> (Barnett 1982)

Such ludicrous incidents are mercifully rare, but all ministers have difficulty in balancing their departmental and collegial roles. Hurd, reflecting on Cabinet life in the 1990s, worried that too many ministers were now unable or unwilling to comment on an issue unless they had previously held the post responsible for it (Hurd 1997). Crossman reflected on his position as Minister for Housing and Local Government:

> With a ministry this size it is very much easier to remain the kind of minister who doesn't play much of a role in Cabinet. It keeps my reading of Cabinet papers down. For example, I don't often look at the Foreign Office telegrams…I don't really look at Ministry of Education or Social Security matters.
>
> (Crossman 1975)

Barbara Castle at Health and Social Services lamented:

> How does one solve the problem of finding the time to equip oneself to be a fully effective member of Cabinet? I work sixteen to seventeen hours a day non stop and there is still not enough time.
>
> (Castle 1980)

The survival of ministers' collegiate role

The picture is not all one-sided. As pointed out in previous chapters, the sense of collegiate responsibility remains resilient. If their interest is captured, ministers can and do make time to read their papers and speak up at meetings. Macmillan, who made his name as a successful and industrious Minister of Housing, may have dealt with departmental paperwork whilst sitting in Cabinet, but he listened to important debates with one ear and made telling interjections (Horne 1989). Healey did the same when Defence Secretary. One of the most telling entries in Crossman's diaries comes 6 months after he took office: wishing to make a telling intervention on Vietnam, he jettisoned his departmental work and spent some hours reading the Foreign Office papers, declaring 'Today I decided to become a Cabinet minister'. Emboldened by success he participated in debates on incomes policy, pay increases for civil servants and diplomacy towards France (Crossman 1975).

Sometimes ministerial interest is prompted by constituency concerns. In ten years in Mrs Thatcher's Cabinet Norman Fowler held mainly social portfolios, but he represented a West Midlands seat and so paid attention to industrial papers and commented from personal experience. As Chancellor, Callaghan showed great interest in leasehold reform which greatly affected his Cardiff constituents (Crossman 1975). Edward Short when Chief Whip fought a long battle against turning Ullswater near his home into a reservoir (Short 1989). Personal friendship can also prompt an intervention. Before the Falklands crisis, the Foreign Secretary Carrington wanted to stop the Ministry of Defence from withdrawing the ship 'Endeavour' which patrolled the south Atlantic and persuaded Prior, the Employment Secretary, to raise it in Cabinet to demonstrate that concern was not just felt in diplomatic circles (Prior 1986)

Some ministers are temperamentally adverse to 'departmentalism', their energies and interests taking them beyond the confines of their own departments. The 1970s Labour Cabinets included such figures as Crosland, Shore, Benn, Dell and Castle who were as interested in overall government policy as in their own departments and who on occasion would reject their own officials' advice and side with 'opponents'. Hailsham, Howe, Prior and Tebbit did the same in the early years of Mrs Thatcher's government.

Politicians can also draw to some extent on their own backgrounds to question colleagues' ideas. Bevin, although Attlee's Foreign Secretary, remained much involved in labour questions, chaired the Cabinet committee on manpower, served on the economic policy and nationalisation committees, effectively spoke for the unions at Cabinet and was frequently consulted by colleagues on all matters, including the budget (Bullock 1983). By the end of his career Rab Butler had enough assorted experience to intervene on most issues. Jenkins, although out of economic posts in the 1970s, could speak with authority on the economy from past departmental experience. Under Mrs Thatcher, Heseltine retained his concern about urban decline long after moving from being 'Minister for Merseyside' to Defence, and no initiative in Northern Ireland would be taken without consulting the one-time Secretary of State, Whitelaw.

Some matters have such ideological importance for ministers that they will drop almost everything to brief themselves. Britain's proposed membership of the EU aroused strong feelings amongst both Labour and Conservative ministers. The decision to postpone raising the school leaving age in 1968 raised near-theological passions in the Labour government, George Brown and Michael Stewart being more vocal against it than the Education Secretary on purely egalitarian grounds (Castle 1984, Crosland 1982). Benn and Shore both produced papers advocating alternative economic policies in the 1970s (Benn 1989). Prior, Walker and Gilmour similarly argued for a different economic strategy in the 1980s. Mrs Castle's diary shows her speaking out on subjects as diverse as military and financial links with Chile, an amnesty for illegal immigrants, Concorde, nuclear tests, industrial relations, overseas aid and MPs' pay (Castle 1980).

Such interventions are sporadic and unpredictable. Mrs Castle was sometime too tired or too busy to speak effectively; she and her colleagues often lacked time to read their papers. Yet when an issue stirred their conscience, touched a personal or constituency nerve, or troubled a political instinct, they often found the time and energy to intervene. In a Cabinet of two dozen, if enough ministers will intervene occasionally, there is a good chance of a questionable proposal being challenged.

The fragmentation of the Cabinet system

As governments have been forced increasingly to resort to committees, a partial fragmentation of the Cabinet system has become apparent. This phenomenon can be detected in an impressionistic kind of way in the diaries and memoirs of ministers: for example, in the 1960s Michael Stewart confirmed that, as Foreign Secretary, he saw far more of the Prime Minister, the Defence Secretary and the Chancellor of the Exchequer than of other colleagues, and clearly he saw little of economic or social matters (Stewart 1980). The same tendency is implicit in subsequent accounts of ministerial life. This fragmentation is confirmed by the analysis of the operation of the Cabinet committee system under Major and Blair in Figures 3 and 4 (using the structure at February 1994 and January 1998 respectively).

This shows a Cabinet system fragmenting into three policy spheres corresponding to the functional divisions of the Cabinet Secretariat: foreign and defence issues, economic issues, and domestic issues (to which last, under Blair, should be added constitutional issues).

This is a rather arbitrary exercise (for an alternative line of analysis, see Burch and Halladay 1996) and in some places it is slightly deceptive (for example, the only committees attended by Blair's Defence Secretary outside the overseas sphere are on freedom of information and human rights, which affect internal Ministry of Defence matters). However, several broad observations are common to both diagrams. In the Major government fragmentation appears worse: almost half of Cabinet ministers serve on committees only in one policy sphere and one-third in two spheres. The Blair government seems at first sight better integrated with ten Cabinet ministers serving in all three spheres, and eight more in at least two spheres. But the Blair government is heavily influenced by the fact that seven ministers serve in the overseas and defence sphere only in the sense that they serve on the Ministerial Sub-Committee on European Affairs – which actually deals with domestic policy, albeit in an overseas context.

These diagrams show a tendency, not a rigid demarcation; and the pattern redraws itself every time the committee memberships change. Nonetheless, the underlying tendency suggests that fragmentation will be a long-term phenomenon.

This fragmentation tends to deprive a minister engaged mainly in one sphere of the opportunity to intervene in another sphere. Indeed, he may come to the unspoken assumption that he has only a limited right to express an opinion on these other spheres. This should not be over-magnified. It would be an exaggeration to suggest that, say, the Scottish Secretary feels that he has no right to express disagreement on foreign policy, but fragmentation reduces the occasions on which he will be consulted and may lead to an implicit assumption, by both him and the Foreign Secretary, that this is not really his business.

Such pressures do not cause the Cabinet system to come apart at the hinges, but there is, inevitably, a loss of articulation and a diminution of collegiate spirit. The sense of joint commitment to policies must be attenu-

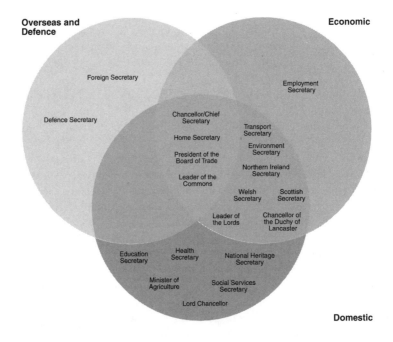

Figure 3 The Cabinet committee system under John Major
Note: Figures 3 and 4 omit the Prime Minister, who attends few committees but is appraised of business across the system. The Chancellor of the Exchequer and Chief Secretary are placed together because they tend to box and cox, attending all committees between them. The figures cover only standing committees and sub-committees with a policy-making function, and so omit: the two 'process' committees, dealing with legislation; the public expenditure allocation committee (EDX/PX) which has an eccentric membership; and Major's committee on science and technology, which is difficult to classify.

ated if members of the government begin to drift out of touch with policies outside 'their sphere' even though, formally, they remain collectively responsible for them.

Prime Ministers' attitudes towards this problem are difficult to analyse. A Prime Minister may not realise that fragmentation is taking place. And if he does, his attitude is likely to be ambivalent. On the one hand fragmentation enhances the premier's position: he becomes one of the few who knows what is going on in all areas of government. Indeed, from his viewpoint it is an advantage that the three areas into which business fragments – foreign affairs, economic affairs and domestic policy – correspond to the three main areas of business between which the modes of policy-making vary, as described in Chapter 5: mainly bilateral in foreign and economic matters, more collective in domestic matters. The fragmentation of the Cabinet probably makes it easier for the Prime Minister to maintain these different patterns of policy-making. On the other hand, some premiers have recognised the dangers inherent in this trend and have fostered Cabinet cohesion as a counter to it. Wilson, supreme manipulator of the committee system, still took pains to involve the Cabinet in major ques-

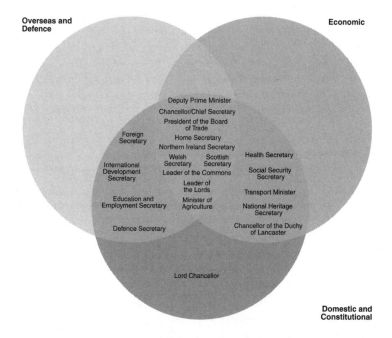

Figure 4 The Cabinet committee system under Tony Blair

tions, for example the 1968 defence cuts. Callaghan did likewise. Heath, for all his semi-presidential style, held regular Cabinet reviews of overall government strategy and created the Central Policy Review Staff as an independent briefing mechanism for his colleagues. At best, however, such efforts have retarded fragmentation, not halted it.

Pressures on collective responsibility

The principle of collective responsibility has taken a battering in recent years. First, the Crossman and Castle diaries show how common and profound disagreement between ministers can be. Second, ministers' increased propensity to leak details of current disagreements makes the pretence that all ministers stand by the final decisions increasingly implausible. Third, Mrs Thatcher's relative lack of concern to cultivate a sense of collegiality amongst her colleagues, leading to protracted episodes of public dispute between ministers, gave rise to suggestions that government could no longer be called collegial.

Fourth is the phenomenon that Nigel Lawson has called 'creeping bilateralism': the fact that ministers find it convenient to clear their proposals privately with the Prime Minister and leave him to circumvent the procedures for collective agreement. When Heseltine resigned he excoriated Mrs Thatcher's neglect of collegiality, yet only a year before had used the threat of resignation to force her to overrule a Cabinet committee decision on the planning of an order for new ships (Lawson 1992). For that matter, as Dell (1994) points out, Lawson and Howe's famous joint resignation threat to force Mrs Thatcher towards the ERM showed no regard for the Cabinet's collective interest.

Dell's critique of collective responsibility

After the Callaghan government fell in 1979, three former Labour ministers of divergent outlooks criticised collective responsibility as unworkable: Edmund Dell, William Rodgers and Tony Benn. [1] Dell, in particular, delivered a detailed and penetrating critique of collective responsibility as a myth no longer credible. Ministers, he maintained, no longer observe its restrictions and leak to disassociate themselves from unpopular measures. It causes delay and overburdens ministers with meetings on matters outside their departmental responsibilities. It requires too many matters to be brought to committee; yet this does not constitute true collective responsibility because few of them can be referred on to Cabinet due to sheer pressure of business. Ministers are ill-informed and ignorant about matters outside their own concerns: more often than not, they side with their friends rather than judge an issue on its merits. Collective decision-making imposes illogical, ill thought out compromises on departments, often with too much regard for short-term political expediency.

Furthermore, the Prime Minister's powers are such that he usually gets his way in Cabinet or committee anyway, making the entire exercise pointless. Thus the twenty-six Cabinet meetings held on the IMF loan terms in 1976 were in Dell's eyes 'a dangerous farce' because ministers knew that they would have to accept the package. They were staged mainly to allow spending ministers to claim that they had put up a fight.

Dell advocates replacing collective responsibility with two interlinked principles: collective purpose – that is, a general strategy for the government – and collective tolerance, by which ministers would refrain from undermining each others' policies in public if they can avoid it. Procedurally, these principles would be implemented in three ways:

1 Collective decision-making, by which an issue falling within the purview of several ministers would be decided jointly by them alone, the Prime Minister adjudicating in the event of disagreement.
2 Consultation, under which colleagues would be consulted by a minister on his most important proposals, but would have the right only to express opinions, not to force their views on him.
3 A more presidential role for the Prime Minister – as Dell points out, a prerequisite for this system.

This has many attractions. It omits much pretence and semi-transparent fiction. It is clear-cut and simple. It would offer a fragmented system of clear areas of responsibility held together by a strengthened centre in the person of the Prime Minister, and ministers would have a real and more independent responsibility to Parliament. However, it is itself open to criticism.

First, it is a managerial critique of an essentially political institution. As stressed in earlier chapters, the Cabinet and its committees are not primarily meetings of experts or technocrats. They consider proposals primarily from a political standpoint, and from a wider viewpoint than that of the lead minister, whose ideas may make sense within the narrow confines of his department but may run counter to the wider purposes of the government. There is a strong case for giving ministers better briefing on matters outside their own departmental concerns, but that flaw derives from inadequacies in their sources of information, not in collective responsibility.

Second, this attack ignores two aspects of the political culture within which ministers operate. The 'us' and 'them' mentality of party rivalry, expressed daily in parliament, holds the government together. And collegiality is essentially implicit; it is not only a doctrine, but a cultural expectation. Ministers take it for granted. Like the electricity supply, they assume that it will always be there and only worry about it when it breaks down. That is why it only gets discussed at moments of crisis.

Third, collective discussion provides the Prime Minister with the opportunity to educate colleagues in the problems and constraints with which the government must come to grips. Seen from that point of view, the lengthy Cabinet discussions about applying to join the EU in the 1960s were essentially an exercise in political education, and the long debates over the IMF terms that Dell so deprecates brought the Cabinet slowly to terms with the enormity and intractability of the economic problems they faced. Seen from that angle, collective discussion is actually a tool of Prime Ministerial leadership.

Fourth, Dell's principle of consultation, to be substituted for committee decision-making, will mean little if infrequent and perfunctory; if frequent and thorough, it will not relieve the burden on ministers or speed decision-taking. In the former case ministers will not take it seriously. In the latter they will become frustrated because, however strong their objections, the responsible minister can always override them – and that is likely to happen often since Dell's system would entrench ministers more firmly in their departmental redoubts. Nor is collective tolerance – avoiding criticising each other – terribly realistic. Ministers are forever exposed to appear on television programmes and asked questions about government policy outside their own department. What do they do then? Moreover, if they disagree with the policies of their colleagues at health or education, what are they to say to disgruntled patients or angry parents at their constituency surgeries?

Dell acknowledges that a prerequisite for his proposed system would be a more presidential Prime Minister. In fact, as a former Cabinet Secretary (Hunt 1994) has observed, it would mean much more. It would genuinely replace Cabinet government with Prime Ministerial government. It would lead to a system very similar to that in France and Germany – both worth glancing at to grasp how very different they are from the British arrangement. In the German Federal Republic – both pre- and post-reunification – the dominant relationship has been between the Federal Chancellor and the departmental minister. Policy initiatives are worked up by one or two departmental ministers in meetings with the Chancellor – whose responsibility for the oversight of policy is stated by the constitution – and perhaps officials from the Chancellor's Office. Formal Cabinet committees as such are few, meet infrequently and have little influence. The Cabinet meets weekly but usually only nods through decisions already approved by the

Chancellor. The traditions of ministerial autonomy and strong Chancellorship rule out any significant role for the Cabinet (Muller-Rommell 1988).

The position in France is complicated by the coexistence of a Prime Minister and an executive President, but in its essentials it is like the German system. Policy proposals are initiated by departmental ministers and amended or rejected by the Prime Minister. There are no ministerial committees. When two ministers disagree they submit their cases to the Prime Minister who issues a binding decision. The weekly Council of Ministers is only a formal meeting that registers decisions rather than taking them (Thiébault 1988). In both countries, where collegiality is only skin deep, the process and nature of decision-making are strikingly different from the British system. If the British collegiate ethos had withered away the Cabinet system, ever adaptable and flexible, would have turned itself into something similar to the German or French pattern. As it is, discussion of policy between British ministers remains real, frequent and often leads to the amendment or rejection of proposals. Only if that ethos of substantial discussion withers would a shift to the system advocated by Dell become viable.

The final and politically strongest argument against Dell's ideas is that once a major conflict arises ministers will be more likely to fight out their differences at least semi-publicly. This is illustrated by an example used by Dell himself. In 1975 the Chrysler car company asked for a government subsidy to keep open its plant at Linwood in Scotland. The Scottish Secretary, William Ross, threatened resignation if the government did not provide the money; the Industry Secretary Eric Varley threatened resignation if it did. Both threats leaked to the press and both sides fought an unusually public battle. Varley lost and, although persuaded not to resign, his career was stopped in its tracks. Worse happened in the Westland affair: two Cabinet ministers fought openly to the extent of contradicting each other in the Commons and undermining each other in public correspondence. This ended in the resignation of them both and severe damage to the Prime Minister's authority. In both cases, other members of the Cabinet were horrified, the Opposition made hay in the Commons, and the damage was immense, since the electorate expects ministers to show a reasonable degree of agreement on the running of the country.

The difficulty of allowing open dissent is well illustrated by the example of France where serious political embarrassment is regularly caused by ministers disagreeing openly with one another (for a catalogue of incidents, see Wright 1989). In the Socialist government of Mauroy in 1981 – after a particularly open argument over police powers between the Interior Minister and the Justice Minister – the Prime Minister sought to rationalise matters in a newspaper article entitled 'Gouverner autrement' ('A different way of governing') in which he denounced ministers of previous right-wing governments for their tameness and impotent timidity. Socialist ministers, he observed, had the habit of speaking their minds and such 'positive personalities are not afraid to express and defend their point of view'. Ministers 'should be able to participate in, and even nourish, public discussion' (*Le Monde* 19–20 April 1982). The public was unimpressed, and so was President Mitterand, at whose behest ministerial discipline was tightened up and political embarrassment lessened. It was a public disagreement of the same sort that prompted Prime Minister Juppé to sack his Finance Minister in 1995 for criticising his colleagues' lack of radicalism, declaring 'A government is not a debating society in which each can play his own tune' (*Le Monde* 29 August 1995).

The advantages of collective responsibility

Collective responsibility has never been a 'pure' doctrine. Ministers are ambitious and highly political. The obligations of collective responsibility are only tolerable if there is a safety valve. For as long as collective responsibility has been accepted as a constitutional principle – roughly the past hundred years – ministers have surreptitiously leaked information and signalled their dissent to newspapers and backbenchers. It is hard to resist the world-weary conclusion of Patrick Gordon Walker, himself a former minister:

> The doctrine of collective responsibility and the unattributable leak grew up side by side as an inevitable feature of the Cabinet in a mass two-party system. In every Cabinet the leak will be deplored and condemned; but paradoxically it is necessary to the preservation of the doctrine of collective responsibility. It is the mechanism by which the doctrine of collective responsibility is reconciled with political reality. The unattributable leak is itself a recognition and acceptance that members of a Cabinet do not disagree in public.
>
> (Walker 1972)

Collective responsibility is no fail-safe guarantee of a good policy. As Lawson points out, the poll tax was hammered out at innumerable meetings of a committee consisting of two-thirds of the Cabinet, which was provided with the fullest information, and was approved by the Cabinet as a whole (Lawson 1992 and 1994). However, it does give ministers a sense of sharing in the exercise of power, which generates a sense of joint acceptance of the result. If a minister is asked for his views but is told that the responsible minister and the Prime Minister will ignore those views if they feel like it, he will hardly feel himself bound to the eventual decision. On the other hand, if he goes into Cabinet or committee knowing that he can stop the proposal if he can persuade enough colleagues to back him, he will feel some sense of obligation to abide by the decision if he loses. This may not sound entirely logical but it does appear to be true. As Peter Shore said of the 1976 IMF spending cuts – which he opposed – 'no-one resigned: at least in part because no-one could say that his or her case had not been fully and seriously examined' (Shore 1993). Collective responsibility does not stop ministers entirely from leaking to the press but it probably minimises it. More often than not it is effective in concealing divisions. If it were not, given the number of controversial decisions taken every month by ministers, there would be far more leaks in the newspapers than there are.

In the end, the reason why collective responsibility is likely to endure is that politicians invented it in the mid-Victorian era and, for all they chafe at its restrictions, they still find it politically essential. Why else would they preserve it (James 1994)? As Mrs Thatcher's Cabinet Secretary put it, if collective responsibility did not exist, it would have to be invented (Armstrong 1986a).

The Prime Minister's duty to foster collective responsibility

Yet, if collective responsibility is to survive as a useful collective defence, Prime Ministers must themselves resist the temptation to leak. Under some Prime Ministers, notably Wilson and Mrs Thatcher, No. 10 has leaked more than any other part of Whitehall. And collective responsibility is not just an obligation imposed on ministers, but also a sense of collegiate solidarity that the Prime Minister must foster, particularly by ensuring that they feel that they have been able to discuss key issues. For example, when Callaghan insisted that his Cabinet approve the 1977 expenditure White Paper page by page (Barnett 1982), and Wilson took his Cabinet in detail through the 'Tiger' agreement with the government of Rhodesia (Crossman 1976) it was to prevent colleagues from distancing themselves from the decisions. Both premiers were then on rock solid ground when they warned wayward colleagues that any breach of collective responsibility would lead to dismissal. Collective discussion is, in short, a form of political insurance for the Prime Minister.

The failure of Mrs Thatcher's non-collegiate style

A cautionary tale regarding the consequences of neglecting to cultivate a sense of collegiality is Mrs Thatcher's premiership. Her ill-concealed impatience with the Cabinet, brusque treatment of colleagues, intolerance of dissent and unsubtle interventions in the work of departments dismayed and dispirited ministers. When she fell out with colleagues a whispering campaign was conducted against them: a string of ministers – Walker, Carrington, Biffen, Jenkin, Pym and Moore – found their reputations tarnished by this insidious operation. Inevitably, collectivity crumbled. Even loyalists like Nott and Parkinson complained in public of the loss of collegiality (BBC 1986b).

It was a high risk way to run a Cabinet and led to three major crises, the last of which destroyed her. Whatever the truth of the 1985 Westland affair (the best account is Linklater and Leigh 1986), its root cause was the lack of any sense of collective responsibility amongst ministers who believed it legitimate to campaign publicly against one another. Two ministers resigned (Michael Heseltine and Leon Brittan) and Mrs Thatcher, who at one stage feared having to resign herself,* was at elaborate pains for some while afterwards to consult colleagues on any matter that might concern them (Armstrong 1994).

This solicitude wore off after the 1987 election. Trouble broke out between her and Chancellor Lawson's ambition to take sterling into the European exchange rate mechanism (ERM). Off and on throughout 1988 and 1989 they contradicted each other in public. Set this example, the Foreign Secretary and other senior ministers joined the public argument with barely coded expressions of support for either side. Several times a compromise formula was patched together, and several times No. 10 reopened the wound. A commitment to join the ERM in the long term was eventually given only after the Foreign Secretary and Chancellor jointly threatened to resign.

The Chancellor's resignation eventually came after the Prime Minister's economic adviser, Alan Walters, attacked the EMS as 'half-baked'. Lawson demanded Walters' dismissal. Mrs Thatcher refused. Lawson went but, as he said in his resignation speech 'the article written by Sir Alan Walters was of significance only in as much as it represented the tip of a singularly ill-concealed iceberg, with all the destructive potential that icebergs possess' (quoted in Lawson 1992).

Mrs Thatcher was immediately criticised by two usually loyal ex-ministers, Norman Tebbit and Lord Hailsham, for undermining Cabinet collectivity (in separate articles in the *Evening Standard* 30 October 1989). Lawson in his resignation speech said pointedly:

For our system of Cabinet government to work effectively the Prime Minister of the day must appoint ministers that he or she trusts and then leave them to carry out the policy. When differences of view emerge, as they are bound to do from time to time, they should be resolved privately and, wherever appropriate, collectively.

(Lawson 1992)

So the rot was well advanced by the time Sir Geoffrey Howe's resignation precipitated Mrs Thatcher's overthrow. By this time she had reluctantly agreed to join the ERM, and debate had changed to a common European currency, which she resisted despite strong business pressures. Another prolonged semi-public row with her new Chancellor and Foreign Secretary followed. When eventually a Cabinet compromise was patched up – with difficulty – in the shape of the 'hard ecu' plan, the Prime Minister promptly pooh-poohed the idea in a Commons answer. Howe resigned and in the resignation speech that precipitated Mrs Thatcher's downfall he bitterly criticised her public undermining of Cabinet agreements:

Cabinet government is all about trying to persuade one another from within....The task has become futile, trying to stretch the meaning of words beyond what was credible, and trying to pretend that there was a common policy when every step forward risked being subverted by some casual comment or impulsive answer.

(Commons debates 13 November 1990, Howe 1994)

This sparked the revolt that swept Mrs Thatcher from office.

Two lessons flow from this. First, by neglecting – if not actively corroding – her government's sense of collegiality, Mrs Thatcher did not immediately occasion her own downfall. She got away with it for some years. However, second, over time it became a risky way to run a government because it diminished the political cohesion of her Cabinet. Led by someone who played fast and loose with collective responsibility, ministers responded either by resigning in despair or, as in the Westland affair, breaking loose of all restraint. The Cabinet is not just a mechanism for taking decisions: it is a means of nurturing political loyalty between colleagues. The Prime Minister, as chairman and leader, cannot afford to neglect this side of its work, and it is no coincidence that the contenders for the Conservative leadership in 1990, including the successful Mr Major, called for a return to the traditional spirit of Cabinet government (*The Times* 26 and 27 November 1990).

Briefing for the Prime Minister

Overseas observers marvel that the Prime Minister's office has only fifty administrative staff and the same number of clerical and typing assistants. This is smaller than any other leading country: the figure runs up to 500 in Germany and 5,000 in France. No. 10 boasts only a small private office supplemented by occasional special advisers and, since 1974, a policy unit of up to fifteen staff. The slenderness of these arrangements is based on the realistic assumption that the Prime Minister's primary adviser on any issue will be the minister handling it, who runs the policy and has the expertise and data at his disposal. The drawback, as described by Lord Hunt, Cabinet Secretary from 1973 to 1979, is that ministerial advice is 'advice from one point of view only – and one which is inevitably more concerned with the particular problems of the department concerned than with the government's overall strategy' (Hunt 1983). But if the Prime Minister feels dissatisfied with the approach, or wants to explore other options, he can effectively be blocked by an uncooperative departmental minister. As a frustrated Wilson complained in 1967: 'I'm sick of asking for this or that suggestion to be followed up only to have Michael or Jim's officials report back three weeks later that nothing could be done' (Castle 1980).

Hence successive premiers' search in the past three decades for alternative sources of analysis and advice. Hunt recalls

> During my seven years as Secretary to the Cabinet under four Prime Ministers I found myself gradually spending more and more of my time trying to help the Prime Minister of the day in this way...But often I was conscious that, while the briefs were served up on time, the resources available to produce them were thin and often stretched to the limit. Indeed I can readily remember at least two occasions under different Prime Ministers (but which I do not intend to reveal) when instinct made me raise a warning flag that a particular decision would be inconsistent with the government's strategy, when there was neither the time not the resources to demonstrate that this was so, but when with hindsight this was undoubtedly the case.
>
> (Hunt 1983)

Berrill, head of the Central Policy Review Staff which advised the Cabinet in the 1970s, echoed this: 'At issue is whether a Prime Minister should have a support system with time to work on problems in some depth across the width of government activities. At present the advice is given and very presentably too, but the depth is inevitably patchy' (Berrill 1985).

The lack of briefing for ministers at Cabinet and committee

If the Prime Minister's briefing support is limited, that for ministers in their Cabinet role is non-existent. Robert Carr, Home Secretary under Heath, recalled:

> I was amazed and dismayed to find how relatively poorly Cabinet ministers were briefed on matters outside their own departmental responsibility.... [and] were less well briefed in breadth and depth than the directors of a well-managed company on matters of major policy on which they were expected to take collective responsibility.
>
> (letter to *The Times* 23 April 1998)

The judgement that ministers are asked to pass on their colleagues' projects is political rather than expert, but political judgement still requires an appreciation of the facts and ministers should take decisions on the basis of the best information available. Yet if a matter lies outside a minister's departmental concerns, his officials will not brief him on it. He has nothing to rely on except the papers submitted by the ministers in contention. These will not be unprejudiced in their presentation of the issues. The two protagonists will argue the case primarily in terms of their own departmental concerns and it is quite possible that the discussion will fail to touch on some of the main relevant consequences of the proposal.

Crossman, a year after first taking office, was struck by this deficiency at a meeting of the Economic Development Committee:

> The main item was Fred Peart's marketing scheme and, apart from myself, [Crossman was a weekend farmer] nobody had any basis on which to comment unless he had been given a departmental brief. And no department will prepare a brief for its minister on any issue outside the departmental purview.
>
> (Crossman 1975)

The consequences of such a situation were demonstrated during the 1967 farm prices review, when the Agriculture Secretary asked for an increase in the milk subsidy of 2d a gallon, against a Treasury offer of ½d. The Cabinet's Agriculture Committee compromised at 1½d; the Treasury appealed to Cabinet. In fact, the farmers would have regarded 1½d as a generous settlement, but this was not vouchsafed to the Cabinet, which pronounced that the Committee's decision should stand as a fair compromise (Crossman 1976).

So, for example, when in 1970 Wilson's Economic Policy Committee rose in revolt against a paper from the Chancellor that they felt was unnecessarily pessimistic on the prospects of economic growth, there was no alternative source of analysis with which the Treasury could be challenged. Despite the unhappiness of the committee, the Chancellor escaped with only minor changes to his plans (Castle 1984). Again, during the 1976 IMF saga a majority of the Cabinet strongly criticised the Chancellor's proposals but, in the words of the dissentient Peter Shore:

> what the critics of the orthodox Treasury view lacked was the back-up of a departmental structure of papers...so that they would be able to take account of all the arguments which the Treasury is in a position to deploy.

The then Permanent Secretary of the Treasury, who was on the opposite side in that contest, agreed:

> however desirous the other Cabinet ministers are to participate in strategic thinking, they don't have the staff at present, and they didn't then, to do any collective thinking...consequently when a strategic matter arises, the ordinary Cabinet minister is in the hands of the particular departmental minister who is bringing the issue to Cabinet'.
> (*Listener* 2 February 1984)

There have been some attempts by departments, at the request of ministers like Callaghan, Heseltine and Rodgers, to prepare briefing on items outside the departmental purview, but without much success (for example, Callaghan 1987). A computerised system called CAB-E-NET accessible to all ministers' private offices was set up by Michael Heseltine in the latest years of the Major government, but it gave news mainly of ministers' engagements and described current policy proposals only in very general terms. As David Willetts, the minister who oversaw its implementation, admitted, ministers wary of central control by No. 10 put only 'sanitised' information on the system (*Sunday Telegraph* 29 June 1997).

The difficulties of policy coordination

There is a perpetual conflict between efficient administration, which relies on division of functions and specialisation, and effective coordination of policy which, in real life, cuts across administrative frontiers. The British tradition of ministerial government and autonomous departments favours the former at the expense of the latter. As described in Chapter 3, the

Whitehall system is good at policy coordination when one department is clearly in the lead, and where there is not a major conflict of interest between departments. However, because the hold of individual departments on policy is so strong, when several departments are in contention, or where a policy requires a pooling of resources, coordination tends to be confined to the minimum possible to avoid needless conflict.

The problem is of long standing, but was highlighted from the very top by the 1997 incoming Labour Government. Peter Mandelson put it bluntly not long after becoming Minister without Portfolio:

> On the whole [government departments] have been good over the years at developing policy where the issues have related to their own responsibilities and when they have received strong political leadership. On the other hand, even the most loyal Whitehall groupie will accept that they have been less good at developing policy where, as is becoming increasingly common, it affects a number of departments more or less equally. All too often the results have been ineffectual – because rooted in the lowest common policy denominator – or incomplete, because bogged down in bureaucratic turf wars.
>
> (Mandelson 1997)

Lord Lester, who had worked as a special adviser twenty years earlier, put it more bluntly: inter-departmental initiatives were 'like rowing in treacle: cumbersome, laborious and in the end wholly ineffectual' (Lords debates 9 July 1997, col. 690).

The lack of strategic capacity in the Cabinet system

From the preceding chapters it is clear that the Cabinet has not at any time since the nineteenth century (if then) been a strategic body. It deals with casework across the span of government but rarely pauses to relate these individual decisions to the government's overall programme. When each minister fights his own corner, there is an obvious danger that collective direction becomes little more than the aggregate of ad hoc settlements of these arguments. In his Reith lectures Douglas Wass, former Head of the Treasury, mused on this inadequacy:

> The machinery that exists within departments to give ministers a perspective of their activities, a set of suggested objectives and a ranking of priorities, is missing in the collective forum of the Cabinet. Ministers in Cabinet rarely look at the totality of their responsibilities,

at the balance of policy, at the progress of the government towards its objectives as a whole…the general thrust of the government's policies is seldom if ever reviewed and assessed by Cabinet; strategic changes of course in response to substantial shifts in circumstances are not subjected to collective consideration; and the ordering of priorities is discussed only in the most general terms. I am not saying that these matters are never reviewed by governments: I can recall several important changes in the field of economic management which governments have made as the result of a deliberate reassessment. But these were not usually Cabinet reviews; and none of them was the result of a systematic study.

(Wass 1983)

Nor do Cabinet committees provide a forum for discussion of government strategy (Wass 1983). Like the Cabinet, committees' discussions are limited to the issues set out in the papers before them. Prime Ministers occasionally write the word 'strategic' into a committee's name – Wilson and Mrs Thatcher both created Economic Strategy Committees in the 1960s and 1970s – but this has not often meant much.

The absence of strategic purpose was painfully evident as the Macmillan and Wilson governments drifted through the 1960s. This was true not only in broad terms – the lack of any sense of direction – but also in contradictions between their few declared general aims and their actual decisions. Hence the Macmillan Cabinet's approval of the postal workers' pay claim which breached the national pay policy was given quickly and without thinking through its practical consequences (Kogan 1971), while Wilson's government proclaimed its opposition to industrial monopolies yet encouraged mergers which fostered monopolies that did not increase competitiveness (Ponting 1989).

As Lord Hunt, the former Cabinet Secretary, put it:

There is no systematic way, other than the general philosophy of the party in power, whereby the benefit from resources for, say, defence, health or motorways can be compared and evaluated. Thus unless the Cabinet can provide a clear strategic oversight over the policies of getting on for thirty departments of state – let alone the other bodies for which the government is directly or indirectly responsible – there is an in-built risk that decisions may be taken in an arbitrary, uncoordinated or even contradictory manner'.

There is in short 'a hole in the centre of government' and a purposeful strategy is needed to fill it.

(Hunt 1983)

Allocating public expenditure: the lack of a systematic overview

One facet of the lack of strategy was for many years the absence of a rational overview of the way in which public expenditure is allocated between departments. Douglas Wass summarised the main dynamics of the system as 'He who has the muscle gets the money' and 'As things are, so broadly shall they remain' (Wass 1983). This was well illustrated by the memoirs of the former Chief Secretary Joel Barnett and the former Chancellor Niger Lawson. In negotiations over public spending, a minister's personal clout counted for almost as much as the intrinsic value of the programme at issue. Inevitably, public expenditure arguments were about 'spending at the margin': whether a department should get 1 per cent more or less. The drawback was the lack of any review of the existing distribution of the bulk of expenditure to see whether or not it matched the government's objectives. Ministers never got a chance to consider the Government's overall priorities. Conservative Cabinets inherited the spending patterns of Labour governments without demur, and vice versa. Furthermore, under any government the pattern of public spending is changed under pressures from outside; for example, external factors pushed up social security spending under the Thatcher and Major governments from a quarter of total expenditure to a third of the total. Partly, as a consequence, spending on infrastructure – notably transport and housing – was squeezed (Darling 1997) but the detailed implications of these shifts were not considered by ministers.* In short, a government needs actively to manage priorities. In the past, this has not happened frequently or systematically across Whitehall.

The Commons Select Committee on Treasury Affairs looked at the system in 1984 and observed that the Cabinet seemed poorly informed on spending matters and that the machinery appeared inadequate to take an overall view of the relative merit of various departments' programmes. There was little or no discussion of the priorities to be accorded to different areas of government activity. The Committee recommended a review 'with particular reference to the need to improve the allocation across departments' (*The Times* 7 December 1984). This report summarised a concern felt for long by many officials and some ministers though, as Lawson points out with justification, cost benefit analysis is much easier within areas of activity than between them (Lawson 1992). Various ministerial committees had been created since the 1950s to review the allocation of spending between departments: all proved short-lived, overwhelmed by the political difficulties of effecting seismic shifts in the distribution of public spending.

The 1990s have seen two promising experiments that seem to be helping to develop a more sophisticated review of the 'balance of spending'. The Ministerial Committee on Public Expenditure (EDX) created in 1992 by Major and his first Chancellor Lamont differed in four ways from Mrs Thatcher's ad hoc Star Chamber of non-departmental ministers. It was a permanent body, chaired by the Chancellor, which strengthened the Treasury. It was given additional political muscle by the addition of senior ministers – at various times Heseltine, Clarke, Howard, Lang, Waldergrave, some of whom had large departmental budgets (notably, Waldergrave as Minister for Agriculture and successively Clarke and Howard as Home Secretary). The presence of such senior colleagues could have caused friction, and indeed in EDX's first year Lamont stalked out of one meeting after senior colleagues, led by Clarke (then Home Secretary) criticised his handling of the economy (Seldon 1997). When Clarke himself became Chancellor the following year he gave EDX a more dynamic role: it met more frequently, and its cycle of meetings began earlier than in previous years with discussions on the broad priorities to guide the Chief Secretary in his discussions with departments. This changed the role of the Chief Secretary: he was less independent, less of a protagonist, and more the agent of the committee's priorities, acting, as it were, as 'counsel to the inquiry'.* It also marked a strong movement towards greater collective involvement in the annual public expenditure survey (Wakeham 1993). Instead of a rather arbitrary allocation of spending priorities, a sub-Cabinet of senior figures imposed a set of priorities and weighed the relative merits of programmes.* It did so, of course, in pretty general terms, perhaps recognising that it is difficult to weigh the relative merits of, say, defence and transport, which must in the end be a political judgement; but, for example, in 1992 EDX (with Major's blessing) deliberately protected capital spending as important to the economy (Seldon 1997).

Even the EDX initiative was limited to deciding which departments would get the largest increase at the margin. The initial signals from the Blair government did not suggest a radical change in priorities: the Public Expenditure Committee (now PX) reverted to a membership of non-departmental ministers and the government undertook to adhere to the spending plans of the outgoing Conservative government for the first three years. However, in June 1997 the Chief Secretary, Alistair Darling, announced an ambitious series of 'comprehensive spending reviews'.

> Every Department will scrutinise its spending plans in detail from a zero base, and ask, how does each item contribute to the Government's objective as set out in our manifesto? Why are we

spending this money? Do we need to spend it? What is it achieving? How effective is it? How efficiently are we spending it?...its conclusions will inform a new set of public spending plans for the rest of this Parliament – a set that reflects our priorities.

(Commons debates 11 June 1997, col. 1144)

The outcome, announced in July 1998, was a substantial shift in spending priorities over the coming 3 years: towards education, health and capital expenditure in transport and housing, and away from defence, agriculture, the diplomatic service and the legal system (Commons debates 14 July 1998, cols. 187–94; see also the excellent analysis in the *Financial Times* 15 July 1998). Departments were allocated funding for three years in advance, rather than one year (although since the Treasury announced that the third year of one cycle would be the first year of the next, this effectively lengthened the cycle to two years only). In exchange, departments were to reach public service agreements with the Treasury to include clear objectives. PX was given the role of ensuring these objectives were met and overseeing subsequent negotiations for future cycles.

The arrangements represent the most ambitious re-engineering of the public expenditure system for several decades, shifting the emphasis away from annual negotiations and their emphasis on inputs, and towards objectives and outputs. The implications for the Cabinet system will be intriguing: the acceptance by ministers of externally monitored policy objectives erodes their autonomy, although stability of funding over three years is a compensation which, the Chancellor implied, would make it easier for ministers to re-order priorities within their departmental budgets. The enhanced role of PX signifies both an enhanced role for the Chancellor as its chairman and further assertion of 'semi-collective' control of the spending allocation process, for PX will decide whether departments have fulfilled their targets and authorise the release of funds to them. The dynamics of the new arrangements will take some years to establish themselves, but choosing the membership of PX is likely to prove one of the Prime Minister's most significant organisational decisions.

This chapter surveyed of the problems within the system. The next chapter looks at some of the institutional changes that have sought to remedy them.

7 Advice at the centre

This chapter examines the central machinery that has long existed to support the Prime Minister and Cabinet ministers: the Cabinet Secretariat, and the Prime Minister's Office, including its shifting cast of incidental advisers. It then examines three innovations of recent decades: the Prime Minister's Policy Unit, special advisers to Cabinet ministers, and the now-defunct Central Policy Review Staff.

The Cabinet Secretariat

Structure and purpose

Since 1945 the only permanent central unit designed to support ministers collectively in policy matters has been the Cabinet Secretariat. Its name causes some confusion. The term 'Cabinet Office' is often used, although by it most people actually mean the Cabinet Secretariat, the two dozen officials who service the Cabinet and its committees and manage the channels through which all major decisions are made. The Cabinet Office proper embraces many wider responsibilities including the Civil Service, machinery of government and propriety issues. (In 1998 these various functions were more closely integrated – see Chapter 8.) The coordination of government policy, however, lies with the Cabinet Secretariat.

The basic configuration of the Secretariat changes little from government to government: the core structure is four Secretariats, dealing respectively with defence and overseas questions; economic and domestic issues; European affairs; and – since 1997 – constitutional matters. Each is headed by a grade 2 (deputy Permanent Secretary). In addition, the Joint Intelligence Organisation synthesises for senior ministers the data gleaned from intelligence sources and the Ceremonial Branch manages the honours system (*Civil Service Yearbook* 1997, second edition, Cabinet Office 1997b, Central Intelligence Machinery 1993).

The Cabinet Secretariat performs four types of function. Its core task is to provide secretarial support to ministerial committees; in the words of Burke Trend, Cabinet Secretary from 1963 to 1972,

> to be an effective administrative apparatus, responsible for circulating the relevant papers in good time, for arranging and recording discussions, and for ensuring the prompt and efficient implementation of decisions.
>
> (Trend 1981)

But servicing these meetings takes up a small proportion of the Secretariats' time and, on its own, would not justify employing so many senior staff. Most time is devoted to the second function, policy management: bringing matters to a state where they are ready for consideration by ministers. This includes keeping track of issues and spotting those which need to be brought before ministers; establishing likely future business through the regular 'forward look' exercise mentioned in Chapter 3; advising departments where a matter should be handled – at Cabinet, committee, at an ad hoc group, or by correspondence – and most important by bringing departments together to sort out policy issues where departments are in disagreement (Cabinet Office 1997b).

Typically, when a thorny problem arises, the secretaries of the appropriate committee will ring the departments most closely concerned to find out their respective stances, and commission a draft paper from the lead department and circulate it at official level for comment. If this reveals serious disagreement, one of the secretaries will chair a meeting of the official committee that shadows each ministerial committee. This may go some way towards resolving differences – often, the simple act of convening a meeting makes departments decide which points they will fight on, and which they will concede – so that, at least, the paper for ministers can be redrafted to map the areas of agreement and highlight the areas of dispute. This then puts the secretaries in a good position to brief the chairman of the ministerial committee on the stance that different ministers will take, and suggest a possible solution.

Third, the coordination of certain functions is entrusted to the Cabinet Secretariat. Most significant among these is the coordination of policy towards the EU by the European Secretariat (described below); the coordination of the future legislative programme; the coordination of the work of the Ministerial Committee on Public Expenditure (PX, formerly EDX) which meets intensively in the summer; and the work of the Civil Contingencies Unit (part of the Economic and Domestic Secretariat) which lays plans for civil emergencies.

Fourth, additional units are occasionally located in the Secretariat. Some, like the Enterprise Unit headed by Lord Young, are billeted there for lack of a better base and are soon hived off to departments. Most, however, are there because their work, even though ephemeral, is a core part of government business. Notable examples are the units established in the 1960s to handle reform of the House of Lords, and in the 1970s to handle devolution. Much of the work of the Constitution Secretariat set up in 1997 to handle the Blair government's reform programme was of a one-off nature, but this body itself will probably have some continued existence, not least to coordinate relations between the new Scottish, Welsh and Northern Irish administrations.

The Cabinet Secretariat is staffed by secondees. The Cabinet Secretary himself is its only permanent senior member; all the staff working for him on policy issues are borrowed from departments for two or three years. Consequently, the Secretariat's ethos is neutral. It exists to coordinate policy, not to pursue objectives of its own. When the courses of departments collide it intervenes as an impartial, conciliatory force. It cannot impose its own perspective but must work within the framework of other departments' views. One consequence, which shows that the Cabinet Secretariat is broadly trusted, is that Cabinet Secretariat officials almost always take the chair of inter-departmental official committees that prepare matters for discussion by ministers. This bestows influence but absorbs a lot of time. A former head of the European Affairs Secretariat reckoned that he chaired about 100 meetings a year and attended at least as many again (Stapleton 1985).

Those few Secretariat staff who have described their work have done so in very similar terms. 'All we do is try to collect together people to get things done. Somebody's got to do it' (Sampson 1971). 'My job is to help settle inter-departmental disputes before they get out of hand' (Heclo and Wildalsky 1981). 'One of the things I think we are very emphatic on is that the Cabinet Secretariat doesn't and shouldn't sort of develop its own policies...but there is often a role for us to do, knocking departmental heads together' (C. Campbell 1983).

Intriguingly, one function not carried out by the Cabinet Secretariat is monitoring the implementation of decisions – a function exercised by analogous organisations in other European countries (Burch and Halliday 1996). It is a signal tribute to Whitehall that this omission causes no problems: the ethos that 'what a ministers says, goes' is deeply engrained, and there is a strong culture in government departments of honouring commitments. It is a sharp contrast to some Asian and African Cabinet systems where up to three quarters of decisions are simply not implemented.

Chapter 5 dwelt on 'segmentation' – the fact that policy is made in different ways in different sectors of the Cabinet system. This affects the *modus operandi* of the Secretariats. In the Overseas and Defence sphere, the infrequent meetings of committees resulting from the frequent absence abroad of key members point to the transaction of much business bilaterally or through correspondence. In the economic and domestic sphere, in contrast, committees meet more often – as witness the facts (a) that most leaks from committees are on domestic matters, and (b) that virtually all the ad hocs created by Major and Blair since 1992 were in the domestic sphere (if you are going to handle the business informally or by correspondence, you don't need to create a MISC or GEN). The European Affairs Secretariat's work is done mainly in official committees: the one ministerial committee deals mainly with casework, and the bulk of EU business – often complex and detailed – is handled through its official shadow, and through offshoots dealing with such issues as legal matters, personnel issues and EU enlargement. (Useful expositions of the 'networks' of these different policy spheres appear in Burch and Halliday 1996.) The bailiwick of the Constitution Secretariat under the Blair government has been an example of old fashioned government by committee, due mainly to the sheer degree of politically sensitive detail that had to be processed against tight deadlines: the Devolution Committee met twenty-two times in its first eight months (Irvine 1998) and the sub-committee on reform of the House of Lords – whose meetings, unusually, were signalled to the press – met four times in the first three months of 1998.

Cabinet Secretariat advice to committee chairmen and the Prime Minister

The Cabinet Secretariat has multiple lines of responsibility: to ministers collectively, to the chairmen of committees, and to the Prime Minister. For most practical purposes, however, secretaries will look to a committee's chairman for direction on its business: what should be considered, when, and – if ministers disagree – what line of resolution the chairman favours. The chairman will usually lean heavily on the advice of the secretary. When an issue is being cleared by correspondence, the secretaries will advise the chairman on the degree of agreement reached, the extent to which the chairman can impose a decision in fields of disagreement (usually not much) and how to resolve outstanding points of disagreement (often by convening a meeting of departmental officials or ministers).

Similarly, when it comes to a meeting, the secretaries prepare for the chairman a 'handling brief'. This is mainly procedural; in Hunt's words:

mainly a brief about the background, about the papers before him, the points that are likely to come up, and the issues to be settled. It is not primarily a brief of political advice; it is a chairman's brief.

(Expenditure Committee 1977)

It suggests useful questions to ask, indicates areas of weakness to be probed, provides courteously phrased prompts in a certain direction and a draft summing up to use if the discussion goes as anticipated. The Cabinet Office 'Guide for departments' states 'we are bound to brief impartially' (1997b) , but adds that the brief will contain an assessment of the options available. For instance, the secretary to the 'Star Chamber', which decided public spending disputes in the 1980s ,'assisted the Chairman in devising compromises' (Lawson 1992). And as the heads of both the CPRS and the Prime Minister's Policy Unit in Hunt's day confirm, that sort of assistance can amount to policy advice (Berrill 1985, Donoughue 1987). The chairman will not always follow the secretary's suggestions and is free to ignore them entirely, but there is a good chance that the brief will provide the first draft of the committee's conclusions. For this reason departments sometimes discreetly lobby the Secretariat by phone to find out what the brief will say and perhaps try to influence the content (Barnett 1982).

While the Cabinet Secretariat takes seriously its responsibility to ministers collectively, it has a particular responsibility to the Prime Minister as chairman of Cabinet and head of the government. In Callaghan's words:

The conventional role of the Cabinet Secretariat is to serve all members of the Cabinet, but if the Prime Minister chooses, as almost all of them do, to work closely with the Secretary to the Cabinet, then it becomes an instrument to serve him above the others.

(Callaghan 1987)

Working closely with No. 10 makes sense, for simple reasons of administrative coordination, and because it attunes the Cabinet Office to the premier's preoccupations and No. 10 to what is happening in departments. Wilson's observation (1976) that the highest proportion of work at No. 10 is carried out in intimate collaboration with the Cabinet Secretariat remains true.

The Cabinet Secretary and heads of Secretariats

In the absence of a Prime Minister's department the Cabinet Secretary becomes – in the words of Burke Trend, Cabinet Secretary in the 1960s – the Prime Minister's Permanent Secretary (Wilson 1967), seeing him two or three times a day and briefing him on all important meetings. If the Prime Minister has a problem the Cabinet Secretary is the person most likely to be able to help. He knows everybody who matters. He can arrange for matters to be rushed forward for decision or can delay consideration if he thinks the timing is wrong. He can persuade, advise and cajole ministers and their senior advisers. He can cut through procedure to help a department in difficulties. He can perhaps have a word with the Treasury to overcome some difficulty they have put in a department's way. In short, he is a remarkably useful person to have on your side.

Post-war Cabinet Secretaries have been influential advisers to No. 10, although the role varies with personality and circumstance. The austere Norman Brook served four premiers and acquired immense power, especially when underpinning the failing Churchill. Macmillan proclaimed him 'a tower of strength' and he became deeply embroiled in Macmillan's summitry, his application to join the EU and Commonwealth relations. A measure of his influence was his successful backstage pressure to introduce life peers to the House of Lords (PREM 11/2029).

His successor, Burke Trend, was a remarkably self-effacing, donnish character but Wilson greatly valued his opinion and he played the same crucial supporting role as Brook in pulling the government's act together, especially in a crisis such as the 1967 devaluation (Crossman 1976). In contrast, John Hunt was openly energetic and ambitious, moving the Cabinet Secretariat to centre stage in the crises of the 1970s, joining forces with the CPRS to challenge the Treasury during the IMF crisis, securing Cabinet Secretariat control of the coordination of ministerial decisions on public expenditure, chairing official committees on unemployment and nuclear reactors, and taking a strong interest in social policy (Donoughue 1987).

Hunt's activism, however, was concealed behind the facades of Whitehall; he contrived to keep his public profile low. His successors – Robert Armstrong in the 1980s, Robin Butler in the 1990s – would have liked to do the same, but the decision was taken in 1982 to combine the post of Head of the Civil Service with that of Cabinet Secretary (as it had been under Brook). These new responsibilities dragged Armstrong into the limelight to be interrogated by an Australian court on the government's attempt to ban *Spycatcher*, and by a Commons Select Committee on his investigation into the Westland affair. The question of whether one person can satisfactorily combine the roles of principal policy factotum to the government with the ethical responsibilities of the Head of the Civil Service is still periodically raised. But Butler argued that this gave the Head of the Civil Service access to the Prime Minister that he would otherwise lack (Butler 1997) and the posts remained combined when Butler was succeeded by Sir Richard Wilson in 1998.

Although Cabinet Secretaries' anonymity has faded, they continue to offer strong policy advice: Armstrong, for instance, successfully urged on Mrs Thatcher measures against AIDS, although he was less successful on Britain's contribution to the EU budget and trade union membership at GCHQ (Jenkins 1989). He played a crucial role in negotiating the 1986 Anglo-Irish Agreement with his Irish counterpart, and successfully sold the outcome to Mrs Thatcher (FitzGerald 1991, Howe 1994). But time constraints have become significant: Butler reckoned that his role as Head of the Home Civil Service took up between a quarter and a half of his time (Treasury and Civil Service Committee 1988), even if many duties could be performed when Parliament was in recess and political pressures reduced. The Cabinet Secretary still attends Cabinet and those committees chaired by the Prime Minister, approving the Prime Minister's briefing and authorising the minutes. And on certain key issues he still plays a leading role – for example, Butler took over the baton from Armstrong in Anglo-Irish relations (Howe 1994). But like other Permanent Secretaries, the Cabinet Secretary has tended to become more of a policy coordinator and director than direct protagonist.

This, allied to the greater devolution of authority to committees, has caused greater responsibility and autonomy to pass to the senior officials who head the component Secretariats of the Cabinet Office. Successive heads of the Overseas and Defence Secretariat have assumed a discreetly significant role, for example being sent to the US in 1979 to discuss acquiring Trident missiles (Callaghan 1987), playing a pivotal role during the Falklands campaign, and pushing through the 1986 Anglo-Irish agreement (Young 1989). Since 1994, the head of the Overseas and Defence Secretariat has also chaired the Joint Intelligence Committee. The head of the Economic and Domestic Secretariat is periodically drawn into managing major crises – for example, the BSE crisis of 1996 – and, since the abolition of the Central Policy Review Staff, has on occasion headed investigations into problems referred to him by ministers (Seldon 1990). And the head of the European Affairs Secretariat has become the Prime Minister's principal adviser on EU matters – he briefs the Prime Minister before, and accompanies him to, European Council meetings – reflecting the unusually dynamic role that his staff play in policy management.

The European Affairs Secretariat

It is worth dwelling on the work of this group of staff because, atypically for the Cabinet Secretariat, they have been drawn into a proactive role by the need to influence initiatives germinating within the European Commission, and to coordinate negotiating positions for EU meetings to very tight deadlines. In all EU countries this is a tricky task, made difficult by competing interests between different departments (for a survey of EU member states see Middlemass 1995); in comparison with other countries, the British are very effective at getting their act together.

The core task of the European Affairs Secretariat is to pull together the contributions of domestic departments, the Foreign Office and the UK permanent representative (UKRep) in Brussels; to act as a broker in resolving disagreements over negotiating stances and tactics; and to keep a watching brief on areas where problems may arise. As described in Chapters 2 and 3, it operates mainly through a pyramid of official meetings: roughly 200 a year, with some 300 documents circulated (Bender 1991). A high point of its weekly schedule is the regular meeting between the head of the Secretariat, the UK permanent representative and senior officials from Whitehall departments to review developments and discuss current issues. The variety of subjects is amazing: a former head of the Secretariat recorded that in two sample months from his diary,

> I took meetings dealing with subjects as varied as the protection of workers from noise, extra-territorial jurisdiction, state aids, counterfeit goods, customs duty on aircraft, and origin marking...But other Secretariat meetings I wished I could have attended discussed considerably more intriguing items such as the taxation of firearms and horses and the importation of obscene life-size rubber dolls.
>
> (Stapleton 1985)

More than other Secretariats, the European Affairs staff must take the initiative, rather than just react to external events, in anticipating developments in Brussels and pulling departments together to coordinate the British stance. Given the hectic, high pressure pace of EU business and the Secretariat's unique overview from the junction between ministers, departments and Brussels, it gets drawn into evaluating different courses of action and advising on strategy and tactics: how to play the hand, when to take initiatives, when to compromise. It becomes deeply engaged in all long-running issues within the EU (for many years in the 1980s the gloomy topic of Britain's EU budget contribution dominated its work). There is a delicate balance between providing that leadership and preserving its impartiality between departments: its neutrality was the reason for the insistence of home departments, particularly Agriculture, that coordination be led by the Cabinet Secretariat and not by the Foreign Office. But at bottom the European Secretariat, and particularly the deputy secretary who leads it, are in the business of policy advice and management as well as coordination (Bender 1991, Seldon 1995, Stack 1983).

The Cabinet Secretariat's limitations as a source of advice

The Cabinet Secretariat is held in high esteem by officials and ministers alike: even by that cheerful sceptic Gerald Kaufman – 'the Cabinet Secretariat is a Ferrari, built for speed and action…if it is on your side, you have a possibly conclusive advantage' (Kaufman 1980). But the principle of neutrality sets clear limits to its role. In a couple of areas where complex issues straddle departmental boundaries – notably EU policy and Anglo-Irish relations – the Secretariat may take the lead. But for the most part, as long as one department feels strongly about an issue – and one usually does – there is little scope for the Cabinet Secretariat to impose its own perspective. As one former Cabinet Secretary told the Expenditure Committee, the whole point of staffing it with secondees is to stop it from developing its own policies (Expenditure Committee 1977).

Yet its central position, with the main strings of policy-making passing through its hands, gives it influence. It can query proposals put up by departments or urge them to explore other options; it can prompt the Prime Minister or committee chairman to query or object. By its management of the agenda it can slow down or speed up a decision, or help to shut off or open up a particular option. Its senior staff can murmur guidance to a committee chairman. But it cannot impose its own view and any attempt to do so will rebound on it. Its influence is used to produce coherent, acceptable policies, not to challenge departments on their own ground.

Burch and Halliday argue (1996) that its potential for influencing policy has increased since 1974 as its size has grown and it has more actively managed the flow of business. This is questionable on three grounds. First, the Cabinet Secretariat, which remains small, should not be conflated with the Cabinet Office, whose numbers have often been inflated by other (and often temporary) functions. Second, the Secretariat channels the flow of business, but cannot determine its volume or content. Third, the Cabinet Secretariat before 1974 should not be under-estimated.

However, the Secretariat has to some extent filled the gap left by the demise of the CPRS, leading studies of inter-departmental questions, occasionally on its own initiative but more usually at the request of the Prime Minister or a Cabinet committee (Armstrong 1986). One such was the review of policy on admitting and caring for refugees in early 1991.* Another was the group established in the summer of 1989 under the head of the Economic and Domestic Secretariat, Richard Wilson (later Cabinet Secretary), including Treasury and Environment officials, government lawyers and a member of the Prime Minister's Policy Unit, to draw the sting of the poll tax (Butler, Adonis and Travers 1994). In such a case the Cabinet Secretary or one of his deputies will take the lead but, as Robert Armstrong acknowledges,

> he can't hope to do much more than eliminate avoidable differences and reduce the thing to the kernel of irreducible differences. What the Cabinet Secretariat isn't so good at is what the CPRS used to do which was to take a non-departmental view...to take account of all the conflicting considerations with particular reference to how things fitted in with the government's strategy.
>
> (BBC 1990a)

Callaghan discovered this in 1977 when he tried to resolve a conflict between his Chancellor, Healey, and the Energy Secretary, Tony Benn, by asking the Cabinet Secretariat to draft a White Paper on 'the challenge of North Sea oil'. The outcome was sound but bland and had to be redrafted by the No. 10 Policy Unit to give it a more positive inflexion and political bite (Donoughue 1987).

So, although the potential influence of the Cabinet Secretariat is great, it can be exercised only in limited circumstances. Its interventions occur at that moment when an important decision is imminent, but its recommendations are likely to fall somewhere within the spectrum of views held by competing departments. The Cabinet Secretariat, bound by its ethos of conciliation, cannot easily take on a more dynamic role if it is to remain trusted by ministers and their departments.

The Prime Minister's advisors

The private office

This comprises half a dozen officials seconded for two or three years, who between them cover foreign affairs, economics, domestic policy and parliament. Their two cramped offices by the Cabinet room are the link between the Prime Minister and the rest of the world (Jones 1973, Wapshott and Brock 1983).

However, they are secretaries, not policy advisers:

> They coordinate [the premier's] engagements; take responsibility for assembling material for his speeches and usually have an important hand in drafting them; ensure he is properly briefed before Cabinet and other meetings at home and when paying official visits overseas;

become his eyes and ears by maintaining a close liaison with other ministers' private Secretariats.

(Callaghan 1987)

Often a close relationship develops; Macmillan said of one of his secretaries: 'He understands the way my mind works. I don't have to explain everything to him' (Evans 1981). They may become companions with whom he can relax and unburden himself.

Their influence lies in their control of access to the Prime Minister and of the timing of decisions. Sometimes the Prime Minister may seek their personal view on a subject, but they lack the time or resources to prepare much briefing. And, like the Cabinet Secretariat, if private secretaries become embroiled in policy wrangles they lose the trust of departments. Macmillan's two main private secretaries Bligh and de Zulueta used his authority too freely and caused strains with the Treasury and Foreign Office; Bligh even advised on party matters (Evans 1981, Horne 1989). Mrs Thatcher's long-serving foreign affairs Private Secretary, Charles Powell, 'overstepped the line between the official and the political domains' (Cradock 1997) and became involved in rows with Foreign Secretaries.

Occasionally, Prime Ministers have added an outside chief of staff to their office. From 1979 to 1985, David Wolfson was essentially Mrs Thatcher's major-domo, his main function to ensure access for the Prime Minister's political advisers (Ranelagh 1991). Then the post lapsed (although Major toyed with reviving it) until Tony Blair in 1997 appointed Jonathan Powell, a former diplomat and, ironically, the brother of Mrs Thatcher's private secretary. Downing Street described his task as 'to coordinate the political and non-political work of No. 10' (*Financial Times* 1997) and, although press stories that he would also become Principal Private Secretary proved groundless, the Civil Service Order in Council was changed to gave him authority to issue instructions to civil servants (*Independent on Sunday* 11 May 1997).

The political office

All Prime Ministers since the 1950s have brought in party assistants to handle party liaison; Wilson regularised this as the Political Office. They nurture relations with the party machine and influential supporters, and contribute to speeches, but even the most famous holders of the office – Marcia Williams under Wilson, Douglas Hurd under Heath – have little influence on policy (Williams 1973 and 1983, Hurd 1979).

Press secretaries

The press secretary's job is unusually sensitive: that is why Prime Ministers, unusually, are allowed to change them pretty much at will, and to make external appointments if they wish. The sixteen postholders since 1929 have been four journalists and twelve civil servants (listed in Harris 1990).

Most press secretaries have confined themselves to briefing the press on the government's view of the world and have not influenced policy. Perceptions of the post have been coloured by the 11-year stint of Bernard Ingham, whose activities in briefing against other ministers were notorious (see for example, Harris 1990, Gilmour 1992). But although his influence with his premier was immense, there is evidence only of his influencing one decision in eleven years: the withdrawal of trade union membership at GCHQ (Howe 1994). Indeed, the only press secretary to influence policy regularly was Joe Haines, under Wilson, who became involved in subjects like incomes policy, housing and Northern Ireland (Donoughue 1987, Haines 1977).

On the whole, though, press secretaries' influence has been on presentation rather than content – although as presentation has increasingly come to be seen as an integral part of the policy process, that is still an influential role: there were political repercussions to Ingham's role in influencing public perception of Mrs Thatcher, which in turn influenced her perception of herself and what she could achieve (for example, over Europe).

Special ministers

Sometimes Prime Ministers appoint non-departmental ministers as personal advisers. They enjoy the advantages of political standing and access to ministerial meetings and papers. But they need a specific job to do, otherwise they will dwindle away without purpose.

Special ministers who work on policy are rare. Lord Mills was personal adviser and trouble shooter on industrial matters to Macmillan, had influence (he talked the Prime Minister into backing Concorde) but was something of a crony (Bruce-Gardyne and Lawson 1976). More high-powered was Harold Lever, Chancellor of the Duchy of Lancaster and personal economic adviser to Wilson and Callaghan in the 1970s. He investigated an extraordinary variety of economic problems: silicon chips, the textile industry, housing finance and oil. He fixed the deal to save Chrysler's Linwood plant against Treasury and Industry Department opposition, and went as Callaghan's personal envoy to Washington during the IMF crisis (Callaghan 1987). Chancellor Denis Healey conceded that despite some friction, 'I normally accepted about one in four of his suggestions – a high average for any external consultant' (Healey 1989). But ministers with great expertise and little ambition are rare.

More often, special ministers are given a remit for press relations. There were a string of these in Conservative governments: Charles Hill, Bill Deedes, Angus Maude – all uniformly unsuccessful. A more successful appointment was Blair's appointment of Peter Mandelson as Minister without Portfolio in 1997, with responsibility for policy coordination and presentation. This attracted extraordinary press interest since he was widely credited with transforming Labour's public image. Mandelson played down his presentational role, referring to his task as checking the quality of government decisions and 'seeing round corners' (*Daily Telegraph* 17 November 1997, *Observer* 17 August 1997). It worked well, but Mandelson, as ambitious as the next man, sought and received his own department in Trade and Industry. The truth is that ministers with special skills are rare and those without personal ambition – like Lever – rarer still.

Outside policy advisers

Prime Ministers have at various times introduced external advisers to advise them alone. An early experiment was Wilson's introduction to No. 10 in 1964 of a small group of economists led by the brilliant theorist Thomas Balogh. He bombarded Wilson with memos on every subject: transport, gas, housing, defence, transport, family allowances and pensions. But apart from reinforcing Wilson's opposition to devaluation, his impact on economic strategy seems to have been small. He opposed EU member-ship and advocated economic expansion and planning – to no avail in each case. It may well have been a matter of personality, for Balogh's antago-nism towards the civil service clashed with Wilson's essentially conservative temperament. Significantly, Wilson does not mention Balogh in his memoir of the 1964–70 government (Crossman 1975, 1976 and 1977, Castle 1984, Contemporary Record 1988b).

More influential was Sir Alan Walters. His monetarist and free-market views and gift for illustrating his arguments with vivid real-life examples caught and held Mrs Thatcher's attention, providing analysis and argu-ments to back up her instincts in her battles with the Treasury and spending departments (profiles in *Sunday Times* 24 July 1988, *Evening Standard* Magazine September 1988).

He had impact, for example, on the 1981 budget, bus and coach dereg-ulation and scotching elaborate railway electrification plans. Some economic ministers criticised his judgements as simplistic (Howell 1987, Bruce-Gardyne 1986) and sometimes his advice was politically insensitive: for these reasons his more radical advice – to cut the rail network severely or close BL motors – got nowhere (Fowler 1991, Edwardes 1983). But he held Mrs Thatcher's confidence and his spell from 1981 to 1983 must be reckoned a success.

He continued to advise Mrs Thatcher from the United States, encouraging her hostility to the European Monetary System, and returned to work for her in 1989. But unlike his earlier spell in No. 10, when he had maintained good relations with the Chancellor, he now engaged in factional infighting by stoking up the Prime Minister's opposition to Lawson's managed exchange rate policy (Lawson 1992). In the virulent, prolonged struggle that followed, with Prime Minister and Chancellor quarrelling semi-openly, Walters was foolishly loose-tongued and wrote an article that boasted of his influence and dismissed the EMS (favoured by Lawson) as 'half-baked' (*Independent* 26 October 1989). Tory backbenchers demanded Walters' resignation and eventually so did an exasperated Lawson. Mrs Thatcher refused; Lawson resigned, obliging Walters to go too. It was an unnecessary debacle, needlessly damaging the concept of Prime Ministerial advisers which, had he been more restrained, his activities would have enhanced.

Special civil service advisers

A third option is drafting in senior officials as special assistants. At very senior level, the precedents are unhappy. In the 1930s Chamberlain embroiled Sir Horace Wilson, Chief Industrial Adviser to the Government, in his appeasement of Nazi Germany; then, in 1939, Chamberlain made him head of both the Treasury and the civil service. Wilson became deeply committed to appeasement, accompanied Chamberlain to Berchtesgaden, Bad Godesberg and Munich, and undertook a personal mission to Hitler during the Sudetenland crisis. On Churchill's accession his star was instantly eclipsed and he retired quietly (Petrie 1958, Armstrong 1986, Gilbert 1982).

The same happened to William Armstrong, the gifted Head of the Civil Service who became over-identified with Heath's economic policy. What started as an organisational task – managing Heath's prices and incomes policy – became an obsession: Whitelaw recalled 'He became more a minister than a civil servant. He was even making political statements at our meetings' (*Sunday Times* 29 February 1976). With tragic fortuity, his health broke and he retired early, later reflecting 'I was always determined not to be another Horace Wilson, but that's what happened' (Hennessy 1989, Heath 1976).

Mrs Thatcher tried the more successful alternative of recruiting less senior officials as personal advisers on foreign affairs and defence. The defence adviser was frozen out within a year: 'Michael Heseltine, then Defence Secretary, simply forbade Ministry staff to take his telephone calls' (Cradock 1997). In contrast, Sir Anthony Parsons, former Permanent Representative at the United Nations, excelled in the foreign affairs post. His functions were to anticipate crises and to see that the Prime Minister was briefed in advance of having to take quick decisions on Foreign Office recommendations; and to interpret to the Foreign Office what was on the premier's mind. He gained her trust, while scrupulously respecting Foreign Office sensibilities and much improved Mrs Thatcher's relations with that department (Jenkins and Sloman 1985). He was succeeded first by Percy Cradock, former ambassador in Beijing, then Rodric Braithwaite, former ambassador to Moscow, who worked variously on East–West relations, the Middle East and South Africa. Both combined the post with the chairman- ship of the Joint Intelligence Committee. But the post was primarily the product of Mrs Thatcher's mistrust of her Foreign secretaries and the Foreign Office. Major enjoyed an easier relationship with both, and under him the post lapsed.

Overall, a single outsider or a specially appointed minister may have an effect if he has specialist knowledge, gains the premier's trust and does not antagonise other ministers or departments. But people like Harold Lever do not grow on trees, and the fundamental drawback to single advisers is that they can only handle a small volume of work and a narrow range of subjects. In contrast a unit of advisers can encompass a multitude of subjects.

The Prime Minister's Policy Unit

The Unit's episodic history

Hence Wilson's creation in 1974 of the most durable of post-war innova- tions in central government: a Prime Minister's Policy Unit intended 'to extend the range of policy options from which the Government – and particularly the Prime Minister as head of the Government – has to choose' and to 'propose and pursue policies to further the government's political goals' (Wilson 1976). It has become a permanent feature of central government, although not easy to chart because it wisely eschews publicity. The Policy Unit serves the Prime Minister alone and its members change when he does: its personnel changed radically when John Major replaced Mrs Thatcher's outside appointees with his own centre-left Conservatives.

Consequently, its history is episodic: what follows is, therefore, a chronology of successive Units, each obliged to reinvent its own aims and modes of operation, followed by some analysis of trends in composition, *modus operandi*, and relations with the rest of Whitehall.

The history falls into five phases.

1 The Labour government of 1974–79

Under first Wilson, then Callaghan, the political scientist and former journalist Bernard Donoughue led seven specialists in economic and domestic policy, all with Whitehall experience (Jones 1974, Donoughue 1987). Inevitably its work was dominated by pragmatic reactions to the crises of those years, particularly by economic and industrial trauma, although the Unit ranged across the whole span of domestic policy, including housing, education and health. Both Wilson and Callaghan valued its work and, crucially, it gained acceptance as a permanent component of the government machine.

2 Mrs Thatcher's first Policy Unit: 1979–82

Surprisingly ill-prepared for government, Mrs Thatcher had not thought through what she wanted from her Policy Unit. She appointed as its head John Hoskyns, an ex-soldier turned computer consultant, who had advised her in Opposition. He was fatally handicapped by having only two assistants, which made it difficult to achieve anything but superficial criticism. Hoskyns' principal influence was as one of that group of advisers, including Wolfson and Walters, who bolstered Mrs Thatcher's nerve in her difficult early years in office. The Policy Unit, in conjunction with Alan Walters, could lay a good claim to exercising a radical influence on the 1981 budget (although Howe disputes this) and on trade union reform, on which Hoskyns had urged a strong line since Opposition days (Ranelagh 1991). But beyond these issues, the Unit's impact was limited (Stephenson 1980, Keegan 1989). Hoskyns became ever more hostile to Whitehall and to what he saw as Mrs Thatcher's unmethodical and non-strategic mode of working, and left in disillusion after three years, firing off virulent attacks on Mrs Thatcher, her government and Whitehall (Hoskyns 1982 and 1984, BBC 1982).

3 A stopgap operation: the Mount Policy Unit 1982–83

Hoskyns' successor, the journalist Ferdinand Mount, was recruited mainly to prepare the manifesto for the 1983 election – in the event, a slender affair. Author of a book on family values, he invested much effort in a Family Policy Group that canvassed radical options such as encouraging working women to stay at home and introducing education vouchers (Blackstone and Plowden 1988). It had little influence, confirming Mount's reputation for being more theoretical than practical (Ranelagh 1991). Mount's main service to the Unit was to increase its size to half a dozen high-calibre staff who began systematically to send comments to the Prime Minister on proposals coming up from Whitehall departments.

4   The Redwood/Griffiths epoch, 1983–90

The Unit moved up a gear with the appointment of the radical, energetic John Redwood, a former merchant banker and fellow of All Souls, passionate free-marketeer, pensions expert and enthusiastic privatiser who in time went on to serve in Major's Cabinet (Stothard 1984, Gimson 1985). The moment was opportune; the CPRS's demise in 1983 (see page 233) left the Policy Unit a monopoly of think-tank activities in Whitehall: it inherited several of its staff, although staffing expanded only slightly. Redwood reverted to Donoghue's practice of assigning staff to shadowing groups of policies and departments. His team focused on economic rather than social matters, becoming a dynamic force behind the privatisation programme, which accelerated dramatically, and behind overhauls of social security, education and health. This was, perhaps, the period when the Policy Unit exercised most influence within Whitehall.

After two years Redwood was succeeded by Professor Brian Griffiths, monetarist Dean of the City Business School (profiles in *The Times* 27 August 1985; *Guardian* 30 October 1989). He never had the same clout as Redwood (Seldon 1997), and his influence waned as the Thatcher premiership ran into trouble. His hostility to European monetary union found a willing audience in Mrs Thatcher, although often overshadowed by Walters' off-stage commentaries. His main impact may have been to broaden the focus of the Unit's work to certain social issues: he kept up a running critique of Baker's education reforms, and provided much radical advice which she imposed on the ill-fated broadcasting legislation of 1990 (Lawson 1992).

5   The Policy Unit under Major

Under Major, the Policy Unit perpetuated the Redwood/Griffiths *modus operandi*, but in a visibly ageing and embattled administration this phase of the Unit's existence more than most saw long-term ambitions crowded out by short-term crises. The financial journalist Sarah Hogg, in charge from 1990–95, found herself perpetually absorbed in crisis management as well as the big issues to which the government was compelled to respond: the replacement for the poll tax, the Uruguay GATT round and the Maastricht negotiations. The management consultant Norman Blackwell, her successor for Major's last two years, worked mainly on pre-election strategy and struggled to develop new themes for a 17-year-old government in the run-up to an increasingly hopeless election (Riddell 1997).

6 *The Policy Unit under Blair*

The Policy Unit instituted by Blair in 1997 included only one civil servant. By mid 1998 it numbered eleven members who, mostly in their 30s or older, tended to be slightly older than the departmental special advisers. All were generalists and only two had previous Whitehall experience. Predominantly their background was as advisers to Labour frontbenchers in opposition, several with links to left-leaning think tanks like Demos and the Institute for Public Policy Research (*New Statesman* 30 May 1997, Draper 1997).

The practice of Unit members shadowing particular departments continued to take up most of their time (*New Statesman* 24 July 1998), but there were closer working links with the Cabinet Office (Mandelson 1997), exemplified in the creation of the Social Exclusion Unit (see Chapter 8). For a year attempts were made to find an external head for the unit – the job was reputedly refused variously by the heads of British Airways, the CBI and the Welsh Office (*Guardian* 6 June 1997, *The Times* 3 June 1997) – until Miliband was eventually confirmed as head.

The Policy Unit's size, staffing and expertise

All phases of the Policy Unit have had certain features in common. In each of them, the Unit covered all areas except foreign policy. The Unit saw all domestic papers going to the Prime Minister and, while practice has varied, its Head, and on occasion other members, had access to most Cabinet committees and some Cabinet meetings – for example, a member of Mrs Thatcher's Unit attended her ministerial group on health service reform in 1988 (Donoughue 1987, BBC 1982, Lawson 1992). Its staff were, in Wilson's phrase, the premier's 'eyes and ears' (Donoughue 1987), alerting the Prime Minister to dangers, drawbacks and omissions in departments' policies and giving him the ammunition to argue back effectively.

It had to shadow the thinking of thirty or so departments. Consequently, Hoskyns' two assistants were not enough – in fairness, Hoskyns in time realised this but expansion was blocked by the Cabinet

Secretary on the grounds of economy, although Donoughue had had twice as many staff (Kandiah 1996). Half a dozen staff is the absolute minimum needed to be viable, and Blair's dozen is closer to the ideal.

Staffing policies have varied. Roughly speaking, there have been three phases. Donoughue recruited only high quality outsiders, mostly academics, but two from commerce. Most remained for five years. The Thatcher and Major Units 'borrowed' staff for two or three years, usually including a couple of civil servants. The latter's presence, as in the CPRS, worked well, providing useful contacts in Whitehall. Most outsiders came from business, some with legal or accounting experience and – unlike the civil servants – were expected to be political sympathisers. Personal expertise counted less in Mrs Thatcher's Unit, which sought to out-argue departments not by superior grasp of detail but by applying the fresh mind and different perspective of an intelligent outsider to the department's concerns. Thus, a secondee from Trade and Industry found himself shadowing Environment, someone from Shell covered transport as well as energy, and a management consultant covered trade, the EU, employment and agriculture (two useful snapshots of the Unit's composition appear in *The Times* 6 November 1984 and Willetts 1987). Both Donoughue and Hogg preferred people who had previously worked as special advisers in departments.

While the Unit in its post-1979 incarnation was not composed of experts, its members compensated for this by exploiting their outside contacts far more than Donoughue had done. Redwood and Griffiths encouraged their staff to get out of the office one day a week to visit factories, hospitals, schools and other workplaces (Willetts 1987), picking up useful information and making valuable contacts on whom they sometimes drew to supplement or out-argue the Whitehall machine. Particularly prolific sources of ideas in Mrs Thatcher's time were right-wing think-tanks like the Centre for Policy Studies (Stone 1996, Kandiah and Seldon 1996) but many outside individuals helped the Policy Unit: pioneering Conservative council leaders gave advice on privatisation, a London professor of surgery worked with Griffiths on the 1988 NHS review, a radical educationist advised on pupil appraisal and merchant bankers at N.M. Rothschilds advised on rail electricity privatisation (*Observer* 8 January 1989, *Independent* 21 May and 18 August 1988). It also drew on a group of independent experts during a fierce dispute between defence contractors and the Navy over rival frigate designs (*The Times* 10 June 1985).

The Unit is – and has to be – politically partisan: Wilson at the outset specified a 'strong political commitment' (Wilson 1976). All ' of Donoughue's staff had been involved with Labour in Opposition. The

Thatcher and Major Units required no party affiliation, but a strong political empathy. The Blair Unit is definitely 'New Labour', albeit with several returnees from the disbanded SDP. This requirement for some affinity of outlook, at the very least, put pressure on the impartiality of the small number of civil servants drafted into the Policy Unit under the Thatcher and Major governments. One, David Willetts of the Treasury, left the civil service to head the free-market Centre for Policy Studies and later became a Conservative MP and minister, although he maintained that other officials could serve in the Unit as part of a normal Whitehall career (Willetts 1987). Certainly, other officials who served in the Unit under Thatcher and Major later returned to normal Whitehall duties. However, a civil servant is unlikely to be seconded unless his mind is attuned to the government's approach: the first civil servant added to Mrs Thatcher's Unit was appointed because he put a paper to the Industry Secretary questioning the value of subsidies to industry (Norton Taylor 1985).

The Policy Unit's reactive and proactive work

The Unit's work has taken four forms. First, because the policy initiative in Whitehall lies with departments, the Unit must vet and comment on proposals coming up from Cabinet ministers. Units which have not done this systematically – those of Mount and, particularly, Hoskyns – miss a lot of tricks. In the first six months of Redwood's stewardship a well-informed newspaper article recorded the Unit's work commenting on, amongst other things, the cost of drugs prescribed by doctors, electricity prices, subsidies for the 'Airbus' project and oil-rig construction in Scotland (Stothard 1984). Sometimes, the advice questions the proposal's premises, or the consistency of its arguments, or its failure to consider broader implications. Here, the Unit's outside contacts and regular 'site visits' to outside locations and organisations provide useful ammunition. Sometimes it questions the proposal's compatibility with the government's objectives and – in the case of Mrs Thatcher's unit – asks whether a cheaper or less interventionist course could be taken (Willetts 1987).

Second, on a small number of issues, the Unit may work very closely with departments on the detail of a policy. The Hogg Unit became deeply involved in discussions with the Department of the Environment on a replacement for the poll tax and influenced the system by which properties would be assessed for the new Council Tax (Hogg and Hill 1995, Seldon 1997).

Third, the Unit has a 'proactive' role in putting up its own ideas. Occasionally the Prime Minister unexpectedly asks for a briefing.

Callaghan often did this – for example on the European Monetary System – asking the Policy Unit not to let the relevant department know what he was thinking about (C. Campbell 1983), just as Mrs Thatcher in 1984 asked her Policy Unit to investigate whether tax cuts really would be spent mainly on imports. More often, the Unit originates an idea itself. Donoughue catalogues a series of initiatives: trying to devise a coherent family policy, attempts to improve legal services and to reform the engineering profession (Donoughue 1987). Hogg has described the extraordinary effort the Unit put in to devising and launching the Citizen's Charter (Hogg and Hill 1995). Launching a new idea is not easy. The Prime Minister, who has enough worries already, must be persuaded that the problem exists. It helps if the Unit simultaneously provides the germ of a solution, although this need not be too long: some of the memos that launched Mrs Thatcher's major reviews of social policy were no more than two pages long.*

It does not always work. Sometimes the Prime Minister rejects the advice: Mrs Thatcher, after many discussions, vetoed various plans from her Policy Unit for a school voucher scheme. Sometimes Cabinet colleagues block it: Mrs Thatcher's colleagues vetoed proposals for decontrolling rents and 'de-privileging' farmers (*Guardian* 2 October 1985, *The Times* 16 and 21 February 1984), both mooted by the Policy Unit. But if the Prime Minister is persuaded, the Unit then provides him with the arguments to make the departmental minister take the problem seriously and produce a detailed answer, to be discussed between the department, Policy Unit staff and the Prime Minister.

However, the Prime Minister and Policy Unit are reliant on the responsible department to do the spadework. At that point, resistance may set in. Mrs Castle ignored the Unit's ideas on one-parent families (Donoughue 1987) and Prior at Employment doggedly resisted the radical reform of trade union immunities that Mrs Thatcher urged, egged on by Hoskyns' Policy Unit. Assuming, however, that the Prime Minister will induce the minister at least to look at the idea, the Policy Unit often tried to involve itself in this work. For instance, Donoughue worked alongside Department of the Environment officials on his ideas for 'life-lease' for council tenants (Donoughue 1987). Redwood made this his standard method of operation. His staff worked with departmental officials, and often ministers and political advisers, to develop such initiatives as the social services review, the community charge and – after Prior's departure – the reform of employment law, sometimes spending weeks in the department.

Finally, the Policy Unit has on occasion aspired to a strategic role. At no time has it attempted the synoptic, far-seeing exercise attempted at one time by the Central Policy Review Staff (see page 229). Rather modest, medium term efforts were made by the Unit for Callaghan and Major when they took over the premiership, trying to identify their main interests and the priorities their governments should pursue (Hogg and Hill 1995, Morgan 1997). Neither was conspicuously successful: the Major Unit's effort amounted to no more than a shopping list of themes like quality of public provision and encouraging voluntary action – partly because the Prime Minister had 'no underlying conviction...pragmatic to a fault' (Seldon 1997), partly because Hogg allowed herself to become absorbed in economic and trade matters to the neglect of the bigger picture, and partly because the administration was increasingly accident prone. Indirectly, however, this initiative did lead to the Citizen's Charter.

The fundamental problem is that the Unit's very proximity to the premier encourages its use for day-to-day fire-fighting, which squeezes out longer-term considerations: Hogg vividly likens her traumatic years after the 1992 election to 'keeping on hammering in the tent pegs round Whitehall while the storm tried to take the tent off the grass' (Seldon 1997).

The Policy Unit's link with the Prime Minister

Because the Unit serves the Prime Minister, its effectiveness relies solely on him. If a Prime Minister does not carry the Cabinet, the Unit's advice gets nowhere. Hoskyns was pushing on an open door when he urged Mrs Thatcher to outlaw secondary picketing but the Cabinet preferred a gradualist approach to reform (Stephenson 1980). Similarly, Keith Joseph as Education Secretary blocked Griffiths' plans for school vouchers (Halcrow 1989). But if the Prime Minister can carry the Cabinet the Unit has a lot of sway.

Obviously the relationship between the Head of the Unit and the Prime Minister is crucial. Donoughue was the only head to serve two Prime Ministers and had a good relationship with both, perhaps because he also acted as an all-purpose political assistant to them: briefing them for parliamentary questions, drafting speeches and running their general election campaigns. Hogg had a similarly close relationship with Major, who had insisted that she lead the Unit and relied heavily on her advice. His confidence in her was a major factor in establishing her credibility within Whitehall (Seldon 1997). Mrs Thatcher overall seems to have had fewer close links with the heads of her Unit, although Griffiths was an old acquaintance and Redwood, while austere, she respected for his intellect. The extent to which other Unit members had direct contact with the premier varied: Redwood encouraged this, making his staff submit memos over their own signatures, encouraging them to develop a lively, distinctive prose style and attend meetings that she chaired on issues they had taken up (Willetts 1987). Otherwise, Prime Ministers seem to develop a rapport with one or two unit members rather than with the Unit collectively: Callaghan greatly respected the advice of the economist Gavin Davies, while Major saw a lot of Nick True and Jonathan Hill.

The Policy Unit's relations with civil servants

At the outset, other Whitehall departments were frankly suspicious, and Donoughue wisely agreed a concordat with the Cabinet Secretary governing relations with officials (Kandiah 1996). In time matters improved; initially Donoughue would always seek a Permanent Secretary's clearance before contacting his department (Jones 1974) but as the Unit became a settled feature of the landscape this became unnecessary and its members developed extensive contacts amongst officials. With only a handful of staff, the Policy Unit relies on departments to do any detailed work at the Prime Minister's behest. This did not stop departments occasionally from being obstructive. The Education Department persistently and successfully opposed a school voucher scheme – on strong practical grounds – and dragged its feet in response to Callaghan's calls – inspired by Donoughue – for educational reforms (Gimson 1985, Donoughue 1987). Officials often ruled out at an early stage options for competition in concerns to be privatised that the Unit wanted to pursue such as electricity, and the Home Office tried in 1978 to preclude radical ideas for broadcasting reform (Donoughue 1987).

An effective way of influencing policy was for the Unit's staff to involve themselves in the development of policy as it was worked up in departments, through a combination of informal meetings with officials and contacts on the political network. The Redwood/Griffiths Unit's more notable achievements were reached through the latter approach, such as the informal meetings with ministers and special advisers on the future of broadcasting in 1988 (*Independent* 12 May 1988, *The Sunday Times* 24 July 1988). Its members, mostly young, could speak to junior officials on friendly informal terms, and get involved in developing the proposal without creating too much of an impression of an overbearing No. 10 presence. In return, the department got an insight into the Prime Minister's outlook and got a litmus test of the Prime Minister's likely reception of the eventual proposals. Indeed, if the Policy Unit is signed up to a proposal, the odds are that the Prime Minister will also back it – giving the department a substantial, possibly conclusive advantage at Cabinet committee stage.

A former Policy Unit member describes this as getting into

the virtuous circle of being recognised as influential, and therefore worth providing with information, which in turn increases one's ability to provide influential advice. The vicious circle, into which the Policy Unit may have fallen in the past, is not to have Whitehall sources of information and thus to lose influence with the Prime Minister and then be further cut out of Whitehall deliberations.

(Willetts 1987)

Hoskyns fell into the 'vicious circle', by-passed by the flow of policy (BBC 1982, Stephenson 1980). Under Redwood the Unit developed almost a complicity with departments, using them and being useful to them. Furthermore if it criticised, it did so privately to the Prime Minister and not – like the CPRS – openly to the Cabinet.

The reactions of ministers to the Policy Unit

In its earlier years the Unit had limited relations with ministers, regarding itself as working for the Prime Minister. Although Donoughue and Hoskyns knew many ministers well from Opposition, their activities were bounded mainly by the No. 10–Treasury–Cabinet Secretariat triangle. But from the days of Redwood onwards, the Unit cultivated Cabinet ministers, energetic junior ministers and special advisers (*The Economist* 8 September 1984, *Spectator* 8 June 1985).

Some of Mrs Thatcher's opponents in her early years such as Francis Pym resented her advisers, especially Hoskyns (BBC 1982, Pym 1984, Holmes 1985). Griffiths also provoked hostility for pressing hard-line free-market monetarism on Mrs Thatcher, and engineering the free-market basis for broadcasting reform in the late 1980s. However, ambitious ministers in the middle ranks of the Cabinet, anxious to impress Mrs Thatcher with their radicalism, worked with the Unit when launching employment reforms, overhauling social security and the health service. By the time of the Major government the Policy Unit was sufficiently part of the landscape for some of its members to attend weekly 'prayer' meetings on some of the departments they shadowed; ministers and senior officials would phone the Unit to ask if the Prime Minister was likely to be happy with a proposed course of action (Seldon 1997). Intriguingly, Blackwell had some success with a series of meetings for ministers collectively – first junior ministers, then Cabinet – for a series of forward-looking seminars, with fertile and lively results (Seldon 1997). For all that, ministers' attitudes varied: one referred to Blair's Policy Unit as 'the spy in the cab' (*New Statesman* 24 July 1998).

Chancellors as a rule have not been keen on the Policy Unit. Neither

Wilson nor Callaghan trusted the Treasury; indeed Callaghan saw the Unit's main function as being to arm him to challenge it (Callaghan 1987). Donoughue's early success in proposing a voluntary pay policy, in opposition to the Treasury's statutory plan, established him as a credible player and thereafter the Unit was consulted on most proposals, including budgets (Donoughue 1987). Throughout Mrs Thatcher's premiership a potentially hostile relationship – Griffiths was a devoted monetarist – was masked by the activities of Walters, but under Major Lamont was suspicious and resentful.

Donoughue refused to be overlord of all advisers in Whitehall, declining responsibility for people over whom he had no control (Donoughue 1987): his contact with them was minimal, to the disadvantage of both. Redwood and Griffiths productively developed contacts amongst departmental special advisers, for example at Employment and Education, getting early warning of what was maturing in departments and forewarning them of the Prime Minister's likely reactions (Gimson 1985). Mount took one special adviser, from Education, into his unit.

The Policy Unit's effectiveness

There are occasional junctures at which the decision is taken at the very top. At a few such moments – the 1975 decision on incomes policy, the 1981 budget – the Policy Unit made a discernible impact. But for the rest, as one former member put it:

> Frequently when you thought you had succeeded in doing something, you might only have been pushing on a door that was already opening. It may have been that you were simply coinciding with advice coming from elsewhere.
>
> (Kandiah 1996)

Ultimately, however, the Unit is the premier's servant and the measure of success is not its influence on policy but his satisfaction with it. By that yardstick it has succeeded. Its usefulness depends on the manner, relevance, quality and political sensitivity of its briefing, with which all premiers seem to have been satisfied.

It is worth noting that, unlike the CPRS and its foreign counterparts which have not lasted, similar Prime Ministerial advisory groups in other countries have survived. New Zealand's Prime Ministerial Advisory Group, modelled closely on the Policy Unit, has survived and succeeded (Boston 1988) and Canada and Australia each have a Prime Minister's Secretariat larger than the Policy Unit but similar in function (Weller 1987, Campbell 1987).

Special advisers

Their role

One of the CPRS's difficulties was its remoteness from the Cabinet ministers it served. An alternative, more personal mechanism for briefing ministers on matters outside their departments is the network of ministerial special advisers (sometimes called political advisers). These were first appointed piecemeal by a few Labour ministers in the 1960s, and later by some of Heath's ministers, almost exclusively to advise on their departmental work. In 1974 Wilson regularised and expanded the practice, allowing Cabinet ministers to appoint two advisers each. Mrs Thatcher in opposition castigated his experiment, but in office continued it. While she initially restricted numbers to one per Cabinet minister, in time her confidence in special advisers grew, particularly when they briefed her for the 1983 election press conferences (Shepherd 1983, Butler 1986), and their numbers expanded again to two per department – although the second adviser was, in theory, assigned to support the ministers of state.

In practice there are two types of adviser: expert advisers (usually a minority), and generalist advisers. Both types are expected to be politically sympathetic to their minister.[1] The experts focus principally on departmental work, giving briefings with which a minister may check or challenge official advice. Prominent examples have been Brian Abel-Smith, a distinguished professor of social policy who assisted Crossman and Castle at the DHSS (see Castle 1980), the economist Adam Ridley who served Howe at the Treasury in the 1980s (Howe 1994) and Sir Jeffrey Sterling, chairman of P&O who throughout the 1980s advised successive Secretaries of State at Trade and Industry.

The generalists may have some expertise in the minister's departmental subject, but are recruited mainly as political aides-de-camp. They are typified by Margaret Beckett and Jack Straw in the 1970s and Michael Portillo in the following decade, young party activists who later became frontbench MPs. Many Labour political advisers were journalists, academics and lawyers; under Mrs Thatcher most were business people or former party headquarters staff.

Data about special advisers is not easy to compile. However, of the thirty-nine appointed by late 1997 to departments (i.e. excluding the Prime Minister's staff) roughly one-third were in their 20s, one-third in their 30s and the remainder in their 40s and 50s. Over two-thirds of them had worked in Opposition for the Labour Party or as advisers to Labour front-benchers (usually the latter). Ten of the thirty-nine – generally the older recruits – could be classified as experts, and they included two university professors – one of education, the other of politics – a former Bank of England official, a regional development expert, a former director of social services, several professional economists and several businessmen (data drawn mainly from the *New Statesman* 30 May 1997).

The appointment of each special adviser is personal to the minister; when he goes, the adviser goes too, although some advisers have followed one minister from one department to another and others have stayed in a department under several ministers (Klein and Lewis 1977, Cardona 1981, Mitchell 1978, Shepherd 1983, Butler 1986).

A significant part of special advisers' work involves dealing with the press. The 1997 review of the Government Information Service acknowledged that 'Special Advisers have for many years, under Governments of both main political parties, taken some part in briefing the media on behalf of their Ministers' (Cabinet Office 1997d). One journalist recalls that, on the day that Major called a leadership election, he was phoned by three special advisers in the space of ten minutes (*Sunday Telegraph* 19 October 1997). As a rule, though, they concentrated on attempting to persuade journalists to put a certain 'spin' on a news story. Under the Blair government, several special advisers seem to have press relations as their primary duty. This was dramatised by an incident in which Treasury special advisers were accused of causing confusion in the currency markets by mis-stating the government's policy on European monetary union (national press 19, 20 and 29 October 1997). But, as the journalist Matthew d'Ancona shrewdly observed,

> the row was about division of labour as much as impartiality. What distinguishes this Government from its predecessors is the belief that presentation is not a secondary activity to be delegated to officials, but the first and most pressing task of every minister. New Labour does not regard news management as an ancillary function of government, but as its very essence.
>
> (*Sunday Telegraph* 19 October 1997)

Special advisers' work within departments

What can special advisers do that civil servants do not? They can handle relations with the party in the country – party officials, MPs and local councillors. In the early 1980s, for instance, the Treasury's special advisers spent hours on meetings and correspondence with Conservative backbenchers worried about economic policy – something that ministers lacked time to do and civil servants could not properly undertake. Special advisers can provide advice to the minister from a party perspective – both inter-party and intra-party – whereas civil service advice, while well attuned to political sensitivities, will not be partisan. Special advisers can say frankly 'This will be the impact on the party in the country, this is how it will affect marginal constituencies'. To policy work they can bring a more adventurous cast of mind. Civil servants are often quite cautious, keen to protect their minister from entering controversial ground. Special advisers, in contrast, are able to suggest things that officials might dismiss as outlandish. They can help the minister to establish a balance between the administrative requirements of the department and the thinking of the party and the manifesto. They provide a politically sympathetic ear with whom the minister can check his own reactions to departmental proposals. And they have the time to work up ideas – the minister's or their own – for new initiatives. Baroness Denton, a former Conservative minister, recalled:

> It is invaluable to have someone who can take up a concept, explore it with those who will be affected (without a meeting for 20 put into the diary for the next month), consider the outline costings on one side of paper, not 40, [and] check it doesn't rock other colleagues' boats without causing the drawbridge to be lifted.
>
> (letter to the *Financial Times* 6 June 1997)

The adviser can attend the same meetings and see the same papers as his minister. Beyond that, his work depends on his minister. As one adviser explained: 'What happens is a process of osmosis. You grow into the role as you feel out the Secretary of State's requirements. You start to think like him' (*Independent* 13 September 1988). The range of possible roles is wide. Most special advisers liaise with the party, write briefs on departmental policies for government backbenchers and deal with constituencies. Many help the minister with public appearances: contributing to the briefing for parliamentary questions and appearances before select committees, drafting speeches and assisting with public statements. Some become informal emissaries to outside groups: Conservatives exploited their links with business to ease problems over the car industry and satellite television (Edwardes 1983, *Financial Times* 28 January 1984); some Labour advisers dealt a lot with trade unions; and David Owen's adviser even went on several missions to overseas countries (Owen 1981).

Within departments they work alongside officials preparing policy initiatives; comment on papers going to the minister; advise him on the political (rather than administrative) dimension of policies, and feed in new ideas. In this field, self-evidently, the expert adviser carries more weight than the political: Professor Michael Barber, an internationally respected expert on school improvement, evidently carried more guns under David Blunkett at the DFEE than Tessa Keswick had carried under Kenneth Clarke, a minister she followed successively from Health to Education, then to the Home Office and finally to the Treasury. The special adviser acts as counsellor, confidant and political ally to a minister surrounded by officials who are – quite correctly – non-political (Peston 1980, Klein and Lewis 1977, Mitchell 1978, Butler 1986, Shepherd 1983).

In particular, the 'expert' variety of adviser can bring to bear knowledge and practical experience which generalist civil servants may not possess. Brian Abel-Smith, often cited as the model expert adviser, contributed greatly in the 1960s to Crossman's national superannuation scheme, a review of health service structure and the development of policy on mental health, work which included redrafting Green and White Papers (Crossman 1977). The businessman David Young successfully applied his commercial acumen to small business development, the management of the Post Office's huge property estate and the privatisation of British Telecom (Young 1990). The lawyer Anthony Lester played a significant part in devising laws outlawing sex and race discrimination (Jenkins 1991).

The impact on policy of special advisers is difficult to assess because they are only one of many voices seeking to influence any particular issue. In one documented instance – the decision to cut income tax in 1986 – the Treasury special advisers provided that extra ounce of persuasion that swung the argument (Lawson 1992). An adviser's impact is more easily discerned if he focuses on a limited number of issues. Roy Jenkins' advisers at the Home Office in the 1970s successfully pressed for an independent element in the police complaints procedure, thereby driving the Metropolitan Police Commissioner, Sir Robert Mark, to resignation (Mark 1978), and produced legislation against sex discrimination despite fierce civil service opposition (Lord Lester, House of Lords debates 9 July 1997, cols. 690–1). David Young was behind a scheme of tax incentives to increase the supply of small business workshops. But advisers' impact always depends on their ability to convince their minister. Kaldor at the Treasury under Healey got through tax relief on stock appreciation but never persuaded his Chancellor of the case for import controls (Healey 1989).

Special advisers' briefing on Cabinet business

For the most part, special advisers advise ministers on their departmental work and so encourage their absorption in their departmental affairs at the expense of collective discussion. However, they also have the potential to address one of the specific weaknesses identified in the last chapter, for on occasion they brief ministers on issues discussed at Cabinet and committee outside their departmental responsibility. Today, as the Cabinet has become a paperless meeting, they can brief only on committee papers, but that is where the action is. This last activity is of most importance to a study of the Cabinet. Briefing on extra-departmental matters is the lesser part of advisers' workloads; some advisers who have written about their work do not mention it at all. Nonetheless, an adviser can find time to study papers by other departments which his hard-pressed minister lacks time to read. Knowing his minister's interests and opinions he can high-light the topics that interest him. The adviser can also draw attention to the party aspects: the likely effect of a proposal on the government's standing in the country, or how it will come across on television, radio and the press (Shepherd 1983).

Although unlikely to be expert on the question, he can draw out the key issues, suggest some pertinent questions to ask and perhaps assemble some critical briefing. During the prolonged 1976 IMF crisis the most important contributions in Cabinet were made by ministers drawing on their special advisers' advice; those without advisers tended to remain silent. Indeed, the No. 10 private office judged that generally under Labour special advisers had widened the scope of Cabinet debate (Donoughue 1987). Examples of this kind of work by special advisers are necessarily rare, but Barbara Castle's diaries record that her generalist adviser Jack Straw briefed her for Cabinet on issues as diverse as EU agricultural policy, the publication of ministerial memoirs and the car industry, and she missed his customary brief when the Cabinet discussed defence (Castle 1980). In contrast, she seems to have ignored CPRS 'collective briefs'. Similarly Tony Benn commissioned his advisers to draft a series of economic papers for Cabinet and committee which became the basis of his 'alternative economic strategy' (Benn 1989).

The special adviser's disadvantage is that he has no link with the Cabinet Secretariat to forewarn him of issues on the horizon, so issues are sprung on him out of the blue. His advantage is that the minister, knowing and trusting him, will more likely read a brief from him than from a more remote source like the CPRS. Yet, although ministers pay more attention to briefing from their advisers than they did to the CPRS, these advisers have fewer resources on which to draw than the CPRS. As one put it:

> If it was a paper on education, I know something about that area so I would look at it, decide whether what was being proposed made sense and offer what amounted to a speaking note for the minister. If he

wished to intervene, he can then make a serious contribution. If it was an area about which I know literally nothing – Concorde, for example – I would say to the minister I don't know anything about the subject, you don't know anything about it either. So here is a synopsis, there are the public expenditure implications, either keep quiet or argue for your department.

(Klein and Lewis 1977)

Special advisers' relations with the civil service

Initially in 1974 many officials viewed special advisers with suspicion, as institutionalised rivals and intrusive nuisances. Some still feel that way; it varies from department to department and official to official (for example, Butler 1986, Lawson 1992). There have been instances where departments have 'forgotten' to copy papers to advisers or invite them to meetings, or alternatively swamped them with paper. Some departments have been reluctant to show special advisers papers before they have gone to ministers, and some advisers have had to work hard to insert themselves into the departmental policy-making chain. But other advisers like David Lipsey under Labour have found officials 'an explorer's dream of friendliness and no enemies to political advisers' (Lipsey 1980). A lot depends on the tact with which advisers set about their – inevitably disruptive – task. Denis Healey said of his advisers at the Treasury that one failed because of 'reciprocal mistrust' of the civil service, while the other succeeded because he could argue with the Treasury without losing its confidence (Healey 1989). Tony Benn's advisers at the Department of Industry in the 1970s got on very badly with the civil service, but then so did their minister (Benn 1989). This author's impression is that overall the civil service has got used to special advisers as an institution but that, as one former adviser has put it, 'Everything depends on the personality, expertise, strength and integrity of the special adviser and developing a healthy, honest, professional relationship with permanent officials and ministers' (Lord Lester, Lords debates 9 July 1997, col. 691).

In time, most officials have come round to the idea. If advisers are carrying out a distinct function – party liaison, briefing the minister for Cabinet and committees, bringing a distinct perspective to bear on policy discussions – they are not duplicating officials' work. Inevitably, their intervention can delay or disrupt the smooth development of policy; routines and understandings have to be devised to minimise friction. But as long as the advisers approach them in constructive spirit, officials accept them as a natural extension of the minister's interest. Indeed, officials may find them useful sounding boards for political opinion: David Young was often asked what the 'monetarist line' on an issue would probably be, or how something should best be expressed in a memo to the minister. Ian Bancroft claimed to be the only Permanent Secretary to persuade a reluctant minister to appoint a political adviser – who proved most successful (Bancroft 1983).

If there is a potential for friction it may equally lie between special advisers and junior ministers, some of whom have resented advisers' access to information and to the secretary of state and their opportunities for influencing policy (for example, Owen 1981). Cabinet ministers choose their special advisers, but not their junior ministers. But this seems to have been a minority problem; generally advisers are wary of the sensibilities of all ministers (Theakston 1987).

There was never liaison between the advisers and the CPRS nor, under Labour, with the Prime Minister's Policy Unit (Donoughue 1987). Under Mrs Thatcher and Major there was some contact with the Policy Unit but it was restricted to the particular department's work; David Young's extensive contacts with the Unit were mainly about privatisation (Young 1990). Links between departmental special advisers were similarly neglected. There was no liaison between them under Labour. Hurd convened some meetings of special advisers in 1973–74 and in the 1980s occasional attempts to establish a network were attempted – briefly by Mrs Thatcher personally, mainly as a means of generating new policy ideas – but none of these initiatives lasted (*Independent* 13 September 1988, Butler 1986).

The Central Policy Review Staff

Purpose and composition

The Central Policy Review Staff (CPRS), alias the 'think-tank', remains particularly fascinating because it addressed a whole range of problems in the Cabinet system: the difficulty of strategic direction, the inadequacy of briefing for ministers and the Prime Minister, and the problem of allocating public expenditure. The CPRS was a small multidisciplinary unit based in the Cabinet Secretariat, created by Heath in 1971 to advise the Cabinet on strategy and policy. It went through three phases, each reflecting successive directors and the governments they served. Led by the research scientist Lord Rothschild under Heath until 1974, it made a considerable impact on Whitehall and was much involved in developing government strategy. Rothschild's successor, the economist Sir Kenneth Berrill, found that under the Labour governments of the 1970s the CPRS was pushed increasingly by economic difficulties and ministerial uninterest into shorter-term reviews of more peripheral issues. Berrill's successor,

Robin (later Lord) Ibbs of ICI, turned it into primarily an industrial research unit. But in this last phase it also became involved in several politically controversial exercises and its last director, the merchant banker John Sparrow (also later knighted) was plagued by leaks. It was disbanded immediately after the 1983 general election, but still seizes the imagination as one of the most instructive and imaginative experiments in central government.

Heath wanted to counteract the tendency of parties, once in power, to lose sight of the objectives set in their manifestos and to become preoccupied instead by immediate problems and by the minutiae of departmental work. His concern coincided with a feeling amongst some senior civil servants that a new analytical capability was needed at the heart of government (Blackstone and Plowden 1988, Pollitt 1984). Their beliefs fused in the 1974 White Paper 'The Reorganisation of Central Government' (Cmnd. 4506) which announced the formation of a 'central capability unit' charged with assisting all ministers

> to take better policy decisions by assisting them to work out the implications of their basic strategy in terms of policies in specific areas, to establish relative priorities to be given to different sections of their programme as a whole, to identify those areas of policy where new choices can be exercised and to ensure that the underlying implications of alternative courses of action are fully analysed and considered.

The civil servants wanted a low-profile backroom research unit, but Heath's appointment of the ebullient Lord Rothschild as its first director presaged something more exciting. A gifted scientist, formerly head of research with Shell International, and a thoroughly independent personality, Rothschild was given to uncompromising analysis and outspoken conclusions (Croome 1972). His working methods were peculiar and sometimes conspiratorial, but under him the Staff thrived. Given a free hand to choose his assistants, he modelled the CPRS largely in his own intellectual image, best exemplified by the 'CPRS style' of investigation and reporting: independent, radical and terse, it was the deliberate opposite of Whitehall circumspection. This reflected Rothschild's stated concept of policy analysis: political impartiality and intellectual honesty, analysing all evidence without concession to ministerial preconceptions, always reaching firm conclusions and never fudging a compromise: 'You cannot have half a Channel tunnel' (Rothschild 1977).

Half the CPRS staff were 'fast stream' civil servants, and half were outsiders from commerce, public corporations, universities and industry.

Most were graduates in their late 20s or 30s, seen as high fliers in their fields, and most stayed for about two years. The mix proved surprisingly fertile: the outsiders encompassed a variety of professional specialisms, had extensive outside contacts and displayed a valuable impatience with over-cautious officialdom; the insiders knew the geography, language and customs of Whitehall but rediscovered in a brief stint of licensed free-thinking a creativity stifled by their civil service upbringing. There was little hierarchy. Teams of between two and six members were set up to handle specific projects, occasionally with help from outside consultants, and dissolved as soon as the project ended.

The CPRS's work

In its early years, the Staff's work took four main forms. The first was strategy review, focused on meetings of the Cabinet, and later of junior ministers, at Chequers every six months to consider the Staff's analysis of the government's overall performance. Douglas Hurd, then Heath's Political Secretary, recalled:

> These were extraordinary occasions. Ministers would gather upstairs at Chequers round a long table. At one end sat Lord Rothschild, flanked by the more articulate members of his team. Taking subjects in turn, they would expound, with charts and graphs, the likely conse-quences of government policy. Their analysis was elegant but ruthless. They made no allowances for political pressures. They assumed the highest standards of intellectual consistency. They rubbed ministers' noses in the future.
>
> (Hurd 1979)

The Staff then followed up any conclusions from these meetings in detail, putting occasional papers on strategy to the Cabinet.

Second, it undertook research projects of varying length and complexity of areas rarely examined by departments and often crossing departmental boundaries, such as the future of London as a financial centre, and the growth of 'cashless pay'. Most were one-off exercises but many industrial problems recurred – for instance shipbuilding and nuclear power – and aspects of both energy and transport were almost always under review. Rothschild's scientific background also allowed the Staff to bring a distinctive technological perspective to economic and industrial problems: energy supplies, computers, nuclear waste, electric cars, govern-ment funding of scientific research and so on.

Third, an attempt was made to provide ministers with fuller briefing on issues at Cabinet and its committees by offering 'collective briefs'. Sometimes these were short-notice analyses of pressing problems: miners' pay, and the sudden collapse of Upper Clyde Shipbuilders were examined in this way. More often, collective briefs tried to tackle ministers' lack of any briefing if their department had no stake in the discussion. CPRS briefs outlined the issues for these 'unconcerned' ministers, highlighting side-effects and drawbacks that the sponsoring minister might play down, and related the proposal to the government's main objectives. About fifty such briefs appeared annually, generally circulated to ministers as a short note, or as a brief list of awkward questions worth asking. However, short notice sometimes meant that these came only as a note for the Prime Minister or committee chairman slotted into his Cabinet Secretariat handling brief (Blackstone and Plowden 1988, Rothschild 1983).

The CPRS also gave constant economic advice during the 1970s and participated in the public expenditure survey, co-writing with the Treasury the economic survey preceding the annual cycle, and later sending further comments to Cabinet as it felt necessary.

The CPRS's relations with the civil service

Surprisingly, relations with officials were good. Although its early style could be bruisingly critical, the Staff needed officials to keep it abreast of developments and to check its facts. Its civil service members knew Whitehall thoroughly and exploited their contacts in departments to effect: despite initial caution by departments, information was hardly ever refused. The CPRS provided the chairman for various inter-departmental committees, for example on the Namibia uranium contract in 1976 (Benn 1989). If anything, by the mid-1970s the Staff was being accused of collaborating too closely with officials (Benn 1980, Mackintosh 1977).

This was partly a matter of style. Rothschild's successor, the economist Berrill, was as independent as Rothschild – as Callaghan for one confirms (1987) – but in his leadership from 1974 to 1980 preferred to work with the grain rather than against it. Nonetheless, it continued to produce reports critical of departmental policy, notably on alcoholism, race relations and the cost of the diplomatic service.

Relations were always rather strained with the Treasury which saw it as 'a challenge to its authority' as Wass, the Treasury's Permanent Secretary put it (*Listener* 2 February 1984). Certainly Berrill crossed the Treasury by advising the Prime Minister during the IMF crisis and later circulating papers calling for reflation. In return the Treasury, which had never liked CPRS involvement in the public expenditure allocation process, ended cooperation in 1977 (Pliatsky 1984). In contrast, the Staff received valuable cooperation from the Cabinet Secretariat, particularly in the 1970s from Hunt who was keen to extend the Cabinet Secretariat's policy role (Expenditure Committee 1976, 1977). When the CPRS was abolished many senior officials, serving and retired, openly deplored this as – in the words of one – 'a sad blow by prejudice against enlightenment' (Bancroft 1984).

The CPRS's influence on ministers

In its earlier years the CPRS took seriously its remit to advise the entire Cabinet. In theory, ministers were to provide the CPRS with its assignments. In fact, ministerial interest in it was sporadic and half-hearted. The Cabinet committee established to devise its work programme soon expired through lack of interest, and although ministerial meetings occasionally referred issues to it the Staff largely chose its own work, subject to Prime Ministerial approval (Blackstone and Plowden 1988).

While most ministers welcomed the Staff's work in theory, in practice they were easily distracted from sustained interest in its activities. Ministers were a myopic and unreliable audience. The Chequers reviews took ministers out of the protective cocoon of their departments and made them a captive audience to a critique of their overall performance. Some appreciated the chance to step back from day-to-day pressures and look at things in the round for once; others thought it a waste of time. One Chequers review in 1972 had great impact in alerting the Cabinet to escalating economic problems (for example, Mrs Thatcher's alarmed reaction recorded in *The Sunday Times* 22 February 1976). One minister recalled: 'The statistics had been available to everyone before but no-one had wanted to see them. Too unpleasant. We needed reminding how serious things were getting' (Pollitt 1984, Prior 1986, Heclo and Wildalsky, 1981). However, as economic trauma grew from late 1973 onwards, the exercises became less frequent. They ceased in 1975 when runaway inflation and sterling crises made forward planning virtually impossible.

The Staff's long-term studies met similar difficulties. Those that tackled intrinsically important and politically uncontroversial matters – for example the influence of multinational corporations or the unsatisfactory relations between central and local government – were regarded by ministers as worthy but dull and did not rouse much interest at Cabinet. Conversely, provocative reports exposing the inadequacies of policy towards race relations or alcoholism and urging expensive or difficult remedies were thoroughly smothered by ministers and their officials (*Guardian* 24 October 1977, *The Times* 27 June 1983). Heath's Cabinet later regretted ignoring prophetic CPRS warnings about the vulnerability of

Britain's oil supplies (Prior 1986) – borne out as oil prices quadrupled in 1973 – just as the Toxteth riots showed Mrs Thatcher's Cabinet that there had been something in the Staff's warnings about the social consequences of unemployment on Merseyside (Blackstone and Plowden 1988).

Reports that confronted politically-live problems uppermost in ministers' minds fired political imaginations but left the CPRS vulnerable to the irrational truth that a departmental minister was more likely to take offence at criticism from the Staff than from any other department. Tony Benn when Energy Secretary showed particular hostility to the CPRS's conclusions on competing designs of nuclear reactor, and there were fierce debates in 1975 over whether to publish the report on over-capacity in the car industry, which coincided with the crisis over the threatened closure of Chrysler's Linwood plant (Dell 1992).

The collective briefs circulated to Cabinet and its committees encountered the same problems: while many ministers found them useful (for example, Dell 1980, Williams 1980) ministers were naturally happier to accept advice that avoided political difficulties – such as 'hiving-in' Rolls Royce and Giro – than advice that invited political difficulties – for example, the reminder that bailing out Upper Clyde Shipbuilders ran counter to declared industrial strategy, or the warning of the expense involved in accepting the 1975 Sharp report on mobility for disabled people (Castle 1980). Understandably, ministers preferred to be advised to take the soft option.

Unlike departments, the CPRS suffered from the disadvantage that its work was not perceived as essential: improved cross-departmental planning and decision-making tended to be seen as optional extras to be squeezed in at the margin of a minister's concerns. Furthermore, unlike almost every other agency in Whitehall, the CPRS had no minister to speak for it in Cabinet. Members of the Staff might attend and speak at Cabinet committees, which helped, but being small the Staff could not always send a representative.

The picture was not entirely negative. All ministers took some interest in Staff reports on key problems such as inflation, unemployment or devolution. Some had personal or constituency interests, or were temperamentally interested in wider issues – such as Antony Crosland, whose advocacy of better 'social monitoring' provided helpful impetus to a project to improve the coordination of social policy (Crosland 1982). But given departments' first claim on their time and loyalty, ministers' attention was at best occasional.

As the 1970s progressed, long-term thinking became increasingly difficult as worsening economic problems repeatedly forced makeshift expedients on the Cabinet. Strategic planning seemed increasingly unreal and, more and more, ministers showed interest only in medium term, single-issue reports on industrial subjects like microelectronics, aircraft manufacturing and the heavy electrical industry. Even work chosen to appeal to the political instinct of a Labour Cabinet – on social policy and on relations with developing countries – failed to hold ministers' attention. Against its will the Staff was used more and more for troubleshooting on immediate or peripheral issues.

It was also squeezed out of economic policy. Callaghan and Healey retreated to the 'economic seminar' of a few ministers and officials: the Staff's surveys of macroeconomics and industrial policy were often circulated only to this group and its reports to Cabinet concerned less central issues. Government became even more personal under Mrs Thatcher: deep divisions within her Cabinet prompted her to circulate CPRS reports only to her small circle of closest advisers: an alarming forewarning in 1981 that unemployment could pass three million was never shown to the full Cabinet.

Sir Robin Ibbs, appointed to replace Berrill shortly after Mrs Thatcher took control of the Secretariat, allowed the Staff to be used increasingly as a research unit to the dominant No. 10–Treasury axis, and it lost much of its independence and imagination. It was excluded from giving public spending and economic advice and made to stick to industry, technology and issues linked to economic regeneration like training and cashless pay. Its scope of interest was much narrower than under Rothschild, when it had studied everything from airships to prisons. When Mrs Thatcher told her colleagues in 1983 that she wanted to abolish it, no one objected, although Howe, for one, regretted its passing (Howe 1994). Wass commented: 'They did not realise it was theirs. They had written it off. It had become more and more the creature of the Prime Minister' (*The Times* 8 November 1983).

The CPRS's relations with the Prime Minister

Consequently, the CPRS was forced to depend on the Prime Minister more than it would have liked. He controlled the machinery of government and, as chief coordinator of the Cabinet, the CPRS's strategic and inter-departmental work concerned him most. He determined the image and purpose of the government and could promote or smother new ideas more effectively than any colleague.

His authority licensed the Staff to put papers to ministers, to attend meetings and request information. All premiers drew on the Staff for personal advice. Heath enjoyed chatting over problems informally with a few of its members. Wilson and Callaghan valued its industrial and economic briefings, especially before international summits, and Berrill attended Callaghan's 'seminar' and advised him during the IMF crisis. Mrs Thatcher used it mainly as a personal industrial research unit, but also received some briefings on youth unemployment. Above all, since the Staff attracted only occasional, even perfunctory interest from ministers, it fell back on the Prime Minister to induce the Cabinet to consider CPRS work or, failing this, to act himself as the Staff's audience.

This enforced reliance on one person had serious drawbacks. If the CPRS lost the premier's confidence it had no audience at all – as happened in 1983. The Prime Minister's opinion of the whole Staff was heavily influenced by his personal relations with its Director; any deterioration could be seriously damaging. When Rothschild made a public speech tactlessly prophesying national decline he badly dented Heath's faith in the Staff, as witness the rejection of a CPRS formula for settling the miners' strike (Whitehead 1985, *The Sunday Times* 29 February 1976). Similarly Ibbs benefited from Mrs Thatcher's obvious confidence in him while Sparrow's links with her were perilously weak.

Furthermore, Heath's successors showed little interest in strategic reviews and used the Staff increasingly as a fire brigade, mainly on economic and industrial issues (Blackstone and Plowden 1988). Within these spheres it scored some notable successes: on the future of the electrical engineering industry, shipbuilding, training and nationalised industries. However, its forays into other areas aroused decreasing interest.

Its style also changed. Under Rothschild it had been light-footed and provocative, raising awkward questions and suggesting possible avenues worth exploring rather than becoming immensely expert. Ibbs tried to make it an expert body. Recruitment was slanted accordingly. It developed specialisms in several fields, notably nationalised industries and removal of obstacles to a free market. In these areas it scored solid successes (for example, Edwardes 1983). But transferring this solid reliable style to other areas produced reports paradoxically both detailed and superficial which Mrs Thatcher scorned as 'guffy stuff, like Ph.D theses' (quoted in Blackstone and Plowden 1988). Being engrossed in detail also made it slower-moving and less able to respond to problems of the moment (Willetts 1987).

The CPRS also lost its political sensitivity, perhaps due to its narrower, more specialist cadre, and suffered from a rash of press leaks. Sparrow unwisely became involved in the Family Policy Group, a Conservative manifesto-drafting exercise promoting self-reliance and family life (*The Times* 1 May 1983). Such controversial papers made their way to the press: the Family Policy Group exercise leaked, and so did a survey of public spending which canvassed radical plans like privatising higher education and health care and cutting welfare benefits, which even Treasury ministers reckoned were 'radical to a fault' (*The Economist* 9 October 1982, Fowler 1991). This last episode led to what Lawson called 'the nearest thing to a Cabinet riot in the history of the Thatcher administration' (Lawson 1992) and did much to undermine Mrs Thatcher's faith in the Staff. Sparrow unwisely made matters worse by producing plans for scrapping the state earnings-related pension scheme (SERPS) in the run up to the 1983 election: an irate Mrs Thatcher ordered the obliteration of the report (Blackstone and Plowden 1988). Cumulatively, these incidents sealed the Staff's fate.

Its leadership style also changed, not necessarily for the better. Rothschild had faults, but under him the Staff had zest. Under Berrill it still had bite, but he cultivated a less collective style and was more 'respectable'. Ibbs and Sparrow allowed greater specialisation and the collegial style declined further. The Staff became less dynamic, more conventional and less happy (Hennessy, Morrison and Townsend 1985, Blackstone and Plowden 1988). Its scientists thrived, but theirs was a somewhat separate activity anyway (Ashworth 1985).

Some of the Staff's problems were of its directors' making. However, more blame attaches to Heath's successors who never thought out what they wanted. They never gave it the support needed to make an impact on Cabinet thinking. If ministers would not use it, it relied on the Prime Minister. If in turn he lost interest, it became redundant. Mrs Thatcher in particular subjected it to 'malign neglect' (Bancroft 1984). As Rothschild observed: 'If the Prime Minister of the day does not feel the need for a think-tank, or does not think its existence is worth the cost, the sooner it is disbanded the better' (Rothschild 1983).

The CPRS: success or failure?

Similar experiments in other countries proved very short-lived. Is it because advising the Cabinet collectively is inherently unviable? The Australian Priorities Review Staff, created in 1973 in deliberate imitation of the CPRS, faced the same problems – lack of consistent ministerial interest, political instability undermining strategic work, and hostility from officials (greater than in Whitehall) – but its fatal weakness was that Prime Minister Gough Whitlam lost interest in his own creation. It was abolished after three years (Boston 1980). A planning division set up in the West German Chancellor's Secretariat also lasted for only three years, mainly because it created too abstract and elaborate a system of forward planning, in which ministers were little interested, and did not take sufficient trouble to cultivate good relations with departments (Dyson 1973 and 1974). In

Italy, the Spadolini government's programme-monitoring unit, created to track the government's overall performance and carry out research on key policy issues, was swept away by Spadolini's fall after a year (Hine and Finocci 1991). The symptoms of decline are not the same, but the pattern of death is alarmingly similar.

At least the CPRS survived for thirteen years, and that was no mean achievement in a difficult climate. It made some impression on most areas of government, and some – notably energy and industry – were profoundly changed by its intervention. Even if rejected at the time, many of its reports later became the basis for new policies, including the study of the car industry, the review of overseas relations and the social effect of unemployment. But the CPRS drew little credit from altering the agenda in the long term, and suffered in the short term from the rejection of its advice.

It offers valuable lessons. First, its hybrid composition and informal structure were highly effective: it provided the model for several subsequent experiments, including the Prime Minister's Policy Unit and the Blair government's Social Exclusion Unit. Second, it demonstrated the immense difficulty of providing a briefing service to ministers collectively – a problem it never satisfactorily resolved, and that may defy resolution. Third, it showed that a central unit of this type would to a large degree depend on the Prime Minister for its work, its survival and its success. Fourth, it tried to solve too many problems in the Cabinet system in one go. Apart from anything else, its size was inadequate to the tasks it set itself: its directors sensibly refused to expand it above twenty members, because size would induce hierarchy and erode the informality and cohesiveness that made it swift-moving and flexible. Consequently, it overstreched itself by striving towards too many disparate goals. But it highlighted many inadequacies in the Cabinet system and pioneered some solutions. While not all should necessarily be tackled by a single organisation, it provided many lessons, tactical and methodological, for any future unit to draw on.

Conclusion

Two recurring themes in these accounts are access and confidence. Access means physical proximity and time. Because the civil service controls access, the Prime Minister's private office and the Cabinet Office have an inbuilt advantage. Other advisers do not. It is now accepted practice across Whitehall that a special adviser should be located next to his ministers: one, appointed to the Treasury in 1979, was assured by every official he met that he would have a room near to the Chancellor (Cardona 1980). Similarly, the Prime Minister's Policy Unit occupies bedrooms straddling

Numbers 10 and 11 Downing Street (Willetts 1987) and Sir Alan Walters made a point of insisting on an office in No. 10 (Walters 1986). For the CPRS to be physically located in the Cabinet Secretariat gave them proximity to the two sources they most needed to work with. Conversely, a milestone in the decline of its Australian counterpart, the Priorities Review Staff, was its move out of the Prime Minister's office to premises a mile away (Boston 1980).

Time is a crucial constraint, especially for the Prime Minister. Mrs Thatcher's private secretary records of her foreign affairs adviser, Cradock,

> for a No. 10 up to its neck in operational matters, finding time in the Prime Minister's crowded day for even the sagest advisers was a perpetual problem. We could not fit them in as frequently as we could the dentist, let alone the hairdresser. In the end we decided that policy advisers merited equal time with the aromatherapist, as a desirable luxury.
>
> (Powell 1997)

At his first Cabinet meeting in November 1990, Major promised senior colleagues a meeting on strategy but, almost incredibly, and despite pressure from his Policy Unit, the Gulf War prevented him from doing so for four months (Seldon 1997). This is why the Cabinet Secretary insists on a regular weekly meeting on forward business with the Prime Minister.

Finally, the politician must express confidence in the adviser, or he will find that access dries up. Alan Walters, Harold Lever, Peter Mandelson and successive heads of the Policy Unit all clearly commanded their premiers' confidence, and received access accordingly. This can even trump the problem of geographical proximity: Macmillan paid much attention to regular letters from the outside economist Roy Harrod 'on whose judgement I placed great reliance' (Macmillan 1973, Horne 1989), while Sir Alan Walters had much influence on Mrs Thatcher even during his absence in the United States (Lawson 1992). If the Prime Minister loses confidence or interest, the adviser becomes redundant – as witness the demise of the CPRS.

8 Conclusion

To sum up: since 1945 the British Cabinet system has moved from being a highly unified machine, in which business was marshalled through the Cabinet and its committees according to strict procedures, to a more diffuse system. Today the Cabinet is essentially a discursive body; decisions are taken variously in committee, in ad hoc groups and bilaterally, and the modes of decision-taking vary according to the area of policy, the Prime Minister's preferred business methods and the circumstances of the moment. But the core of the decision-making system remains its battery of ministerial committees.

This system is fissiparous. The predominant forces within it encourage its divisions and seem likely to continue doing so. Workload and ambition press ministers to entrench themselves in their departments, putting pressure on the wider concept of collective responsibility. The Cabinet fractures into different policy spheres, devolving functions to committees and ad hoc groups, and diluting its own role. Momentary convenience encourages the use of ad hoc groups. The sense of joint responsibility and collegiality often comes under heavy pressure, although it is far from dead. In this more disparate system, emphasis falls increasingly on the Prime Minister to hold things together. Although his relationship with ministers remains essentially one of mutual dependence, his policy role is considerable: continuous and vital in economics and foreign affairs, more selective but still important in other spheres. In contrast, the Cabinet has always had limited influence in foreign and economic spheres and, while domestic issues have traditionally taken up the bulk of its time and energies, the onus for decision in this sphere has passed to committees and other smaller gatherings.

The existing system is still workable, but is developing faults catalogued in Chapter 6. The traditional machinery described in Chapter 7 fills the gaps only to a certain extent. The Policy Unit and Cabinet Office between them now provide stronger support to the Prime Minister. To a lesser extent, special advisers are advising ministers on issues outside their departments. The Major and Blair governments' measures to improve the rationality and collegiality of public spending allocation look promising. The remainder of this chapter looks at other reforms to the Cabinet system that have been mooted: measures that might reinforce Cabinet collegiality; possible ways of developing the Cabinet's involvement in strategic matters; the idea of ministerial 'cabinets'; the oft-suggested idea of a Prime Minister's department; and several interesting institutional changes, whose development will be worth watching, made by the Blair government.

Bolstering Cabinet collegiality

Collegiality is essentially a state of mind and the key to fostering it lies with the Prime Minister. If he wants his colleagues to think and act collegially, he must ensure that they are consulted on key issues, show a good example by not leaking to the press, remind them of their duty to respect collective decisions, and instil in them a sense of joint responsibility. Institutional arrangements alone cannot achieve this state of mind: it must lie with the Prime Minister constantly to cultivate it.

Nonetheless, there are three institutional changes open to the Prime Minister. One possibility is to restore to the Cabinet a more substantial role in policy discussions. This could be done by using the Cabinet Office's forward look and the Prime Minister's contacts with committee chairmen to identify issues sufficiently significant to merit full Cabinet discussion, even if previously agreed at committee. Only a few issues could be dealt with in this way, but their political significance would probably be more important than their number.

A second option is to restore the practice of one-day seminars of the whole Cabinet at Chequers focusing on specific issues. These were popular in the 1960s and 1970s when, ironically, the Cabinet was pioneering the concept of the 'awayday' now so fashionable in both public and private sectors. Such meetings could either focus on particularly important issues of the moment – Wilson's Cabinet went to Chequers to discuss devolution, economic strategy and EU membership (Castle 1980, 1984) – or could, like Heath's Cabinet, consider more strategic issues (a point considered further below). Three preconditions exist for the success of such meetings, however: a relatively united Cabinet (even at his most collegial, Major would not have invited his Cabinet for a day at Chequers to discuss Europe); preparation beforehand by the Cabinet Office or Prime Minister's Policy Unit of material to inform discussion; and full-hearted participation by the Prime Minister.

A third possibility is to borrow from abroad the concept of informal Cabinet gatherings. Swedish ministers lunch together every weekday, not discussing much of great importance but giving them time for political gossip and some informal inter-departmental business. The meeting helps to keep up a sense of collective purpose (Larsson 1988). Cabinets in The Netherlands used to have a similar weekly dinner gathering (Andeweg 1988). The Finnish Cabinet meets on one evening a week, informally but with an agenda, a gathering which plays an important role in coordination and policy formulation, and helps to reinforce the collegiate ethos (Nousiainen 1988).

One problem that appears to be beyond resolution is the issue of briefing for Cabinet ministers on matters outside their departments. The collective briefs attempted by the CPRS were a brave and rational effort, but their tepid reception suggests that this approach is not worth reviving. It seems that the system must rely on the sporadic briefs offered to ministers by their special advisers, and on the Cabinet Secretariat's prompting of Cabinet committee chairmen to ask pertinent questions.

Government strategy: the weakness of the Cabinet and the crucial role of the Prime Minister

The engagement of the Cabinet in any attempt to give strategic direction to the government is not crucial, but it is advisable; for strategy is stillborn if it is not translated into the policies of individual departments, and both policy and strategy are matters of crucial interest to the Cabinet. However, a Cabinet of two dozen members is not ideally designed for the task, and is not supported by any strategic analytical capability to concentrate minds on the long term. Consequently, any initiative must be impelled mainly by the Prime Minister, the only person who can take the initiative to organise meetings, require colleagues to attend, set a framework for discussion, commission background papers, and above all guide and structure the discussion so that arguments ranging over the diverse activities of thirty or so departments can be marshalled to coherent conclusions. All this takes time, energy and fixity of purpose, and consequently it is rarely done. Today's crises crowd out next year's plans: Major, for example, promised his first Cabinet meeting a wide-ranging policy discussion; but thanks to the Gulf War, it was four months before he could keep his promise (Seldon 1997). In addition, the Prime Minister may be tempted not to bother because if the Cabinet does not concern itself with strategy, responsibility for it devolves by default onto him. This may suit him: Mrs Thatcher, for one, was happy to keep strategy in her own hands because many colleagues' scepticism of her economic and social programme was obvious. The problems arise if colleagues bridle against a strategy imposed on them.

Yet Cabinets are capable of a strategic role, as several European examples show: every month or two the Spanish Cabinet holds special meetings to discuss political strategy and particularly important issues (Bar 1988), and once or twice a year the Irish and Swedish Cabinets hold meetings lasting two or three days to discuss future policy (Larsson 1988, Farrell 1988). For that matter, the six-monthly meetings organised by Heath worked: the Cabinet just had the misfortune to hold these at a time when economic and political upheavals made strategic foresight impossible. Events, not flaws in conception, undermined these exercises.

There are, however, two necessary preconditions. First, the Prime Minister must be fully committed to engaging the full Cabinet in a strategic initiative; without this the attempt will founder. Second, there must be some analytical support from the central government machine. While the CPRS's coherent and systematic approach merits revival, particularly if strategy is linked to public expenditure plans, it does not necessarily require a separate staff: it could be carried out by the Policy Unit if it were boosted with additional strategic capability.

There is, however, one highly significant disincentive to this kind of exercise. As Howe records, in the early 1970s the Cabinet could hold strategy sessions at Chequers without seeing the results splashed over the press the next day. A decade later, the danger of leaks is high.

'Cabinets ministériels'

One idea occasionally suggested by politicians or political commentators is the introduction of the system known by the French name of 'cabinets ministériels'. The usual prompt for this is the observation that, although special advisers have proved a durable success, ministers are restricted to one or two advisers each. Few other countries are so restrictive: Norway and Finland are rare examples of countries that limit their ministers to one political assistant. Eyes therefore turn to Western Europe, where 'cabinets ministériels' are to be found in France, Spain, Italy, Portugal and Belgium, amongst other countries. These staff usually comprise outsiders from various backgrounds and officials seconded from their original departments. Their function is to serve the minister, advise him and take the lead in inter-departmental relations. (Thuiller 1982, Neville-Jones 1983, Fournier 1987, Schrameck 1995, Timmermans 1994).

British advocates of 'cabinets ministériels' are usually under the delusion that this change would amount to giving ministers a larger group of special advisers to draw on. In truth, it would deeply affect the structure and workings of departments and lead to a substantial politicisation of civil service functions. While the functions of 'cabinets ministériels' vary according to the minister they serve, common experience overseas is that they siphon policy development and decisions upwards from the rest of the department, leaving the permanent officials responsible essentially for administrative tasks. The Spanish arrangement is typical: the under-secretary who heads the permanent officials in a department is essentially in charge of logistical support; the Gabinete dominates policy-making. One reason why this system works in France is that there are no Permanent Secretaries as such, only heads of individual policy divisions reporting to the minister and his 'cabinet'. Indeed, these units often develop a considerable degree of authority – formal or informal – over departmental officials. They also take responsibility for inter-departmental coordination of policy.

What would the impact be of transplanting this system to Whitehall? Ministerial private offices would wither away. The policy-making functions of civil servants would not be entirely superseded, but their advice would be liable to be re-written by the unit of personal advisers before going to the minister. The overall level at which decisions are taken within departments would probably rise as officials cleared their lines with the 'cabinet' rather than risk being challenged at a later date. The civil service itself would not be politicised, but one of its most substantial functions would. Such units would be likely to become barriers between the Secretary of State and junior ministers. Existing arrangements between officials for inter-departmental coordination would be confined largely to administrative matters, with a parallel circuit of policy-making between ministers' personal advisers handling policy matters. Given that political appointees would be driven by the political agenda more directly than permanent civil servants, inter-departmental conflict would be more likely to arise and would be pushed further up the political chain.

It would probably be possible to transplant such a system to Britain if a government were dead set on it. But it has developed to suit the needs of a wholly different political and administrative culture: more adversarial, less collaborative and, above all, one where the civil service to is to some degree politicised. Indeed in Belgium, the bloated size of 'cabinets ministériels' is to a large extent an attempt to impose control on the turmoil caused by a combination of political appointments and frequent changes of government.

A Prime Minister's department?

In Britain the idea of a Prime Minister's department has been considered by every Prime Minister since 1964 (for example, Bruce-Gardyne 1974, Donoughue 1987, Hennessy 1989). Most recently it was floated in a book by two Labour party advisers close to Blair in the run-up to the 1997 election (Mandelson and Liddle 1996).

A common solution to this problem in other comparable countries is to roll all these functions together into a central department under the command of the Prime Minister. Australia, Canada and New Zealand each have a department that services both Prime Minister, Cabinet and committees, but with more explicitly active roles in policy coordination – for example leading inter-departmental task forces and general troubleshooting – in addition to keeping a watching brief on developments in departments so that they can keep the Prime Minister briefed (Weller 1985).

Germany and France have slightly different requirements since their Cabinets are weaker and individual ministers more autonomous. The German Chancellor's Office has a staff of several hundred who, in addition to servicing the Cabinet, shadow the work of departments to keep the Chancellor in touch and are actively involved in inter-departmental coordination. In the French system in addition to the personal 'cabinets' that both President and Prime Minister maintain, there is a Secretariat-General to the Presidency that is involved in policy-broking between departments and a Secretariat-General to the Government which is more of a technical and secretarial organisation (Plowden 1987, Fournier 1987).

The idea tends to be discussed in the abstract in Britain, without considering what functions it might actually discharge. The following list sets out the functions carried out in all or some of the Prime Minister's offices of Germany, Spain, France, Italy, Canada and Australia with, in parentheses, the government departments that carry out these functions in Britain:

1   Secretarial support for the Prime Minister (No. 10 private office)
2   Party liaison (Prime Minister's political office)
3   Press relations and communications (Prime Minister's press office)
4   Secretariat to Cabinet and its committees (Cabinet Office)
5   Constitutional affairs, including relations with devolved administrations (Cabinet Office and Home Office)
6   Intelligence services coordination (Cabinet Office)
7   EU policy coordination (Cabinet Office)
8   Senior civil service management (Cabinet Office)

9   Parliamentary relations (Offices of the leaders of the Commons and Lords, and whips' offices)

10 Legal advice (Law Officers' Secretariat)

11 Statistics (National Statistical Office)

12 Policy advice units, covering foreign affairs, economic matters, domestic issues, etc. (Policy Unit and Cabinet Office, to a limited extent)

13 Units concerned with policy issues which cross departmental boundaries (Policy Unit and Cabinet Office, to a limited extent)

14 Units dealing with planning of the government's programme (Cabinet Office, to a very limited extent)

This analysis focuses the argument rather better. Proponents of a British Prime Minister's department have not been much concerned with the first eleven functions, which are well integrated (all but two are located in the Cabinet Office–No. 10 complex) and arouse little criticism. It is the last three areas, all concerned with policy, that have been the focus of calls for a Prime Minister's department; and they are the areas in which the Prime Minister has limited support and relies on the relatively slender resources of his Policy Unit and the Cabinet Office.

Why have successive Prime Ministers' shied away from this idea? Many objections have been raised to the idea of a Prime Minister's department, and were rehearsed in an exchange between Professor Patrick Weller (1983) and Professor George Jones (1983). Some objections are not terribly convincing. Claims that it would forfeit the flexibility of existing arrangements underestimate the proven flexibility of central government departments like the Cabinet Office and ignore the fact that overseas Prime Ministers' departments tend to be constellations of units that wax and wane as required. The German Chancellor's Office is a good example of this. There is more to the worry that it would swamp the Prime Minister with more material than he could cope with, but this underestimates the skill of the private office in controlling the flow.

On the constitutional front, objections from politicians like Francis Pym (Channel Four 1982a) that it presages a presidency or undermines the Prime Minister's ability to cultivate consensus amongst his colleagues are based on a distortion of his role. While part of his job is to foster Cabinet collegiality, another part is to give a lead, to question and query, 'to make his own waves' as Callaghan put it (Callaghan 1987). The Prime Minister who does not lead fails his Cabinet, as Douglas-Home did. Having his own department might increase his propensity to intervene, although not dramatically since Prime Ministers are hardly reluctant to intervene now.

There are, however, three serious arguments against the idea. First, the fear that it would inexpertly challenge expert departments, although it would address the point that departments see policies from their own perspective while a central department would view them from a wider, more strategic angle, and that departmental premises often merit challenge, like the Treasury's 1970s addiction to statutory incomes policies. Second, there is the tendency to accumulate functions – as witness the Italian Prime Minister's office, swollen by bodies as varied as the Italian central office of information, the equal opportunities commission and the commission for conserving the leaning tower of Pisa.

The final and most substantial argument against a Prime Minister's department is not that it would concentrate power in the Prime Minister's hands but that ministerial and official fears of such a concentration, however groundless, would cause dissension and suspicion. This was the argument put forward by the more thoughtful critics of Mrs Thatcher's flirtation with the idea. A loyal former minister, Francis Maude, warned that 'it would add to the tensions and frustrations, not only inside Downing Street but in the government machine as well' (Channel Four, 1982b; see also Lord Thorneycroft quoted in the national press 19 November 1982). While a Prime Minister's department could work, the apprehension and resentment, justified or not, that its creation might generate outweighs its advantages.

The idea is likely to remain on the agenda: future Prime Ministers, like their predecessors, are likely at least to toy with the idea. If they do, they need to bear in mind a final danger: that such a department may be created for the wrong reason, by a Prime Minister in trouble, as a headline-grabbing way of re-asserting control. Departments created as gimmicks rarely come to any good, as Wilson's ill-fated Department of Economic Affairs proved.

The Blair government initiatives

In the event, the Blair administration did not opt for a Prime Minister's department, but introduced several significant changes to the machinery of central government in 1997 and 1998, focusing on policy coordination and review. At the time of writing, these were in their early stages. But at first blush they appeared potentially as significant as the creation of the CPRS and the Prime Minister's policy unit in the 1970s. Certain initiatives – the establishment of over 150 task forces, and the comprehensive spending review described in Chapter 6 – were one-off exercises. But two institutional innovations will be worth observing as they evolve: the Social Exclusion Unit and the Performance and Innovation Unit.

Announcing the creation of the Social Exclusion Unit in December 1997, Blair defined social exclusion as:

> a shorthand label for what can happen when individuals or areas suffer from a combination of linked problems such as unemployment, poor skills, low income, poor housing, high crime environments, bad health and family breakdown. The Government has polices that are targeted at reducing all of these individually, but Government programmes have been less good at tackling the interaction between these problems or preventing them arising in the first place. The purpose of the unit is to help break this vicious circle and coordinate and improve Government action…by promoting solutions, encouraging cooperation, disseminating best practice and, where necessary, making recommendations for changes in policies and machinery or delivery mechanisms. The unit will not cover issues that are of interest to one department only, or duplicate work done elsewhere. It will focus on areas where it can add value and address the long term causes of exclusion.

A deliberate attempt appeared to have been made to learn from the experience of the CPRS: the Unit was given strong institutional and political backing, its work steered by the Prime Minister personally, assisted by a network of junior ministers in the departments most affected by its work (Commons written answer, 8 December 1997). In institutional terms, it was part of the Economic and Domestic Secretariat of the Cabinet Office, which gave it powerful allies within Whitehall, and its members were a combination of seconded civil servants and outsiders: a social services director, a probation officer, a police chief superintendent, a banking executive and a (part time) member of the No. 10 Policy Unit (Social Exclusion Unit 1997). It was one of the most original institutional initiatives of recent decades, to some extent based on the models of the CPRS and the No. 10 Policy Unit.

Its early work led to action. Its first report – on pupils excluded from schools – led to government plans 'to target more resources on preventative work with children at risk of exclusion' and to a range of measures to set targets for truancy and exclusion reductions and strengthen police powers to pick up truants (Lords debates, written answer 11 May 1998, cols 93–5). Its second report led to a package of measures to end 'sleeping rough' in major cities, including appointment of a homelessness 'tsar' (national press, 8 July 1998).

Its task was a tall order. William Plowden, a former head of the CPRS social policy unit, opined: 'sooner or later any attempt to tackle apparently discrete problem groups...will mean altering some ministers' spending priorities, or asking them to do something inconsistent with current priories' and 'most serious programme changes would call for additional resources, at least in the short run' (Plowden 1998). Still, the Unit made a convincing start, with strong political backing, and is an initiative well worth watching.

The following year, the Prime Minister announced a re-organisation of the Cabinet Office, following a review by the Cabinet Secretary. The personnel and policy management sides of the Office were merged to 'help ensure that concerns about policy implementation are properly analysed in the process of developing policy, and help contribute to more effective follow-through when policies are agreed'. A Cabinet minister, Jack Cunningham, was placed in charge of all Cabinet Office functions (except the Secretariat) with a remit 'to ensure the Prime Minister's objectives and the Government's programme is running right across Whitehall' (Prime Minister's spokesman, quoted in the *Independent* 28 July 1998).

One significant element of these new arrangements was the creation of a new Performance and Innovation Unit to 'focus on selected issues that cross departmental boundaries and propose policy innovations to improve the delivery of the Government objectives' and to 'select aspects of government policy that require review, with an emphasis on the better coordination and practical delivery of policy and services which involve more than one public sector body (Commons written answer 28 July cols 132–4, Cabinet Office 1998). The Performance and Innovation Unit was to conduct a rolling programme of policy reviews that cross departmental boundaries, each to be carried out by a small team assembled temporarily for the purpose drawn from the civil service and outside. It was also to review aspects of policy and service delivery involving more than one public sector body. The first group of projects to be carried out by the Unit included studies of the government's presence in cities and the regions, and of how older people can play a more active role in the community).

These initiatives were intended to be mutually reinforcing. The Performance and Innovation Unit drew explicitly on the experience of the Social Exclusion Unit, and both were required to work closely with the economic and domestic side of the Cabinet Secretariat. The Performance and Innovation Unit was to draw its work programme in part from the Ministerial Committee on Public Expenditure, and the Social Exclusion Unit was to feed into the expenditure allocation process any recommendations for redirections of priorities.

The need for 'continuous revolution'

A Prime Minister's Department, revival of a Cabinet strategy staff, more special advisers, more units like the Social Exclusion Unit: no one of these solutions automatically excludes all the others, nor is there any single correct solution. There is no platonic ideal for the arrangement of functions at the centre. Besides, Prime Ministers are wont periodically to re-order the central machinery of government because of its highly personal nature: much depends on the needs of the moment, the personalities in the government and the Prime Minister's own working habits. This points to a flexible constellation of small, free-standing units as at present. No solution will be definitive; even a Prime Minister's department which, once created, might be seen as a definitive innovation, could easily see its functions increased and decreased over time, as has happened in Canada, Australia and Italy.

There is another good reason for not pronouncing in favour of one optimum arrangement. To keep central sources of analysis and advice creative they need changing every so often. A degree of originality and radicalism is expected of policy units and advisory staffs. Inevitably over time they risk losing their bite: the grit in the machine is worn smooth. It happened to the CPRS and several times to the Policy Unit. Sometimes advisers get out of tune with their clients, like Balogh's economists. Sometimes for no clear reason it just fizzles out.

This, together with the ease with which Prime Ministers can remodel the machinery that surrounds them, suggests that the advisory apparatus at the centre will always have an experimental element about it. Some degree of 'continuous revolution' seems likely and desirable. And indeed the actual organisation of advisory units is not the most important consideration. What matters above all is that they show flair and energy and that they target their efforts on the structural flaws in the Cabinet system.

Conclusion

Cabinet government is not a subject that lends itself to a pithy summing-up. The system, always in a state of perpetual evolution, lost a number of its familiar points of reference in the 1970s and 1980s, and may not yet have settled on its new course. In particular, the relationship between Cabinet collegiality and Prime Ministerial leadership is still working itself out.

Instead, I will conclude with two observations about the cabinet system. One, relevant to the advisory mechanisms discussed in the last two chapters, is that teams of advisers producing high quality analysis are all very well, but they can only be as good as ministers will allow them to be. In particular, institutional tinkering cannot remedy problems of collegiality. Which leads to the second observation: that at the heart of the system lies a dilemma centred on the Prime Minister. The ethos and expectations of the British political system, both at ministerial and parliamentary level, are that the system will operate in a fundamentally collegiate manner. Yet most of the tendencies – and the temptations – in the system encourage the premier to cut corners with collective decision-making. Too much concern for collegiality, and he is accused of weakness; too little, and the dangers of long-term disintegration, as witnessed in the Thatcher government, loom. The odd paradox to which this leads is that Prime Ministers need to use the powerful advantage that their authority gives them to maintain a genuinely collective style of government.

Further reading

This short guide is intended for students who want to read further on specific aspects of the Cabinet system. Full bibliographical details are given in the Bibliography.

In the first edition of this book I bemoaned the paucity of writing on Cabinet government. Things have improved slightly, but so many crucial documents remain unpublished that I suspect some authors of wilful obscurity. Amongst notable omissions, Lord Hunt's 1983 lecture on 'the hole at the centre of government' remains unpublished, Sir Robert Armstrong's 1986 lecture explaining the work of the Cabinet Office (the only one by a serving Cabinet Secretary) appeared in print only in French, and John Barnes' essay on the symbiotic model of Cabinet government was for years available only in the transactions of the National Parliament of Peru.

A student's starting point should be the material published by the Cabinet Office itself. The list of Cabinet committees is updated every six months or so by means of a parliamentary written answer by the Prime Minister, but is most easily available in Vacher's Parliamentary Companion (published quarterly) or on the No. 10 Downing Street website at http://www.number-10.gov.uk/index.html. Otherwise the latest list can be obtained by writing to the Secretary of the Cabinet, 70 Whitehall, London SW1A 2AS. From the same address you can obtain 'Cabinet Committee Business: a guide for departments' (latest version 1997) and the Ministerial Code; a charge of £5 is made for the latter. The Cabinet Office website at http://www.open.gov.uk/cohome.htm was due to be revamped in early 1999 and should now carry much of this material. Wakeham's lecture on Cabinet Government must have been vetted by, if not written by, the Cabinet Secretariat and so can be taken as having quasi-official status.

Studies of the Cabinet by political scientists are rare. One is the reader by Rhodes and Dunleavy which contains several useful theoretical chapters, Dunleavy's quantitative analysis of Cabinet committees and several good case studies. Another welcome newcomer is Burch and Halliday's *The British Cabinet System*, which stresses the informal character of Cabinet government, although I think it overstates the concentration of power at the centre. Dell's attack on collective responsibility is essential reading. Other works tend to be historical. Mackintosh's textbook is the definitive history up to 1945 but the post-war section is terribly outdated. *Cabinet* by Peter Hennessy is memorable for its brilliant exposé of the middle years of Mrs Thatcher's premiership and also has good chapters on Cabinet committees and nuclear policy, but has dated. A useful mine is the dry, discreet but workmanlike account of the Cabinet in the 1960s by Patrick Gordon Walker, a Labour Cabinet minister. In contrast, Harold Wilson's *Governance of Britain* is stylish but should be approached warily: it omits as much as it includes. Early appraisals of the Blair premiership by Hennessy and Riddell are listed in the bibliography.

There is no definitive study of the Prime Minister, although Graham Thomas' textbook synthesises for students the work of other authors. Anthony King's reader remains valuable and includes King's own percipient essay on Mrs Thatcher and George Jones' milestone 1965 article on the Prime Minister's power – although Brown's 1968 article remains the crispest summary of the latter subject. A historical study of the office of Prime Minister by Peter Hennessy is imminent.

Prime Ministerial memoirs are usually dull. The extended memoirs of Macmillan and Wilson are mainly catalogues of events; those of Callaghan and Thatcher are slightly better written (the latter by many 'assistants') but reveal little of interest. Livelier than any of these are the eye-witness accounts of life at No. 10 by various assistants: John Colville, Harold Evans, Bernard Donoughue and Sarah Hogg – all very readable. And the explosion of political biography has generated many books with useful material on Prime Ministers and their management of their Cabinets: see particularly Campbell on Heath, Morgan on Callaghan (a chapter devoted to the subject), Young on Thatcher, and Seldon's supremely well-informed book on Major. Historical studies of administrations usually yield less on the work of central government: exceptions are Lamb on Eden, Barnes' essay on Macmillan's government, Ponting on the first Wilson government and Stephenson's 1980 book on Mrs Thatcher's first year – a brilliant work of instant history, still worth reading.

Political science has neglected ministers and their departments. The best study, although dated, is Bruce Headey's 1974 *British Cabinet Ministers*, a unique and essential analysis of departmental ministers' roles; see also the chapter by Smith, Marsh and Richards in the Rhodes and Dunleavy reader. Kevin Theakston's book on junior ministers contains a lot about departments generally, and is a model of how to blend written and other sources. Otherwise, the best commentaries are by ministers themselves. Gerald Kaufman's *How to be a Minister* is sharply observed and very funny; it was reprinted before the 1997 election as a primer for new Labour ministers. Jock Bruce-Gardyne's *Ministers and Mandarins* runs it a creditable second for both style and interest. Joel Barnett's *Inside the Treasury* is excellent on the political dimension of public spending battles. Barbara Castle's *Sunday Times* article on mandarin power still repays reading.

The best flavour of ministerial life is to be found in the voluminous diaries of three Labour ministers from the 1960s and 1970s: Castle's are the best, since she kept a shorthand note at the time. (Unfortunately her most interesting volume, 1974–76, has an abysmal index.) Tony Benn is informative, and valuable on Cabinet committees in the 1970s, but his record of ministerial meetings is impaired because he records his own contribution at length and others' too briefly. Of Richard Crossman's diaries his colleague Michael Stewart aptly observed:

> Crossman was not always able to distinguish between what he thought had happened (or wished had happened) and what had actually occurred. When he uses the word 'obviously' he means that this was the impression he formed at the time.

Nonetheless, the first fifty pages of his first volume catch well the bewilderment of a minister new to Whitehall.

The 1980s have seen a veritable blizzard of ministerial memoirs, but few are much use to the student of Whitehall. The exception is Nigel Lawson's *The View from the Treasury*, compelling reading not just on economic policy-making but on many aspects of governmental life. Read it selectively – it is over 1,000 pages long. Dell's various works on economic policy-making in the 1970s are scholarly and interesting. Howe's memoirs are made unexpectedly good reading by his running battle with Mrs Thatcher. Beyond that, there are snippets – but often little more than that – in the memoirs of Boyd-Carpenter on the 1950s, Healey and Jenkins on the 1960s and 1970s, and Prior, Tebbit, Baker, Young and Fowler on the 1980s. The last two, while unexciting as literature, have the most on the work of ministers in their departments. The promised memoirs of Douglas Hurd may be more rewarding.

The best general introduction to the civil service is by Drewry and Butcher, although Dowding's study has a valuable theoretical inflection. Peter Hennessy's *Whitehall* is an indispensable history but very comprehensive: students need to be selective. Young and Sloman reproduce interesting interviews with officials in their three studies 'No, Minister',

'But Chancellor' and 'With Respect, Ambassador'. Holland's RSA lecture gives a lively and attractive insight into civil service life; Part's memoirs are unintentionally revealing of the more tortuous cast of a mandarin mind.

Europe remains a gap in the literature. Hayes-Renshaw and Wallace's book on the Council of Ministers has remedied the worst deficiency, and is best read in conjunction with Butler's valuable if dated practitioner's guide. Bulmer and Wessel's book on the European Council has long been overtaken by events but a second edition is promised. Middlemass' volume is good on the internal politics of the EU. As to ministerial accounts, Kaufman and Bruce-Gardyne offer merrily cynical chapters on the EU, and the otherwise soporific Thatcher memoirs are a treasury of material on the European Council. Tebbit and Lawson's memoirs have a bit as well, but Benn's diaries on his 1977 presidency are a let-down.

The case study approach is catching on. A series of short studies makes up the second half of Burch and Halliday, and a number more appear in James (1997). Longer case studies appear in the readers by Rhodes and Dunleavy, and by Greenaway, Smith and Street. Butler, Adonis and Travers have produced a full-length study of the poll tax débâcle.

A great contribution to comparative studies has been made by Professor Jean Blondel: in addition to his book on ministers around the world, he has edited with Muller-Rommel two readers on West European Cabinets, of which the 1988 volume of essays on individual countries is perhaps of more use to British students than the 1993 *Governing Together* (London: Macmillan) which dwells on the consequences of coalitions, as does the edited collection by Laver and Shepsle. Sadly, the latter two volumes do not cover Spain, a country with many striking parallels to Britain. There are also good collections on Prime Ministers in Western Europe in the Jones reader and in Westminster model countries in Weller, as well as a comparative collection on Cabinet committees edited by Mackie and Hogwood. Neville-Jones's article on ministerial 'cabinets' illuminates a subject on which British commentators usually talk nonsense; for French 'cabinets ministériels' see the short volumes (in French) by Thuillier and Schrameck.

The meagre literature on advisory mechanisms was revitalised as this volume went to press in 1998 by the appearance of *At the Heart of Whitehall* by Lee, Jones and Burnham, notable especially for Lee on the Cabinet Office and Jones on the Prime Minister's secretaries. Otherwise, on the Cabinet Office, see Seldon's essay and Lee's reply in (eds) Rhodes and Dunleavy. On the Policy Unit, there are three first-hand accounts by Donoughue, Hogg and Hill, and Willetts – the latter being the more analytical. Blackstone and Plowden's book on the CPRS will probably remain definitive even after the public records are opened. The first fifty pages of Cradock's book are essential reading on foreign policy and intelligence advice. Alas, there is nothing good on special advisers. The progress of the Social Exclusion Unit can be followed on its website at www.open.gov.uk/co/seu/seuhome.html.

The Whitehall Programme, funded by the ESRC and encouraged by the Cabinet Office, should from 1999 start yielding publications useful to student of the Cabinet system. Particularly relevant are likely to be George Jones' history of Prime Ministerial advisers; Richard Rose's study of the premiership; Phillip Norton on senior ministers; two studies by M J Smith on 'complexity in the core executive' and central government departments in the policy process; Simon Bulmer on the impact of the EU on British government; Brady, Catterall and Kandiah on Cabinet committees; Kevin Theakston on Permanent Secretaries; and several volumes edited by Vincent Wright on policy coordination core executives in France, Germany, Italy and The Netherlands. To judge by the output of past ESRC programmes, it will be miraculous if all these volumes appear, but just a few of them could move the scholarship of this under-studied area forward considerably.

Notes

2 Ministers and their departments

1 This approach was recommended to Heath by his machinery of government study group in opposition, led by Lord Boyle. A comparison of Barbara Castle's diaries for 1964–70 and 1974–76 suggests that there was some shift towards greater delegation to junior ministers between the two periods, although Wilson's *Governance of Britain* (1976) is silent on the point. I am grateful to John Barnes for drawing my attention to this development.

4 The role of the Prime Minister

1 Most notably Jones' 1969 study. The debate is summarised excellently in Brown's 1968 article. Crossman had begun to modify his argument in his 1972 lectures.

2 There is actually no statutory limit on the number of ministerial appointments the Prime Minister may make. The Ministerial And Other Salaries Act 1975 limits to 110 the number of such appointees who may be paid from the public purse, but non-salaried ministers may be appointed beyond that limit – for example, Lord Simon of Highbury, a businessman who accepted unpaid junior office under Blair. Incidentally, the House of Commons Disqualification Act 1975 limits to 95 the number of paid office-holders in the Commons (the 'payroll vote').

5 The dynamics of collective decision-making

1 This is relatively unusual amongst Western European governments. Muller, Phillip and Gerlich (1993) observe that only in Norway and Ireland are Prime Ministers deeply involved in both foreign and economic affairs: although their survey did not cover it, the same is true of Spain. In France, foreign affairs is famously the domaine réservé of the President, leaving the Prime Minister to attend to economic matters. In Germany and Italy, heads of government are more involved in economic than in foreign matters. In a surprising number of countries the premier shows no deep involvement in either.

6 Problems of the Cabinet system

1 Dell's views were set out in his 1980 lecture to the Royal Institute of Public Administration, Rodgers' in a lecture at the 1986 RIPA conference, which is not in print, and Benn's in his diaries (1989). In contrast ministers who served under Mrs Thatcher have usually argued for a strengthening of collective responsibility.

7 Advice at the centre

1 Two exceptions to the 'political sympathy' rule are the National Drugs Coordinator and his deputy who are, for technical reasons, appointed as special advisers.

Bibliography

Notes

1   * in the text signifies that the reference comes from the LSE Cabinet Government seminar, held under Chatham House rules.
2   Authors are cited as described in their publications, i.e. titles conferred after publication are ignored.
3   References to PREM in the text are to the records of the Prime Minister's Office, held in the Public Records Office at Kew.
4   For reasons of space, references to specific Cabinet committees are not given; for sources, see 'Further reading'.

Printed Sources

Alderman, G. (1992) 'Harold Macmillan's Night of the Long Knives', in *Contemporary Record*, vol. 6 (2), Autumn.
Alderman, G. (1995) 'A Defence of Frequent Ministerial Turnover', in *Public Administration*, vol. 71, Winter.
Andeweg, R. (1985) 'The Netherlands: Cabinet Committees in a Coalition Cabinet', in T. Mackie and B. Hogwood, *Unlocking the Cabinet: Cabinet Structures in Perspective*, pp. 138–54.
Andeweg, R. (1988) 'The Netherlands', in Blondel and Muller-Rommel (eds), *Cabinets in Western Europe*, pp. 47–67.
Andeweg, R. (1993) 'A Model of the Cabinet System: The Dimension of Cabinet Decision-Making Processes', in Blondel and Muller-Rommel (eds), *Cabinets in Western Europe*, pp. 23–42.
Armstrong, R. (1986a) 'Horace Wilson', in Lord Blake and C. Nicholls (eds), *Dictionary of National Biography 1971–1980*, Oxford: Oxford University Press.
Armstrong, R. (1986b) Untitled contribution in Institut Français des Sciences Administratives, Le Secrétariat-Géneral du Gouvernement, Paris: Economica.
Armstrong, Lord (Robert) (1988) 'The Civil Service We Deserve?', Phillips and Drew lecture delivered at the London School of Economics, 10 November.

Armstrong, R. (1994) 'Cabinet Government in the Thatcher years', in *Contemporary Record*, 83 (3), Winter.

Ashworth, J. (1985) 'Giving Advice to Governments: The Role of the Chief Scientific Adviser in the Central Policy Review Staff'. Address to the Royal Signals Institution, 28 November.

Asquith and Oxford, Earl of (1928) *Fifty Years of Parliament*, vol. 2. London: Cassell.

Attlee, The Earl (Clement) (1960) *The Sunday Times*, 27 November.

Attlee, The Earl (Clement) (1969) 'The Making of a Cabinet', in A. King (ed.), *The British Prime Minister*, 1st edn, cit. pp. 69–79.

Bagehot, W. [1867] (1964) *The English Constitution*, London: Watts & Co.

Baker, A. (1998) *A Very Peculiar Process; the Prime Minister, the Cabinet, the Constitution and the Making of Questions of Procedure for Ministers Since 1945*, London: Gresham College.

Baker, K. (1993) *The Turbulent Years*, London: Faber and Faber.

Balen, M. (1994) *Kenneth Clarke*, London: Fourth Estate.

Bancroft, Lord (Ian) (1983) 'Whitehall: Some Personal Reflections'. Suntory-Toyota lecture delivered at the London School of Economics, 1 December.

Bancroft, Lord (Ian) (1984) 'Whitehall and Management: A Retrospect', *Royal Society of Arts Journal*, vol. CXXXII, (5334), pp. 367–79.

Bar, A. (1988) 'Spain', in Blondel and Muller-Rommel (eds), *Cabinets in Western Europe*, pp. 102–119.

Barnes, J. (1987) 'From Eden to Macmillan 1955–59', in Hennessy and Seldon, *Ruling Performance*, pp. 98–149.

Barnes, J. (1999) 'The Prime Minister's Role in Foreign Affairs and Economic Policy: Creeping Bilateralism in Action?' in James, S. and V. Preston, *New Politics, Old Politics: Essays in Political History since 1945*, London: Macmillan.

Barnett, J. (1982) *Inside the Treasury*, London: André Deutsch.

Bender, B. (1991) 'Whitehall, Central Government and 1992', in *Public Policy and Administration*, vol. 6(1), Spring.

Benn, A. (1980) 'Manifestos and Mandarins', in RIPA, *Policy and Practice*, pp. 57–78.

Benn, A. (1988) *Office Without Power: Diaries 1968–72*, London: Hutchinson.

Benn, A. (1989) *Against the Tide: Diaries 1973–76*, London: Hutchinson.

Benn, A. (1990) *Conflicts of Interest: Diaries 1977–80*, London: Hutchinson.

Berrill, K. (1985) 'Strength at the Centre: The Case for a Prime Minister's Department', in A. King (ed.), *The British Prime Minister*, 2nd edn, pp. 242–57.

Blackstone T. and Plowden W. (1988) *Inside the think-tank: Advising the Cabinet 1971–83*, London: Heinemann.

Blondel, J. (1985) *Government Ministers in the Contemporary World*, London: Sage.

Blondel, J. and Muller-Rommel, F. (eds) (1988) *Cabinets in Western Europe*, London: Macmillan.

Blondel, J. and Muller-Rommel, F. (eds) (1993) *Governing Together: The Extent and Limits of Joint Decision-Making in Western European Cabinets*, London: Macmillan.

Boston, J. (1980) 'High Level Advisory Groups: the Case of the Priorities Review Staff in Australia', in P. Weller and D. Saersch (eds) *Responsible Government in Australia*, Richmond, Australia: Drummond.

Boston, J. (1988) 'Advising the Prime Minister in New Zealand: The Origins, Functions and Evolution of the Prime Minister's Advisory Group', in *Politics*, May.

Boyd-Carpenter J. (1980) *Way of Life*, London: Sidgwick and Jackson.

Brown, A. (1968) 'Prime Ministerial power', in *Public Law*, Spring and Summer editions, pp. 28–51 and 96–118.

Bruce-Gardyne, J. (1974) *Whatever Happened to the Quiet Revolution?*, London: Charles Knight.

Bruce-Gardyne, J. (1986) *Ministers and Mandarins*, London: Macmillan.

Bruce-Gardyne, B. and Lawson, N. (1976) *The Power Game*, London: Macmillan.

Bullock, Lord (1983) *Ernest Bevin*, vol. 3, London: Heinemann.

Bulmer, S. and Wessels, S. (1987) *The European Council*, London: Macmillan.

Burch, M. (1993) 'Organising the Flow of Business in Western European Cabinets', in J. Blondel and F. Muller-Rommel (eds), *Governing Together*, pp. 99–130.

Burch, M. and Halliday, I. (1996) *The British Cabinet System*, Hemel Hempstead: Harvester Wheatsheaf.

Burridge T. (1986) *Clement Attlee, A Political Biography*, London: Jonathan Cape.

Butler, C. (1986) 'Special Advisers: A Semi-secret Circle', in *Planet*, 55, February–March.

Butler, D. and Butler, G. (1994) *British Political Facts 1990–9*, 7th edn, London: Macmillan.

Butler, D., Adonis, A. and Travers, T. (1994) *Failure in British Government: The Politics of the Poll Tax*, Oxford: Oxford University Press.

Butler, M. (1986) *Europe, More than a Continent*, London: Heinemann.

Butler, Lord (R.A.B.) (1971) *The Art of the Possible*, London: Hamish Hamilton.

Butler, R. (1993) 'The Evolution of the Civil Service – A Progress Report', in *Public Administration*, vol. 71, Autumn, pp. 395–406.

Butler, R. (1997) 'The Changing Civil Service'. Address to ESRC Whitehall Programme conference and author's note of questions and answers, 24 September.

Cabinet Office (1995) 'Cabinet Committee Business: A Guide for Departments'.

Cabinet Office (1997a) 'Ministerial Code: a Code Of Conduct And Guidance On Procedures For Ministers'.

Cabinet Office (1997b) 'Cabinet Committee Business: A Guide For Departments, Revised Version'.

Cabinet Office (Office of Public Service) (1997c) 'Guidance on the Work of the Government Information Service'.

Cabinet Office (Office of Public Service) (1997d) 'Report of the Working Group on the Government Information Service'.

Callaghan, J. (1987) *Time and Chance*, London: Collins.

Campbell, C. (1983) *Governments under Stress: Political Executives and Key Bureaucrats in Washington*, London and Ottowa, Toronto: University of Toronto Press.

Campbell, C. (1985) 'Cabinet Committees In Canada: Pressures And Dysfunctions Stemming From The Representational Imperative', in T. Mackie and B. Hogwood, *Unlocking the Cabinet*, pp. 61–85.

Campbell, J. (1983) *Roy Jenkins: A Biography*, London: Weidenfeld and Nicolson.

Campbell, J. (1993) *Edward Heath: A Biography*, London: Jonathan Cape.

Cardona, G. (1981) 'One step ahead of "Yes Minister"', *The Times*, 11 November.

Carrington, (Lord) (1988) *Reflect on Things Past*, London: Collins.

Castle, B. (1973) 'Mandarin Power', *Sunday Times*, 10 June. Reprinted in P. Barberis, (1996) *The Whitehall Reader*, Buckingham: Open University Press.

Castle, B. (1980) *The Castle Diaries: 1974–1976*, London: Weidenfeld and Nicolson.

Castle, B. (1984) *The Castle Diaries 1964–70*, London: Weidenfeld and Nicolson.

Castle, B. (1993) *Fighting All the Way*, London: Macmillan.

Catterall, P. and Brady, C. (forthcoming) 'Cabinet Committees in British Governance', in *Public Policy and Administration*.

'Central Intelligence Machinery' (1993), London: HMSO.

Civil Service Yearbook, published annually, London: HMSO.

Clark, W. (1986) *From Three Worlds*, London: Sidgwick and Jackson.

Clarke, A. (1993) *Diaries*, London: Weidenfeld and Nicolson.

Cmnd. 4506 (1971) 'The Reorganisation of Central Government', London: HMSO.

Cole, J. (1995) *As It Seemed to Me*, London: Weidenfeld and Nicolson.

Colville, Viscount (Jock) (1985) *The Fringes of Power: Downing Street Diaries 1939–1955*, London: Hodder and Stoughton.

Conlon, B. (1998) 'How Was It For You?', in *Public Service*, August/September.

Contemporary Record (1988b) '1967 devaluation: symposium', vol. 14, pp. 44–53.

Cotta, M. (1988) 'Italy', in Blondel and Muller-Rommel (eds), *Cabinets in Western Europe*, pp. 120–37.

Cradock, P. (1997) *In Pursuit of British Interests: Reflections on Foreign Policy under Margaret Thatcher and John Major*, London: John Murray.

Criscitiello, A. (1994) 'The Political Role Of Cabinet Ministers In Italy', in M. Laver and K. Shepsle (eds), *Cabinet Ministers and Parliamentary Government*, pp. 187–200.

Croome, A. (1972) 'On being a Grand Vizier', *New Scientist*, 27 February.

Crosland, S. (1982) *Tony Crosland*, London: Jonathan Cape.

Crossman, R. (1963) Preface to 'The English Constitution' reprinted in King (ed.), *The British Prime Minister*, 2nd edn, pp. 175–93.

Crossman, R. (1972) *Inside View: Three Lectures on Prime Ministerial Government*, London: Jonathan Cape.

Crossman, R. (1975) *The Diaries of a Cabinet Minister: Volume One: Minister of Housing 1964–66*, London: Hamish Hamilton and Jonathan Cape.

Crossman, R. (1976) *The Diaries of a Cabinet Minister: Volume Two: Lord President of the Council and Leader of the House of Commons 1966–68*, London: Hamish Hamilton and Jonathan Cape.

Crossman, R. (1977) *The Diaries of a Cabinet Minister: Volume Three: Secretary of State for Social Services 1968–70*, London: Hamish Hamilton and Jonathan Cape.

Currie, E. (1989) *Lifelines*, London: Sidgwick and Jackson.

Dalyell, T. (1989) *Dick Crossman: A Portrait*, London: Weidenfeld and Nicolson.

Darling, A. (1997) Darlington Economics Lecture, 14 November. Text released by H.M Treasury.

Defence Committee of the House of Commons (1986), Fourth Report, 23 July.

Dell, E. (1980) 'Collective Responsibility: Fact, Fiction Or Facade?', in RIPA, *Policy and Practice*, pp. 25–48.

Dell, E. (1991) *A Hard Pounding: Politics and Economic Crisis 1974–76*, Oxford: Oxford University Press.

Dell, E. (1992) 'The Chrysler UK Rescue', in *Contemporary Record*, vol. 6(1), Summer.

Dell, E. (1994) 'The Failings of Cabinet Government in Mid to Late 1970s', in *Contemporary Record*, vol. 8(3), Winter.

Derbyshire, I. and Derbyshire, J. (1996) *Political Systems of the World*, London: Helicon.

de Winter, L. (1993) 'The Links between Cabinets and Parties and Cabinet Decision-Making', in J. Blondel and F. Muller-Rommel (eds), *Governing Together*, pp. 153–178.

Diamond, Lord (John) (1975) *Public Expenditure in Practice*, London: Allen and Unwin.

Dickie, J. (1992) *Inside the Foreign Office*, London: Chapman.

Donoughue, B. (1987) *Prime Minister*, London: Jonathan Cape.

Donoughue, B. (1988) 'The Prime Minister's Diary', in *Contemporary Record*, 2(2).

Donoughue of Aston, Lord (Bernard) (1994) 'The 1975 Chrysler Rescue: A Political View from Number Ten', in *Contemporary Record*, vol. 8 (1) Summer.

Dowding, K. (1995) *The Civil Service*, London: Routledge.

Draper, D. (1997) *Blair's 100 Days*, London: Faber and Faber.

Drewry, G. and Butcher, T. (1998) *The Civil Service Today*, Oxford: Blackwell.

Dunleavy, P. (1995) 'Estimating the Distribution of Positional Influence in Cabinet Committees under Major', in R. Rhodes and P. Dunleavy (eds), *Prime Minister, Cabinet and Core Executive*, pp. 298–321.

Dyson, K. (1973) 'Planning and the Federal Chancellor's Office', in *Political Studies*, vol. 31(3), pp. 348–62.

Dyson, K. (1974) 'The German Federal Chancellor's Office', in *Political Quarterly*, vol. 32(3), pp. 364–71.

Eden and Avon, Earl of (Anthony Eden) (1960) *Full Circle*, London: Cassell.

Eden and Avon, Earl of (Anthony Eden) (1962) *Facing the Dictators*, London: Cassell.

Edwardes, M. (1983) *Back from the Brink*, London: Collins.

Edwards, G. (1985) 'The case of the United Kingdom', in C. O'Nuallain, *The Presidency of the European Council of Ministers*, London: Croome Helm.

Egremont, Lord (John Wyndham) (1968) *Wyndham and Children First*, London: Macmillan.

Elwyn-Jones, Lord (1983) *In My Time*, London: Weidenfeld and Nicolson.

Ericksen, S. (1988) 'Norway', in J. Blondel and F. Muller-Rommel (eds), *Cabinets in Western Europe*, pp. 183–96.

Evans, H. (1981) *Downing Street Diaries*, London: Hodder and Stoughton.

Expenditure Committee of the House of Commons (1976), Evidence of Sir Kenneth Berrill and others to the General Sub-Committee, 6 December.

Expenditure Committee of the House of Commons (1977), Evidence of Sir John Hunt and others to the General Sub-Committee, 14 February.

Farrell, B. (1988) 'Ireland', in J. Blondel and F. Muller-Rommel (eds), *Cabinets in Western Europe*, pp. 33–46.

FitzGerald, G. (1991) *All in a Life*, London: Macmillan.

Foley, M. (1993) *The Rise of the British Presidency*, Manchester: Manchester University Press.

Foster, C. (1996) 'Reflections on the True Significance of the Scott Report for Government Accountability', in *Public Administration*, vol. 74(4), Winter.

Fournier, J. (1987) *Le Travail gouvernemental*, Paris: Presses de la Fondation Nationale des Sciences Politiques, Dalloz.

Fowler, N. (1991) *Ministers Decide*, London: Chapmans.

Fulton, Lord (1968) 'The Civil Service', Report of the Committee 1966–68. Cmnd. 3638, London: HMSO.

Garel-Jones, T. (1993) 'The UK Presidency: An Inside View', in *Journal of Common Market Studies*, vol. 31(2), June.

Gilbert, M. (1982) 'Horace Wilson: Man of Munich?', in *History Today*, vol. 32, October, pp. 3–9.

Gilmour, I. (1992) *Dancing with Dogma: Britain under Thatcherism*, London: Simon and Schuster.

Gimson, A. (1985) 'The Guardians of Thatcherism', in *Spectator*, 8 June.

Gladstone, W. (1879) *Gleanings of Past Years*, vol. 2. London: John Murray.

Gormley, J. (1982) *Battered Cherub*, London: Hamish Hamilton.

Greenaway, J., Smith, S. and Street, J. (1992) *Deciding Factors in British Politics: A Case Studies Approach*, London: Routledge.

H. M. Treasury (1997) 'Comprehensive Spending Review: Terms of Reference', 30 October.

Hailsham, Lord (1978) *The Dilemma of Democracy*, London: Collins.

Hailsham, Lord (1987) 'Can Cabinet Government Survive?', the Granada Television Lecture, London: Granada.

Haines, J. (1977) *The Politics of Power*, London: Jonathan Cape.

Halcrow, M. (1989) *Keith Joseph: A Single Mind*, London: Macmillan.

Harris, K. (1982) *Attlee*, London: Weidenfeld and Nicolson.

Harris, R. (1990) *Good And Faithful Servant: The Unauthorised Biography of Bernard Ingham*, London: Faber and Faber.

Hastings, M. and Jenkins, S. (1983) *The Battle for the Falklands*, London: Michael Joseph.

Hattersley, R. (1995) *Who Goes Home? Scenes from a Political Life*, London: Little, Brown and Company.

Hayes-Renshaw, F. and Wallace, H. (1996) *The Council of Ministers*, London: Macmillan.

Headey, B. (1974) *British Cabinet Ministers* London: George Allen and Unwin.

Healey, D. (1989) *The Time of my Life*, London: Michael Joseph.

Heath, E. (1976) 'William Armstrong', in Lord Blake and C. Nicholls (eds), *Dictionary of National Biography 1971–80*, Oxford: Oxford University Press.

Heath, E. and Barker, A. (1977) 'Heath on Whitehall Reform', in *Parliamentary Affairs*, vol. XXI, pp. 363–90.

Heclo, H. and Wildalsky, A. (1981) *The Private Government of Public Money*, 2nd edn, London: Macmillan.

Hennessy, P. (1986) *Cabinet*, Oxford: Blackwell.

Hennessy, P. (1989) *Whitehall*, London: Secker and Warburg.

Hennessy, P. (1996) *The Hidden Wiring: Unearthing the British Constitution*, revised edn, London: Indigo.

Hennessy, P. (1997) 'The Blair Style of Government: An Historical Perspective and An Interim Audit', *Government and Opposition*, 33(1), Winter.

Hennessy, P. and Seldon, A. (1987) *Ruling Performance: British Governments from Attlee to Thatcher*, Oxford: Blackwell.

Hennessy, P., Morrison, S. and Townsend, R. (1985) 'Routine Punctuated by Orgies: The Central Policy Review Staff 1970–83', *Strathclyde Papers on Government and Politics* no. 31. Glasgow: University of Strathclyde.

Heseltine, M. (1987) *Where There's a Will*, London: Hutchinson.

Hill, Lord (Charles) (1964) *Both Sides of the Hill*, London: Heinemann.

Hine, D. and Finocci, R. (1991) 'The Italian Prime Minister', in G. Jones (ed.), *West European Prime Ministers*, pp. 79–96.

Hogg, S. and Hill, J. (1995) *Too Close to Call: Power and Politics – John Major in No. 10.*, London: Little Brown.

Holland, G. (1995) 'Alas! Sir Humphrey. I knew him well', *RSA Journal*, November.

Holmes, M. (1985) *The First Thatcher Government 1979–83*, London: Wheatsheaf.

Horne, A. (1988) *Macmillan: 1894–1956*, London: Macmillan.

Horne, A. (1989) *Macmillan: 1956–86*, London: Macmillan.

Hoskyns, J. (1982) 'Westminster and Whitehall: An Outsider's View', Address to the Institute of Fiscal Studies, 12 October, London: IFS.

Hoskyns, J. (1984) 'Conservatism Is Not Enough', in *Political Quarterly*, vol. 55(1).

Howard, A. and West, R. (1965) *The Making of the Prime Minister*, London: Jonathan Cape.

Howe, G. (1994) *Conflicts of Loyalty*, London: Macmillan.

Howell, D. (1987) 'Review of A. Walters, Britain's Economic Renaissance', in *Political Quarterly*, vol. 58(1), p. 104.

Hunt, Sir John (1977) 'Dos and Don'ts of Chairmanship', in *Management Services in Government*, vol. 32(2), pp. 61–4.

Hunt of Tamworth, Lord (John) (1983) 'Cabinet Strategy and Management', Lecture to the RIPA/CIPFA Conference, Brighton, 6 June.

Hunt of Tanworth, Lord (John) (1994) 'The Failings of Cabinet Government in Mid to Late 1970s', in *Contemporary Record*, vol. 8(3), Winter.

Hurd, D. (1979) *An End to Promises*, London: Collins.

Irvine of Lairg, Lord (1998) 'The Constitutional Reform Programme', Statute Law Society, Conference Proceedings 1997, London: Institute of Advanced Legal Studies.

James, S. (1994) 'Cabinet Government: A Commentary', in *Contemporary Record*, vol. 8(3), Winter, pp. 495–505.

James, S. (1997) *British Government: A Reader in Policy-Making*, London: Routledge.

Jay, Lord (Douglas) (1980) *Change and Fortune: A Political Record*, London: Hutchinson.

Jenkins, K., Caines, K. and Jackson, A. (1988) 'Improving Management in Government: The Next Steps – Report to the Prime Minister', London: HMSO.

Jenkins, P. (1987) *The Thatcher Revolution*, London: Jonathan Cape.

Jenkins, R. (1989) *European Diary 1977–1981*, London: Collins.

Jenkins, R. (1991) *A Life at the Centre*, London: Macmillan.

Jenkins, S. and Sloman, A. (1985) *With Respect Ambassador: An Inquiry into the Foreign Office*, London: BBC.

Jones, G. (1969) 'The Prime Minister's Power', in King (ed.), *The British Prime Minister*, pp. 195–220.

Jones, G. (1974) 'Harold Wilson's Policy-Makers', *Spectator*, 6 July.

Jones, G. (1975) 'Development of the Cabinet', in W. Thornhill (ed.) *The Modernisation of British Government*, London: Pitman.

Jones, G. (1983) 'Prime Ministers' Departments Really Do Cause Problems', in *Public Administration*, vol. 61(1). pp. 79–86.

Jones, G. (1985) 'The Prime Minister's Aides', in King (ed), *The British Prime Minister*, pp. 72–95.

Jones, G. (ed.) (1991) *West European Prime Ministers*, London: Frank Cass.

Junor, P. (1996) *John Major*, revised edn, London: Penguin.

Kandiah, M. (ed.) (1996) 'Witness Seminar: The Number 10 Policy Unit', in *Contemporary Record*, vol. 10(1), Spring.

Kandiah, M. and Seldon, A. (1996) *Ideas and Think Tanks in Post War Britain*, Volumes 1 and 2, London: Frank Cass.

Kaufman, G. (1980) *How to be a Minister*, London: Sidgwick and Jackson.

Keegan, W. (1984) *Mrs Thatcher's Economic Experiment*, London: Allen Lane.

Keegan, W. (1989) *Mr Lawson's Gamble*, London: Hodder and Stoughton.

Keegan, W. and Pennent-Rea, R. (1979) *Who Runs the Economy?*, London: Temple Smith.

Kilmuir, Lord (1964) *Political Adventure*, London: Weidenfeld and Nicolson.

King, A. (ed.) (1969) *The British Prime Minister*, 1st edn, London: Macmillan.

King, A. (ed.) (1985) *The British Prime Minister*, 2nd edn, London: Macmillan.

King, A. (1991) 'The British Prime Ministership in the Age of the Career Politician', in Jones (ed.), *West European Prime Ministers*, pp. 25–47.

King, A. (1994) 'Ministerial Autonomy in Britain', in Laver and Shepsle (eds), *Cabinet Ministers and Parliamentary Government*, pp. 203–225.

Klein, R. and Lewis, J. (1977) 'Advice and Dissent in British Government: The Case of the Special Advisors', in *Policy and Politics*, vol. 61.

Kogan, M. (ed.) (1971) *The Politics of Education: Edward Boyle and Antony Crosland in Conversation with Maurice Kogan*, Harmondsworth, Middlesex: Penguin.

Lamb, R. (1987) *The Failure of the Eden Government*, London: Sidgwick and Jackson.

Larsson, T. (1988) 'Sweden', in Blondel and Muller-Rommel (eds), *Cabinets in Western Europe*, pp. 197–212.

Larsson, T. (1994) 'Cabinet Ministers and Parliamentary Government in Sweden', in Laver and Shepsle (eds), *Cabinet Ministers and Parliamentary Government*, pp. 169–186.

Laver, M. and Shepsle, K. (eds) (1994) *Cabinet Ministers and Parliamentary Government*, Cambridge: Cambridge University Press.

Lawson, N. (1992) *The View from No. 10: Memoirs of a Tory Radical*, London: Bantam.

Lawson, N. (1994) 'Cabinet Government in the Thatcher Years', in *Contemporary Record*, vol. 8(3), Winter.

Lee, J., Jones, G. and Burnham, J. (1998) *At the Heart of Whitehall: Advising the Prime Minister and Cabinet*, London: Macmillan.

Linklater, M. and Leigh, D. (1986) *Not with Honour*, London: Sphere.

Lipsey, D. (1980) 'Who's in charge in Whitehall?', in *New Society*, 24 April.

Ludlow, P. (1993) 'The UK Presidency: A View from Brussels', in *Journal of Common Market Studies*, vol. 31(2), June.

MacDougall, D. (1987) *Don and Mandarin: Memoirs of an Economist*, London: John Murray.

Mackie, T. and Hogwood, B. (1985) *Unlocking the Cabinet: Cabinet Structures in Perspective*, London: Sage.

Mackintosh, J. (1977) *The British Cabinet*, 3rd edn, London: Stevens.

Macmillan, H. (1972) *Pointing the Way*, London: Macmillan.

Macmillan, H. (1973) *At the End of the Day*, London: Macmillan.

Mallaby, G. (1965) *From my Level: Unwritten Minutes*, London: Hutchinson.

Mandelson, P. (1997) 'Co-ordinating Government Policy', Speech to Birmingham University Conference on Modernising the Policy Process, 16 September.

Mandelson, P. and Liddle, R. (1996) *The Blair revolution: Can New Labour Deliver?*, London: Faber and Faber.

Mark, R. (1978) *In the Office of Constable*, London: Collins.

Marsh, R. (1978) *Off the Rails*, London: Weidenfeld and Nicolson.

Maudling, R. (1978) *Memoirs*, London: Sidgwick and Jackson.

Middlemass, K. (1995) *Orchestrating Europe: the Informal Politics of European Union 1973–1995*, London: Fontana.

Mitchell, P. (1978) 'Special Advisers: A Personal View', in *Public Administration*, vol. 56(1), Spring, pp. 87–98.

Morgan, K. (1997) *Callaghan: A Life*, Oxford: Oxford University Press.

Morley, J. (1889) *Walpole*, London: Macmillan.

Muller, W., Phillip, W. and Gerlich, P. (1993) 'Prime Ministers and Cabinet Decision-Making Processes', in J. Blondel and F. Muller-Rommel (eds), *Governing Together*, pp. 223–258.

Muller-Rommel, F. (1988) 'Federal Republic of Germany', in Blondel and Muller-Rommel (eds), *Cabinets in Western Europe*, pp. 151–66.

Neustadt, R. (1985) 'White House and Whitehall', in King (ed.), *The British Prime Minister*, pp. 155–73.

Neville-Jones, P. (1983) 'The Continental Cabinet System: the Effects of Transposing it to the United Kingdom', in *Political Quarterly*, vol. 54(3), July–September

Norton-Taylor, R. (1985) *The Ponting Affair*, London: Woolf.

Nousiainen, J. (1988) 'Finland', in Blondel and Muller-Rommel (eds), *Cabinets in Western Europe*, pp. 213–33.

Owen, D. (1981) *Face the Future*, London: Jonathan Cape.

Owen, D. (1991) *Time to Declare*, London: Michael Joseph.

Page, B. (1978) 'The Secret Constitution', in *New Statesman*, 21 July.

Part, A. (1990) *The Making of a Mandarin*, London: André Deutsch.

Peston, M. (1980) 'A Professional on a Political Tightrope', *Times Higher Educational Supplement*, 11 July.

Petrie, C. (1958) *The Powers Behind the Prime Ministers*, London: Gibbon and Key.

Phillips, R. (1977) 'The British Inner Cabinet', in *London Review of Public Administration*, vol. 10, pp. 5–27.

Pliatsky, L. (1981) *Getting and Spending: Public Expenditure, Employment and Inflation*, Oxford: Blackwell.

Pliatsky, L. (1984) 'Mandarins, Ministers and the Management of Britain', in *Political Quarterly*, vol. 55(1), pp. 23–8.

Plowden, W. (1987) *Advising the Rulers*, Oxford: Blackwell.

Plowden, W. (1998) 'Unit Costs', *Guardian*, 7 January.

Pollitt, C. (1984) *Manipulating the Machine*, London: George Allen and Unwin.

Ponting, C. (1989) *Breach of Promise: Labour in Power 1964–70*, London: Hamish Hamilton.

Powell, C. (1997) 'The Mandarin and his Masters', review of P. Cradock, *In Pursuit of British Interests* in *Sunday Telegraph*, 31 August.

Prior, J. (1986) *A Balance of Power*, London: Hamish Hamilton.

Pym, F. (1984) *The Politics of Consent*, London: Hamish Hamilton.

Ranelagh, J. (1991) *Thatcher's People*, London: Harper Collins.

Redhead, B. (1977) 'James Callaghan', in J. Mackintosh (ed.) *British Prime Ministers in the Twentieth Century*, vol. 2, London: Weidenfeld and Nicolson.

Rees, M. (1985) *Northern Ireland: A Personal Perspective*, London: Methuen.

Rhodes, R. and Dunleavy, P. (eds) (1995) *Prime Minister, Cabinet and Core Executive*, London: Macmillan.

Riddell, P. (1997) 'Cracks in the Cabinet Cement', *The Times*, 10 November.

Riddell, P. (1998) 'RIP Cabinet Government', *The Times*, 5 January.

Ridley, N. (1991) *My Style of Government*, London: Hutchinson.

RIPA (Royal Institute of Public Administration) (1980) *Policy and Practice: the Experience of Government*, London: RIPA.

Rodgers, W. (1984) 'Government Under Stress: Britain's Winter of Discontent 1979', in *Political Quarterly*, vol. 55(2).

Rose, R. (1974) *The Problem of Party Government*, London: Macmillan.

Rothschild, Lord (1977) *Meditations of a Broomstick*, London: Collins.

Rothschild, Lord (1983) 'A Useful Exercise, With Interest', *The Times*, 2 July.

Sampson, A. (1971) *The New Anatomy of Britain*, London: Hodder and Stoughton.

Schrameck, O. (1995) *Les Cabinets ministériels*, Paris: Dalloz.

Scott, R. (1996) 'Report of the Inquiry into the Export of Defence Equipment and Dual-Use Goods to Iraq and Related Prosecutions', HC 115.

Sedgemore, B. (1980) *The Secret Constitution*, London: Hodder and Stoughton.

Seldon, A. (1981) *Churchill's Indian Summer: The Conservative Government 1951–55*, London: Hodder and Stoughton.

Seldon, A. (1995) 'The Cabinet Office and Co-ordination, 1979–87', in Rhodes and Dunleavy (eds), *Prime Minister, Cabinet and Core Executive*, pp. 125–148.

Seldon, A. (1997) *Major: A Political Life*, London: Weidenfeld and Nicolson.

Shepherd, R. (1983) 'Ministers and Special Advisers: Tilting the Balance Away from Cabinet', in *Public Money*, vol. 33.

Shepherd, R. (1994) *Ian Macleod: A Biography*, London: Pimlico.

Shore, P. (1993) *Leading the Left*, London: Weidenfeld and Nicolson.

Short, E. (1989) *Whip to Wilson*, London: MacDonald.

Silkin, J. (1987) *Changing Battlefields*, London: Hamish Hamilton.

Social Exclusion Unit (1997) Leaflet describing the Unit's work, London: Cabinet Office.

Stack, F. (1983) 'The Imperatives of Participation', in F. Gregory, *Dilemmas of Government: Britain and the European Community*, Oxford: Michael Robertson.

Stapleton, G. (1985) 'Beyond the Thin Green Line', in MAFF Bulletin, October, pp. 75–7.

Stephenson, H. (1980) *Mrs Thatcher's First Year*, London: Jill Norman.

Stewart, M. (1980) *Life and Labour*, London: Sidgwick and Jackson.

Stone, D. (1996) *Capturing the Political Imagination: Think Tanks and the Policy Process*, London: Frank Cass.

Stothard, P. (1984) 'Mr Redwood Walks Small', *The Times*, 8 March.

Tebbit, N. (1988) *Upwardly Mobile*, London: Weidenfeld and Nicolson.

Thatcher, M. (1993) *The Downing Street Years*, London: Harper Collins.

Theakston, K. (1987) *Junior Ministers in British Government*, Oxford: Blackwell.

Thiébault, J.-L. (1988) 'France', in Blondel and Muller-Rommel (eds), *Cabinets in Western Europe*, pp. 86–101.

Thiébault, J.-L. (1993) 'The Organisational Structure of Western European Cabinets and its Impact on Cabinet Decision-Making', in Blondel and Muller-Rommel (eds), *Governing Together*, pp. 77–98.

Thomas, G. (1998) *Prime Minister and Cabinet Today*, Manchester: Manchester University Press.

Thorpe, D. (1989) *Selwyn Lloyd*, London: Jonathan Cape.

Thuillier, G. (1982) *Les Cabinets ministériels*, Paris: Presses Universitaires de France.

Timmermans, A. (1994) 'Cabinet Ministers and Policy-Making in Belgium: The Impact of Coalition Constraints', in Laver and Shepsle (eds), *Cabinet Ministers and Parliamentary Government*, pp. 106–124.

Treasury and Civil Service Committee of the House of Commons (1988) 'Duties and Responsibilities of Civil Servants in Relation to Ministers', minutes of evidence by Sir Robin Butler, 9 March.

Treasury and Civil Service Committee of the House of Commons (1994) 'The Role of the Civil Service', fifth report, session 1993–4, Volume 1, London: HMSO.

Trend, Lord (Burke) (1981) 'Norman Brook', in E. Williams and C. Nicholls (eds), *Dictionary of National Biography 1961–70*, Oxford: Oxford University Press.

Wakeham, Lord (John) (1993) 'Cabinet Government', in *Contemporary Record*, vol. 8(3), pp. 473–83.

Walker, P. G. (1972) *The Cabinet*, revised edn, London: Heinemann Educational.

Walters, A. (1986) *Britain's Economic Renaissance*, Oxford: Oxford University Press.

Wapshott, N. and Brock, G. (1983) *Thatcher*, London: MacDonald.

Wass, D. (1983) *Government and the Governed*, London: Routledge and Keegan Paul.

Watkinson, Lord (1986) *Turning Points*, Salisbury: Michael Russell.

Weller, P. (1983) 'Do Prime Ministers' Departments Really Cause Problems?', in *Public Administration*, vol. 61(1), pp. 59–78.

Weller, P. (1985a) *First Among Equals: Prime Ministers in Westminster Systems*, London and Sydney: George Allen and Unwin.

Weller, P. (1985b) 'Cabinet Committees in Australia and New Zealand', in Mackie and Hogwood (eds), *Unlocking the Cabinet*, pp. 86–113.

Whitehead, P. (1985) *The Writing on the Wall: Britain in the 1970s*, London: Michael Joseph.

Whitehead, P. (1987) 'The Labour Governments 1974–79', in Hennessy and Seldon, *Ruling Performance*, pp. 241–273.

Whitelaw, Viscount (William) (1989) *The Whitelaw Memoirs*, London: Aurum Press.

Willetts, D. (1987) 'The Role of the Prime Minister's Policy Unit', in *Public Administration*, vol. 65(4), pp. 443–54.

Williams, M. (1973) *Inside No. 10*, London: Weidenfeld and Nicolson.

Williams, M. (1983) *Downing Street in Perspective*, London: Weidenfeld and Nicolson.

Williams, P. (1979) *Hugh Gaitskell*, London: Jonathan Cape.

Williams, S. (1980) 'The Decision-Makers', in RIPA, *Policy and Practice*, pp. 79–102.

Wilson, H. (1967) 'The Prime Minister and the Machinery of Government', *Listener*, 6 and 13 April.

Wilson, H. (1971) *The Labour Government 1964–70*, London: Weidenfeld and Nicolson and Michael Joseph.

Wilson, H. (1976) *The Governance of Britain*, London: Weidenfeld and Nicolson and Michael Joseph.

Wilson, H. (1979) *Final Term: the Labour Government 1974–76*, London: Weidenfeld and Nicolson and Michael Joseph.

Wilson, S. (1975) *The Story of the Cabinet Office to 1945*, London: HMSO.

Wright, V. (1989) *The Government and Politics of France*, 3rd edn, London: Unwin Hyman.

Young, Lord (David) (1990) *The Enterprise Years: A Businessman in the Cabinet*, London: Headline.

Young, H. (1989) *One of Us*, London: Macmillan.

Young, H. and Sloman, A. (1982) *No Minister: An Inquiry into the Civil Service*, London: BBC.

Young, H. and Sloman, A. (1984) *But Chancellor: An Inquiry into the Treasury*, London: BBC.

Young, H. and Sloman, A. (1986) *With Respect, Ambassador*, London: BBC.

Zuckerman, Lord (Solly) (1988) *Monkeys, Men and Missiles*, London: Collins.

Broadcast and audio sources

BBC (1982) 'David Dimbleby in conversation', interview with John Hoskyns, BBC1 Television, 7 December.

BBC (1986a) 'Talking Politics', BBC Radio 4, 4 January.

BBC (1986b) 'Newsnight', item on Mrs Thatcher's style of government, BBC2 Television, 30 January.

BBC (1987) 'The World This Weekend', interview with Mrs Thatcher, BBC Radio 4, 5 April.

BBC (1990a) 'That inherent weakness', part 5 of 'Sailing Without an Anchor', BBC Radio 3, 28 March.

BBC (1990b) 'Analysis: diminished responsibility', discussion between Denis Healey, Roy Jenkins, Enoch Powell and Peter Hennessy, BBC Radio 4, 22 November.

BBC (1992) 'On the Record', BBC 1 Television, 18 October.

BBC (1998) 'So you want to be Foreign Secretary?', BBC2 Television, 4 January.

Channel 4 (1982a) 'Face the Press', interview with Francis Pym, 7 January.

Channel 4 (1982b) 'The Week in Politics', interview with Francis Maude, 7 November.

Channel 4 (1997) 'The Week in Politics', 11 May.

Channel 4 (1998) 'Now we are one: Blair's year', 19 April.

Hurd, D. (1997) *Letters From a Diplomat*, BBC Worldwide.

London Weekend Television (1986) 'Weekend World', 12 January.

Scottish Television (1997) 'We are the Treasury', ITV 7 October.

Williams, S. (1996) *Snakes and Ladders: A Political Diary*, BBC Worldwide.

Index